Praise for *The Tangled Web of the Civil War and Reconstruction*

"Throughout his distinguished career, David Madden has been 'myriad minded,' as his numerous publications in so many genres show. This book examines the Civil War as depicted in fact and in fiction and from myriad perspectives. Madden's intersecting lines of trajectory give newcomers to the study and experienced historians alike new strands to touch and new reverberations to feel. Imaginative and multifaceted, *The Tangled Web of the Civil War and Reconstruction* is an audacious and genuinely original achievement."

—Allen Wier, University of Tennessee, Knoxville;
author of *Tehano*

"David Madden's *The Tangled Web of the Civil War and Reconstruction* is the record of a first-rate mind and a clear effective writer engaging critically and imaginatively with the central events of the American experience. I haven't learned more about the Civil War since 1967 when I was following Shelby Foote around Memphis State University with a tape recorder."

—James A. Perkins, Distinguished Professor Emeritus
of English and Public Relations, Westminster College

"David Madden has long been one of our most acute and thoughtful commentators on the culture and history of the American South through his fiction, his essays, and his book reviews. Whether discussing such writers as William Faulkner or Robert Penn Warren or analyzing classics of Civil War fiction or meditations on the great conflict, Madden tells the reader more in a few pages than most lengthy historical tomes do in a hundred. These are not essays for scholars only, but they will engage the interest and imaginations of general readers and students alike."

—M. Thomas Inge, Randolph-Macon College;
editor of *Company Aytch: Or, a Side Show of the Big Show*

The Tangled Web of the Civil War and Reconstruction

The Tangled Web of the Civil War and Reconstruction

Readings and Writings from a Novelist's Perspective

David Madden

ROWMAN & LITTLEFIELD
Lanham • Boulder • New York • London

Published by Rowman & Littlefield
A wholly owned subsidiary of The Rowman & Littlefield Publishing Group, Inc.
4501 Forbes Boulevard, Suite 200, Lanham, Maryland 20706
www.rowman.com

Unit A, Whitacre Mews, 26-34 Stannary Street, London SE11 4AB, United Kingdom

Distributed by NATIONAL BOOK NETWORK

Photographs on pages 171, 185, and 186 by Timothy H. O'Sullivan. Courtesy of the Library of Congress.
Photograph on page 176 courtesy of University of Tennessee Video & Photography / Ernie Robertson.
Photograph on page 180 by George N. Barnard. Courtesy of the Library of Congress.
Photograph on page 183 by Alexander Gardner. Courtesy of the Library of Congress.
Photographs on pages 178, 181, and 182 courtesy of the Library of Congress.

British Library Cataloguing in Publication Information Available

Library of Congress Cataloging-in-Publication Data

Madden, David, 1933–
The tangled web of the Civil War and Reconstruction : readings and writings from a novelist's perspective / David Madden.
pages cm
Includes bibliographical references and index.
ISBN 978-1-4422-4348-4 (cloth : alk. paper) — ISBN 978-1-4422-4349-1 (electronic)
1. United States—History—Civil War, 1861–1865. 2. Reconstruction (U.S. history, 1865–1877) 3. United States—History—Civil War, 1861–1865—Literature and the war. 4. Interdisciplinary approach to knowledge. I. Title.
E468.9.M2143 2015
973.8—dc23

2015009219

∞™ The paper used in this publication meets the minimum requirements of American National Standard for Information Sciences—Permanence of Paper for Printed Library Materials, ANSI/NISO Z39.48-1992.

Printed in the United States of America

For James Wharton, who as Louisiana State University chancellor enabled me to create the United States Civil War Center

And to the memory of Larry Crain, my genial guide through the web

"Of wars . . . of legality conferred on crime we sing, and of a mighty people attacking its own guts with victorious sword-hand, of kin facing kin, and . . . of conflict waged with all the forces of the shaken world for universal guilt, and of standards ranged in enmity against standards, of eagles matched and javelins threatening javelins. What madness was this, O citizens?"

—Lucan's *Civil War*, AD 61–65 (Caesar vs. Pompey)

"O what a tangled web we weave . . ."

—Sir Walter Scott, *Marmion*

Contents

Part II. Meditations on the Civil War and Reconstruction by Willis Carr, Sharpshooter

Part III. Lincoln on Remembrance and Perspective

Introduction

"The Vibration Ripples to the Remotest Perimeter"

> Cass Mastern lived for a few years and in that time he learned that the world is all of one piece. He learned that the world is like an enormous spiderweb and if you touch it, however lightly, at any point the vibration ripples to the remotest perimeter, and the drowsy spider feels the tingle and is drowsy no more but springs out to fling the gossamer coils about you who have touched the web and then inject the black, numbing poison under your hide. It does not matter whether you meant to brush the web of things. Your happy foot or your gay wing may have brushed it ever so lightly, but what happens always happens and there is the spider, bearded black and with his great faceted eyes glittering like mirrors in the sun, or like God's eye, and the fangs dripping.

The metaphor of the spiderweb from the "Cass Mastern" Civil War chapter of Robert Penn Warren's *All the King's Men*, my choice of one of the ten or so greatest Civil War novels—a choice that may at first seem perverse—is so apt in my view for the tangled strands of the American Civil War and Reconstruction that I have used—perhaps overused—it often. This collection begs for its use once again because in the essays I have selected from my many pieces, I touch points all over the web, because each is connected in many ways with all others.

The spider metaphor illuminates all my writings—short stories, novels, poems, plays, screenplays, memoirs, creative nonfiction, critical essays, and books. Touch one work, the vibrations set all others in motion. While I chose for each one its own specific bite, variety, not similarity, is the overriding word for what I have created over the past seventy years, starting when I was eleven, attracted even then to all genres. The nonfiction and fiction pieces enhance each other. My expectation is that this intrinsic creative variety will ward off anyone's first-glance charge that this collection is a hodgepodge. I could have settled on this as a title: Readings and Writings on the Civil War and Reconstruction by an East Tennessee Novelist: A Variety of Perspectives on the Causes, Conduct, and Consequences.

It might be helpful if the reader were to keep in mind that I am from Knoxville in divided East Tennessee, trying to pass F. Scott Fitzgerald's "test of a first-rate intelligence: to hold two opposed ideas in the mind at the same time and still retain the ability to function."

"There are two sins for which America can never atone," said Southern novelist and historian Shelby Foote on a panel, referring to both North and South: "slavery and reconstruction." One of Foote's most-remembered remarks comes from the opening episode of the film *The Civil War*, by Ken Burns. In describing the significance of the war, he says, "It was the crossroads of our being, and it was a hell of a crossroads."

We may extend that declaration to all civil wars worldwide throughout history, because the truth of his statement lies in the very nature of civil war. I am currently engaged in a study on that premise.

Deep into research for my Civil War novel *Sharpshooter: A Novel of the Civil War*, I created the United States Civil War Center, the only research institution in literary history to derive from research for a work of fiction. The perspectives explored in the novel cover every aspect of the war and Reconstruction; the Civil War Center was conceived to bring to bear every conceivable academic discipline, profession, and occupation, all the arts, ethnic concerns, women, children, and civilian life in general. The protagonist is haunted for many years by the conviction that he missed the war, even though he fought in battles in many places and most probably shot a famous Union general; that became a premise of the Civil War Center, inspiring the essays in this collection. Back then and ever since, Americans missed the war by failing to study it from every possible perspective.

This book is a collection of pieces not by a historian who wrote a Civil War novel but by the author of ten novels and three collections of short stories, poems, plays, and other nonfiction works, whose interest led him to write a Civil War novel, two scholarly books, and hundreds of book reviews on Civil War, Reconstruction, and Abraham Lincoln as subjects. My immersion in research for *Sharpshooter* began around 1985. So it is as an East Tennessee novelist, more than as a historian, that I write here about my readings and writings, in fiction and nonfiction, about the war and Reconstruction.

"THE VIBRATION RIPPLES TO THE REMOTEST PERIMETER"

"For the New Millennium, New Perspectives on the Civil War and Reconstruction" comes first in this collection because it explores many of the unusual subjects that other pieces take up and the sometimes innovative techniques they employ.

> By understanding the war, we can understand ourselves in the world today, both our dark problems and our bright prospects. We Americans have missed the war by focusing too much and too long on battles and leaders. That focus distracts us from our deeper purpose: to trace back to Reconstruction, to the war itself, and to the antebellum era the origins of the forces at work in our culture today. Among the dark problems today, racism, violence, economic instability, and distrust of government daily stare us in the face. The promising benefits to society of the many technological inventions, medical discoveries, industrial techniques, and business methods that evolved out of the war have been only partially fulfilled or have been postponed, partly because the problems put a drag on the pace of progress.

(Several passages from this essay—and a few others—are repeated verbatim in a few essays and fiction pieces that follow it. I have not omitted repetitions because they directly enhance the essence of various essays and fiction pieces, especially Willis Carr's obsessive perspectives on the war and Reconstruction.)

After the direct and implied complexities of the first essay, a specific piece seems called for. Fletcher Pratt's *A Short History of the Civil War,* originally entitled *Ordeal by Fire* (1935) gives me the opportunity to examine and recommend a style other historians might find instructive.

> Pratt's style is the main indication that he was speaking to the public of the Depression years, imagining his readers to be the same as those he'd had as a reporter and popular-magazine writer of both short stories and articles. His style is slam-bang staccato—as if the James Cagney of *Public Enemy* had taken the reader by the arm and said, "Okay, this is how it's going to be—I talk, you listen—got it?" Pratt's style sounds less like that of Pulitzer Prize–winning historian Douglas Southall Freeman and more like the first-person voices of James M. Cain's Frank Chambers, Dashiell Hammett's Sam Spade, or Raymond Chandler's Philip Marlowe. It is interesting to note that Pratt's contemporary, the Civil War novelist MacKinlay Kantor, wrote one of the first gangster novels, *Diversy* (1928).

My praise and analysis of his tough-guy style argues directly and simply for the superiority of this book over other short and most long histories, and the importance of avoiding the prevalent turgid, cliché-ridden, unimaginative, dull style we experience too often in books about the Civil War—what I call "the storm clouds were gathering" school of rhetoric. Ironically, the many historians who cherish Pratt's book as the first, or early best, history that they read failed to follow his example, missing what makes it so powerfully fast-paced: the 1930s tough-guy narrating voice. It was my own first, and remains my personal choice as the best history of the war, so I'm proud to have persuaded

Dover Books to reprint it after many years as a tattered paperback. My impressions are borne out by a perusal of testimonies on Amazon and Goodreads.

James McPherson is a good example of a later historian whose style is readable but not really distinguished. "On James McPherson's *For Cause and Comrades: Why Men Fought in the Civil War*" is a critical examination of McPherson's choices of reasons and his own reasoning in support of those choices. I discuss the kinds of reasons soldiers' subjective letters and journals are intrinsically unreliable, just as much of the objective reports in the numerous volumes of the official records are, for other reasons, to various degrees, unreliable. "The motives of many volunteers were mixed in ways that were impossible to disentangle in their own minds. McPherson tries to unmix mixed motives and takes up each in separate chapters: conviction and lack of it, cowardice and courage, and so forth. But for the most meaningful results, motives must be examined in their *mixed* state." Psychological considerations must come prominently into play when we attempt to use letters as evidence supporting claims.

In "Classics of Civil War Fiction," I return to a broad subject, commenting on the choices well-known novelists and critics made when asked to write about classic works. I take up the question of what constitutes a classic of Civil War fiction and what would qualify a work to be regarded as among the greatest. Included are *Absalom, Absalom!* by William Faulkner, *The Wave* by Evelyn Scott, and *The History of Rome Hanks and Kindred Matters* by Joseph Stanley Pennell. I examine the many types and facets of novels and stories by both Northern and Southern writers, touching upon the question of the Great American Novel. My own choice is *Absalom, Absalom!* but at one time it was a novel that in many ways resembles Faulkner's—*Rome Hanks* by Pennell. My focus in writing about both is on the achievements in using the technique of point of view and style that is derived from it, along with other techniques as expressions of emotion and meaning.

> In the ideal Civil War novel, the author's vision and purpose emerge out of the complexities of the war experience but transcend them. The novel succeeds in stimulating and engaging the emotions, the imagination, and the intellect to make the war agonizingly alive in the reader. Its point of view, style, and other techniques make the reader a collaborator with the author in creating a conception of the Civil War that will enable the reader, long after the fiction ends, to illuminate his or her experiences. It would be the novel Americans need to stimulate a revolution in our way of feeling, imagining, and meditating on an event that has determined the development of this nation and that continues to affect our behavior in ways we do well to see and understand.

"William Faulkner's *Absalom, Absalom!* Quentin! Listen!" dramatizes my conviction that the most meaningful Civil War novels deal with the war indirectly and richly through implications. We miss the war—and Reconstruction—when we stare at it head-on. All the essays and fiction pieces in this collection express facets of that conviction. Faulkner's myriad perceptions range across a spectrum of aspects of the antebellum, war, Reconstruction, and modern eras, setting the stage not only for the variety of essays that follows but also for the imaginative selection of subjects. I'm inclined to suspect that few will agree with me that William Faulkner's ninth novel *Absalom, Absalom!* (1936) is about the Civil War itself and far fewer that it is the greatest Civil War novel, but I feel confident that many will agree it is a profound antebellum and Reconstruction novel, enhanced by the context of the years 1833 and 1910. Only a few pages are set during the war. In "Quentin! Listen!" I defend the claim that the depiction in 1909–1910 by five storytellers speaking alternately of the antebellum and Reconstruction eras delineates the causes and effects of the "offstage" Civil War years. "Faulkner dramatizes the fact that while the conventional Southern values, which coalesced in the issues and the warrior mentality of the Civil War, fail to produce creative acts in the lives of individual descendants, the legends do stimulate each individual listener's imaginative participation, a value that transcends the ritual teaching function of the South's past. For them the unvicarious life is not worth living; at least they have *that* much of a life." I challenge the focus on plantation slave owner Thomas Sutpen as the protagonist because it distracts our attention to twenty-year-old Harvard student Quentin Compson as a protagonist who listens to all the storytellers and reluctantly retells the Sutpen story, motivated by deep psychological need. The misplaced focus on Sutpen as protagonist and misunderstandings about Quentin's role derives from a general failure among critics to read the novel as a necessarily complex work of innovative art. This essay and the following two make a case for the importance of understanding the authors' use of the technique of point of view to avoid complete misreading of their novels.

"Rediscovering a Major Civil War Novel: Joseph Stanley Pennell's *The History of Rome Hanks and Kindred Matters*" is not only a prime example of the value of actively making an effort to rediscover fine Civil War novels but also, I argue, one of the great ones. It was my choice as the greatest until I read *The Wave* by Evelyn Scott and then reread *Absalom, Absalom!* by Faulkner, so it is one of my three choices. *Rome Hanks* satisfies most of the criteria for greatness that I set forth in *Classics of Civil War Fiction* (1990).

> Many major American novels from *The Scarlet Letter* to the present are novels of meditation on events that illuminate American history, the American Dream, and the American character. The character relationship that embodies that meditative process is the hero-witness relationship. Rome Hanks and Lee's other kin, and Wagnal as well, are heroes who stimulate the meditations of Lee, the witness.

In "The Innocent Stare at the Civil War: Madison Jones's *Nashville 1864: The Dying of the Light*," I wrestle with ambiguities that may border on an apologia for the old plantation way of life. After brief examination of all Jones's fiction, I conclude that he was not an apologist, far from it. His novel was the first winner of the Michael Schaara Award, under the auspices of the United States Civil War Center. I was not one of the judges. Reading it, I was dismayed by the seeming pro-Confederate tone of the elderly narrator, unrelieved by any implication from the author that he, also elderly, disagreed.

> Paradoxically, it is the innocent stare of the very young that sometimes provides a more meaningful view of the antebellum, war, and Reconstruction eras as compared with adults who seem compelled to heap facts, out of a misdirected sense of obligation to authenticity, upon the heads of readers, diluting the impact of direct experience. The adult Steven brings to that past experience no fresh perspectives and derives from the act of memory and memoir writing no significant insights about either his personal experience or the national tragedy. To the extent that the art of fiction fails, all else in a novel fails.

Having reviewed Jones's fiction, most of it overtly antiracist, as context, I take an approach in this essay that is purely in terms of the art of fiction, calling into question my original impression but concluding that the novel was too ambiguous artistically, and thus thematically, to make a judgment. For me, it remains a tangled web.

"O. Henry's Civil War Surprises" argues that O. Henry is primarily a Southern storyteller and that aspects of the Civil War and Reconstruction are often his subjects. He "relished listening to people talk and assumed his readers would too. His powerful, authoritative voice as all-knowing narrator—the engagingly self-conscious voice of a creator of settings, characters, and dramatic events, always with humorous overtones—evolved out of his youthful participation as listener and teller in the Southern tale-telling tradition."

"The Last American Epic: The Civil War Novels of Father and Son, Michael and Jeff Shaara" is a study of a literary phenomenon of huge proportions. Taken together, the Civil War novels of Michael Schaara, *The Killer Angels* (1974), and his son Jeff, *Gods and Generals* (1996) and *The Last Full Measure* (1998), provide unusual examples of Civil War fiction. They constitute a unique epic in scope, and no single novel quite rivals that epic, although Mary Johnston's two novels *The Long Roll* (1911) and *Cease Firing* (1912) and Scott's *The Wave* (1929) come close—Johnson's in scope, Scott's artistically. Artistically, the son is, I argue, the better novelist.

> The use of the term "epic" to characterize the events and the poems, novels, and movies of the Civil War is, for Americans caught up in history, unusually apt. The importance of the accurate use of the term for the historic event

> and as a genuine honorific for novels and movies that deal with the war on a grand scale is that when we feel we are experiencing the magnificent exploits of heroes on a high level, our response to such works is magnified and elevated, and our sense of the war as being relevant to our lives today is deeper.

In "The Simultaneous Burning of Nine Bridges in East Tennessee," I offer an example of the novelist as historian. This is a scholarly, peer-reviewed essay about an actual event. Carefully planned with General William Sherman, President Abraham Lincoln, and Reverend William Blount Carter of East Tennessee, the effort to burn simultaneously nine bridges from Stevenson, Alabama, up the valley of East Tennessee to Abington, Virginia, by nine Unionist guerrilla bands was the most complicated coordinated guerrilla action of the war.

> While the execution of Andrews's raid was indisputably a failure (as had been an earlier raid led by him), Reverend Carter's venture at least produced five burned bridges, with fewer losses. Andrews and seven of his raiders were executed, and fourteen went to prison. None of Carter's raiders was killed in action, and only a few were wounded; five were hanged for burning one bridge, and only four other men went to prison. As a thrilling exploit that captured and has continued to hold the public imagination, the "Great Locomotive Chase" deserves its reputation, but for their own unique venture, Reverend Carter and his raiders deserve more recognition than they have received thus far.

To compare my fictional version of this tangled event with the scholarly version, see the first chapter of *Sharpshooter* (pages 3–22). I wrote the two versions somewhat simultaneously.

Asked to give a performance reading of the poems of Walt Whitman, Carl Sandburg, and Vachel Lindsay at a luncheon, on the occasion of the 133rd commemoration of Lincoln's Gettysburg address, I heard a nocturnal voice implore me to enable Lincoln to give a second address, in November 1996, in which he takes issue with the way historians and others have dealt with the war, talks about our failings in remembering and writing about the war and Reconstruction, and describes what Americans need yet to do. To the dismay of many historians, I performed the Lincoln piece, following Justice Sandra Day O'Connor's controversial speech on Lincoln's suspension of habeas corpus at the supposed site of the address. This piece is provided here in part III titled "Lincoln's Second Gettysburg Address."

> Americans have failed to make the nature of this war and its lessons part of their everyday lives as they deal with America's problems. Let your vision henceforth be not to celebrate the war as an interesting time in history but to meditate on the war as a prelude to action. Let us come to the realization at long last—six score and thirteen years later—that the task, long neglected

> through imperfect understanding, which must now be taken up, is to look at the war through fresh perspectives, through every conceivable perspective. Implore nurses, lawyers, physicians, journalists, dentists, teachers, merchants, laborers of every type, scientists of every type, engineers, geographers, secretaries, politicians, architects, teamsters, and even optometrists to look at the war from their points of view and meditate on, talk about, and publish their visions.

(This is an example of "performance criticism," an innovative form I began developing at Gettysburg earlier that year in May. I performed a lecture on Thomas Wolfe's Civil War, and a Wolfe scholar said to me, "David, I've never heard anyone *perform* a lecture." Ever since then I have called most of my lectures or performance pieces "performance criticism.")

"The Sinking of the *Sultana*: A Meditation on Loss and Forgetfulness" is a revised version of my introduction to the facsimile reprint of a nineteenth-century book of reminiscences by survivors of the sinking of the *Sultana*, America's worst maritime disaster, on a night when Lincoln's funeral train was crossing the northern United States. It occurred on the Mississippi River about seven miles above Memphis at 2:00 a.m. on April 27, 1865, when the steamboat *Sultana*, carrying 2,222 known passengers and crew, exploded and sank. Over 1,500 recently paroled Union prisoners of war were killed by the explosion or drowning; many of the one hundred civilian men, women, and children perished. About two hundred of the 586 who were saved died later of exposure or injuries in hospitals. The combined death toll was over 1,700.

> Readers may strive to imagine the vast, complicated canvas of folly and agony, and then perhaps to ponder the web of implications and absorb into their own consciousnesses the testimony of the survivors. Hopes for a national day of mourning being delusional, even during April, which is Civil War History Month, perhaps national recognition at least may come sometime during the final year of the Civil War sesquicentennial meditation, 2015.

Although I think of my novel *Sharpshooter* as a dramatic meditation (a drama of consciousness), the protagonist, Willis Carr, experiences the sinking of the *Sultana* but does not meditate at length upon that particular event. (Only one copy of the original book about the *Sultana* was for sale online when I recommended that it be reprinted.)

MEDITATIONS ON THE CIVIL WAR AND RECONSTRUCTION BY WILLIS CARR, SHARPSHOOTER

Revised versions of parts of the fictional pieces, except for the last one on Lincoln, were included in the 160-page published version of my novel *Sharp-*

shooter: A Novel of the Civil War (1996), which was two thousand pages in an early stage. All were published separately in literary magazines from 1985 to 2004. Writing vastly different versions over a ten-year period, I wove a tangled web of aspects of the Civil War and Reconstruction. These six fictional pieces show how my fiction spawned the nonfiction perspectives of the essays reprinted here in part I, as well as many others not included.

"Willis Carr, Sharpshooter, at Bleak House, Knoxville" (a performance version) is a transcription of an early, oral version of *Sharpshooter* that I delivered on impulse, as if I were Willis Carr at eighty, in 1984, before a huge audience in my hometown, Knoxville, Tennessee. The radio station at my alma mater University of Tennessee sent me a tape recording, the second half of which had accidentally been recorded over. Remembering the rest, I completed that narrative summary of the novel on the typewriter. What I made up in an hour took me ten years to complete as a novel. This oral version touches upon many aspects of the pieces that follow and of the novel.

In "Willis Carr Meditates on the Act of Sketching: Hair Trigger Pencil Lines," I focus on Willis's talent as an amateur sketch artist as opposed to his talent as a sharpshooter. Having told his story to a live audience of strangers, Willis Carr feels compelled about a year later to tell his story again, to himself, on paper, as a kind of detailed meditation, in the monk-like solitude of his mountain cabin. This version differs from passages included in the published novel. An amateur sketch artist—of moderate talent—Willis Carr meditates upon the nature of sketching as an art and its ways of depicting the war. Along the way, he compares sketching with photography.

Willis explores myriad facets of the war over a long life. The next piece is "Willis Carr, Sharpshooter, Meditates on Photographs." The photograph that haunts Willis most intensely is the famous one of the rebel sharpshooter in Devil's Den at Gettysburg. He first sees this image as a drawing in a newspaper and imagines it as a photograph even before he sees it; meanwhile, he discovers it is a fake but very real in its effect upon viewers. He ponders the relationship between photographer and subject, photograph and viewer.

The innovative, hybrid techniques of "A Fever of Dying: Henrietta Ramsey Lenoir and General William Price Sanders" employ some passages from Dr. James G. M. Ramsey's fascinating autobiography about his daughter Henrietta and General Sanders's reports on military action and on camping at her house in Lenoir, Tennessee, from the *War of the Rebellion: Official Records of the Union and Confederate Armies* (1886). My imagined private, lyrical interaction between Sanders and Henrietta contrast with his stilted report. Willis Carr removes himself almost totally as he meshes imagination—the Henrietta-Sanders relationship—with his (implied) access to the original manuscript of Dr. Ramsey's autobiography (1872) and with the factual record—Sanders's official reports. He is moving toward some degree of human omniscience. (Although Willis says he never read Ramsey's book but only imagines how

Ramsey would have written it, I have drawn upon actual passages, published in 1954. It went out of print at one time, and in 1974 or so, I urged the East Tennessee Historical Society to reprint it.)

"The Incendiary at the Forks of the River" is a short piece about a Union soldier sent by Reconstruction governor of Tennessee Parson Brownlow to burn his archenemy's home place, Dr. Ramsey's estate. Historically, factually, the event happened, but Willis Carr deliberately imagines it as an omniscient narrator.

"Fragments Found on the Field: Parson Brownlow and Dr. James Gettys Ramsey" is Willis Carr's complex philosophical character study of two Knoxville historical personages: Brownlow, a Unionist, who favored slavery and who was nationally famous, and Ramsey, a Confederate well known in Tennessee and in North and South Carolina, whom Brownlow opposed in every way. This story and the preceding three stories were not included in the short published novel. This story recapitulates some of the subjects and themes of the previous fictional pieces and introduces others. By not taking sides with either of the representative men, Union and Confederate, Willis Carr achieves a kind of omniscience. Convinced he has missed the war, Willis may, by now, cause the reader to conclude that he uniquely did not miss it.

For a list of my other Civil War pieces, see http://www.davidmadden.net/ and the journal *Civil War Book Review*.

I

"THE VIBRATION RIPPLES TO THE REMOTEST PERIMETER"

For the New Millennium, New Perspectives on the Civil War and Reconstruction (as of 1997)

Pursuing research for my tenth novel, *Sharpshooter: A Novel of the Civil War*, I gathered around me, over many years, more than 1,500 books, and from those books I gathered thousands of facts about every facet of the Civil War. The first draft was over two thousand pages long; the published book is less than 160 pages short. During the fifteen years between the first long draft and the final short draft, the mere accumulation of facts proved less and less meaningful; but the selection of facts and the placement of facts in contexts that ignite the reader's emotions, imagination, and intellect produced a novel that looks at the war in many unusual ways.

Only thirteen when he took up his rifle, the hero of *Sharpshooter*, at the age of ninety, is still trying to focus the war in his sights. "Why," he wonders repeatedly, "since I was in every battle, East and West, with General Longstreet, do I feel that I missed the war?" The veteran sharpshooter and I had the same mission: to target the facts. But the more facts we got on target the more we felt—he as a participant looking back and I as a space-age American citizen bemused, beguiled, and bewitched by the facts—that we missed the war.

Sharpshooter's theme is that all the participants, soldiers and civilians, missed the war as it happened and in memory. The vision out of which I created and developed the United States Civil War Center derives from the same conviction. Thus, my research for a novel inspired the creation of an institution. Today, individually and collectively, no matter how many books we read or write, we miss the war to the extent that we fail to place the facts we know in the richest possible contexts and to illuminate them by personal emotional involvement, imaginative conceptualization, and complex intellectual implication. Possession of the facts and the artifacts alone is not enough.

And it is not only the dull recital of facts that makes history dry and remote for many American children and adults; it is also dull imagination.

THE ROLE OF THE CIVIL WAR CENTER

The United States Civil War Center's mission was to facilitate the study of the war from the perspective of every conceivable academic discipline, profession, and occupation. I myself am not an academic historian; I am a novelist and a teacher of literature and creative writing in all genres. The center strived to help all American citizens, young and old, North and South, avoid missing the war by urging them to imagine fresh perspectives that would enable them to make the war that most profoundly shaped the American character an integral part of their own individual identities.

The Civil War Center took leadership in this new approach. In the spring of 1996, the U.S. Congress passed and the president signed a resolution designating the United States Civil War Center and its partner, the Gettysburg College Civil War Institute, as the institutions charged with planning and facilitating the sesquicentennial. The long-range implementation of our interdisciplinary mission will materialize in publications, conferences, and exhibits each year up to and through the sesquicentennial in the years 2011–2015. It will be the last opportunity for most adult Americans living today to reflect upon the war and its legacy together.

The events of each decade in American history provide a fresh perspective on the Civil War. Professional historians, amateur historians, and ordinary citizens revisit, rediscover, and redefine this central event of the American experience. Thus, we reflect on the past, experience the present, and enlighten the future by the fitful light of shifting interpretations. The decade of the civil rights movement was a perfect time for a centennial reassessment of the Civil War. In the 1980s, several books, the movie *Glory*, and Ken Burns's PBS documentary *The Civil War* gave us a sharp sense of the role of African Americans and of women in the war.

I am mindful of the fact that to study the Civil War is also to study the antebellum through the reconstruction years as one unbroken series of events. By understanding the war and reconstruction, we can understand ourselves in the world today, both our dark problems and our bright prospects. We Americans have missed the war by focusing too much and too long on battles and leaders. That focus distracts us from our deeper purpose: to trace back to the war itself and to the antebellum era the origins of the forces at work in our culture today. Among the dark problems today, racism, violence, economic instability, and distrust of government daily stare us in the face. The promising benefits to society of the many technological inventions, medical discoveries, industrial techniques, and business methods that evolved out of the war have been only partially fulfilled or have been postponed, partly because the problems put a drag on the pace of progress.

Context is everything. By context, I mean webs of causes and webs of consequences. What if all this nation's historians were to devote a full year to tracking down every fact about the siege of Vicksburg? What would they have accomplished, if that mass of interesting facts did not illuminate our understanding of webs of causes and webs of consequences? Facts alone fail us. Imagination alone fails us. Emotion alone fails us. But emotion, imagination, and intellect acting together make the facts stand up and speak.

The purpose of making data more accessible is to provide the means for research; the ultimate goal of research is to provide the means for understanding and interpretation, for achieving a personal and a public vision, and for seeing how our nation today evolved out of that most crucial event in our history so that we can resolve our problems and realize our prospects more forcefully. The kind of interpretation that seems to us most promising is that which is derived from looking at the war not only through the eyes of the historian but also from the perspectives of all academic disciplines, professions, and occupations, an approach that involves people from all walks of life. The effect is that Americans will gain a more multifaceted view of the war than if they relied solely upon the interpretations of professional historians.

The major tool of the United States Civil War Center's interdisciplinary educational effort was its home page on the Internet, which in its first two years received more than six million visitors. Over fifteen thousand people from all over the world—from Japan to Israel, Germany, and Sweden—from corporations to the military, and from historians to school children "virtually" visited the Civil War Center each day. We linked our visitors to almost three thousand other Civil War organizations. Sixteen organizations gave us their highest rating as a research site. Computer science, as one of the newest disciplines, enabled us to see every facet of the war with great speed and precision.

Throughout history, worldwide, the turning of a century has been taken as an opportunity for reassessment, reaffirmation, and resolution. The year 2000 is only the second opportunity since the birth of Christ for the world to mark the beginning of another thousand years with a heightened consciousness of the lessons of the past and their application in the future. That happened in the year 1000, when the Western world began to loosen the grip of the Dark Ages. If we the living fail to learn and act, the deaths of over half a million soldiers and civilians (about thirty thousand) in the Civil War will have been in vain.

Americans will step over the creaky threshold into the new millennium with the legacy of the Civil War still very much alive in the national consciousness but with major differences from earlier landmark years. In 1900, Americans were far less interested in the history and legacy of the war than they are now. During the four-year centennial commemoration of the early 1960s, academic historians controlled the public's perception of the causes, course, and consequences of the war. While reconciliation between North and South and conciliation among whites and African Americans have not yet been completely achieved, a new and fervent national interest in the war and a new consciousness about it has been developing over the past thirty years or so.

Americans in all walks of life, aware now more than ever before of ways the war has shaped their identity, are looking at it from new and more numerous perspectives. The next major step will be to apply those perspectives to an understanding of how the American Dream and the American nightmare evolved out of the war and how that understanding will enhance the ability of citizens to wake up from the nightmare and turn the dream into reality.

A major question is, What have we learned from our study of the Civil War over the past 130 years that will guide our conduct in the new century and over the next thousand years? Until about 1985, whatever we learned, academic historians were our teachers. In the ways that it is in the nature of historians to pursue, they acquitted themselves very well of their responsibilities. Americans are in their debt. But experts in other disciplines and citizens in other professions and occupations have arrived upon the field, standing shoulder to shoulder with historians. While the ranks of Civil War roundtables and of reenactors have swelled dramatically, devotedly preoccupied with battles and leaders and authentic details, others (e.g., archaeologists) have knelt to the dirt at dawn to dig and have walked away at dusk with the Civil War under their fingernails and artifacts that speak volumes in their hands.

The question *What have we learned?* becomes more pressing and somehow more poignant on the occasion of the sesquicentennial. Will we look back on it as a simple four-year flag-waving celebration, or as a complex meditation with active consequences? One answer is that we have begun to learn that many new perspectives have not yet been brought to bear. Many people in academic disciplines, professions, and occupations have not yet realized that their unique contributions will be to write about the war from their own special perspectives.

"Do *you* have an interest in the Civil War?" I asked my optometrist recently, just after he had declared my vision good. He was, he said, reading the second volume of Shelby Foote's massive history. "Do you ever relate what you read to your own profession?" He answered no. But I saw something dawn on his face. So we talked a long time about the possible effects of faulty vision upon the conduct of the war. Even while reading Foote's narrative, my optometrist had missed the war; now he sees the possibilities.

I ask the same question at every opportunity, and I received similar answers when I asked my insurance agent, my accountant, and my physician. Lawyers have a long and distinguished record of publishing books on battles and leaders, but ironically no book by a lawyer that offers a legal interrogation of the issues and ramifications of the war is in print. Engineers are among the ranks of nonacademic historians who become so entranced with a battle or a leader that they write books, yet no study of the astonishingly crucial role of various kinds of engineers in the war has been published.

As we look back over the four years of the sesquicentennial, will the books reveal a reliance upon familiar approaches and subjects? The discovery of a few facts more than previous writers had at their disposal or a clever angle is too often the historian's justification for writing a new book on a battle or a general, employing a generic narrative strategy ("meanwhile . . .") and style ("storm clouds were gathering"). Knowledgeable readers, however, are already demanding and getting more: an imaginative conception, a distinctive style, and a fresh method. A sampling also reveals that a trend is already under way toward dealing with new subjects and taking, occasionally, new approaches.

Daniel Sutherland's *Seasons of War: The Ordeal of a Confederate Community, 1861–1865* (1995) is a breakthrough study that should influence the way that Civil War books are written from this day forward. In his lively and vivid style, made dramatic by his audacious decision to use the present tense, he places Culpeper, Virginia, on the forestage of history, breathing life into a community's past. Culpeper becomes an active and lingering presence in the reader's mind. Sutherland raises and answers such questions as, What was the class structure of the Culpeper community, and what feuds or other conflicts erupted? What changes did war force upon politics, education, journalism, religion, health care, and the food supply? What effects did the war have upon the farmers, free blacks and freed slaves, merchants, and manufacturers who struggled to keep the community's economy functioning? How did the people of Culpeper behave during federal occupation? How prevalent were lawlessness, guerrilla activity, and fraternization? Sutherland is uncannily adept at placing readers in the midst of it all and activating all of their senses, intertwining the social and the military life to create a prism through which readers can feel, know, and imagine the many facets of the decisive moment in their history.

Sorely missing from the Civil War bookshelf until recently were books on Confederate exiles in South America, on medicine and surgery, on the economics of individual Southern states, on the role of Native Americans and black regiments, and on the role of the Irish, Jews, and other European immigrants, North and South. Several books now provide unusual approaches to the question of why men on both sides fought and how they reacted to battle. Comparative histories show parallels between antebellum Southern planters and European quasi-feudal lords and delineate the European inheritance of the legacy of the Civil War. Serious studies, as opposed to the dominance of sensational potboilers, of military intelligence during the war have appeared. Diaries of women who played various roles—from domestic witnesses to spies, nurses, and soldiers in disguise—are being published with increasing frequency. A few books provide us with an understanding of how Christian rhetoric and symbols were absorbed by the rhetoric and icons of the tradition of the Lost Cause and transmitted to the present day through public education in the South and in popular culture. The United States Civil War Center discovered that many publishers of books for children about the war are more innovative and venturesome than publishers of adult books and encouraged one publisher to plan a series of books for young readers that looks at facets of the war from the geologist's and the geographer's perspective.

The term "historian" should be used in the broadest and most just sense, in reference not only to academic historians but also to men and women who write about historical events after long hours of daily work at a profession or an occupation, passionately pursuing their interest in Civil War history "on the side." But most of them do not yet bring to those interests the perspectives of their own professional or occupational expertise.

Even so, the achievements of some nonacademic historians have added impressive works to the endless Civil War bookshelf. Peter Svenson, an artist, missed the war until he bought a farm and struggled to restore it and work it, and discovered it was a battlefield. Walking the battlefield in his backyard, delving into mysteries of the human spirit, he shows us how to mesh our private lives with our country's public history.

Jerry Ellis, a young man who refuses to miss the war, recounts his adventures, in the twentieth century's final decade, as he follows the route of General William Sherman's fiery march through Georgia.

Arlene Reynolds, an actress, discovered the manuscript of Mrs. Custer's memoir of the war years, and the Civil War Center secured its publication.

Gene Salecker, a campus policeman at Northwestern University and an independent scholar, recounts the sinking of the *Sultana*, the worst marine disaster in the history of this nation: more than 1,500 Union soldiers recently released from Confederate prisons drowned.

The possibilities of interdisciplinary studies have remained unenumerated, perhaps to avoid the charge of improbability or outright absurdity. For instance, imagine the announcement of an all-day, three-day conference on the Civil War that consists of talks by experts in twenty-eight distinctly different disciplines. Even those few who profess the conviction that the more perspectives one brings to a subject, the more invigorating the discourse, might be doubtful, skeptical, and even disinclined to attend, on the assumption that the whole enterprise would be foredoomed to crash in a traffic jam of ideas. To explore the possibilities for interdisciplinary studies, the Civil War Center held such a conference Thanksgiving week in 1996 at Louisiana State University. For participants and the audience, made up of students, teachers, and townspeople, it was a provocative success. It provided a yes answer to the questions, Is a broadly interdisciplinary approach to the Civil War viable, and will it provide Americans with a means of understanding the war's legacy in all its complexities?

Never before had the concept of interdisciplinary studies been applied so broadly to a single, though multifaceted, subject; never before, certainly, had the Civil War been scrutinized by so many disciplines and professions at one time. Not only did we understand the war more fully, but also we understood each discipline more clearly as it was applied to a subject not normally within its domain. And we arrived at a more complex understanding of the dynamics and far-flung possibilities of interdisciplinary study itself.

Having tested our mission in this conference, we planned to test it further, calling on experts from all over the nation to convene in a major city within the next few years. We would publish papers delivered there in the first issue of our annual hardcover publication, *Civil War Perspectives*. Although that plan was not pursued after I resigned two years later to finish my Civil War novel, I refer to it now to illustrate how one concept may propagate others.

In the general public's experience, it is not the historian who dominates the manifold subject of the Civil War but the novelist and the moviemaker. Most historians have a limited audience. James McPherson may be an exception, but in the popular imagination, Shelby Foote, novelist-turned-historian in the 1950s, was our greatest living historian. In the realm of popular culture, of mass communication, the study of the war has always been multidisciplinary if not interdisciplinary. More recently, it has also been multicultural and has thus with some justification come under fire as being politically correct (a particularly complex subject). The spectrum of interest now is educationally, politically, and culturally quite wide, varied, and extremely complicated, rendering simplicity a little overrated perhaps.

For over forty years, we have heard that the interdisciplinary approach to subjects and problems is the wave of the future and that this educational method will compete with specialization. We need both; each reinvigorates the other. The melancholy fact is that while the potential is great and the prospects are very good, the interdisciplinary approach has been conservatively advocated and practiced. The norm is that two related disciplines work together on a given subject or theme. Beyond the classroom, conferences on selected topics seldom bring together experts from more than three disciplines. Why? Logistics? Logistical difficulties may be overcome by determination.

The Civil War Center fired the first shots in a revolution that supplements the basic narrow focus with a very broad range of perspectives that will expand and deepen our nation's varied interest in its Civil War. Having sampled the usual and the slightly unusual Civil War offerings to the American consciousness published in these late years of the twentieth century, let us consider how we might begin to explore relatively new possibilities for books in the twenty-first century. I can expect each reader of this book to recognize his or her own profession in the following list. To illustrate more concretely the possibilities of the interdisciplinary approach, here are a few questions, limited by my own knowledge of these many areas of expertise, that suggest fresh perspectives. Questions for which the Civil War Center as of 1997 had books, conferences, and exhibits planned or under way are marked with an asterisk:

- What were the psychological effects* of the war and Reconstruction upon children?
- What forces in the war were set loose in the realm of commerce and business administration?
- Does some Civil War painting and photography* transcend documentary value to become art?
- How did weather determine the day-by-day conduct of the war?
- How did the war affect the development of American journalism*?
- What was the effect of the war upon the development of the organized labor movement?
- In what ways have Civil War folklore and popular culture acted as a force in society, North and South, then and now?
- What was the war's impact upon the development of public and private education?
- How did sports* affect the mental and physical health of troops during the war?
- How did the Civil War affect the development of railroads in later decades?
- How might linguists show relationships between words and actions?
- How might the zoologist's perspective modify our knowledge of the role of animals in the war?
- In what ways were rivers important in the war?
- How is the influence of religious rhetoric and political oratory seen in diaries and letters of soldiers and civilians, North and South?
- Given the impact of statistics at the end of the war on our sense of its scope, how might today's much more complex and sophisticated statistical tools modify our view of the war?

- Over the past 130 years, how have books written for children* shaped their attitudes about the war's cause and its legacy?
- How did music soothe the savage breast of war or ignite the fire within?
- Was Southern agronomy the undoing of the Confederacy?
- Which special circumstances spurred developments in technology?
- What were some significant and decisive applications of mathematics in the war?
- How is the Civil War still relevant to military science?
- What transient ecosystems did the war create?
- How have fiction, poetry, theater, and film* shaped our vision of the war?
- How did the war stimulate developments in the science of chemistry?
- What was the effect of poor nutrition upon military performance?
- How did the common study of classical languages* affect the thinking of generals on both sides?
- How may the American Civil War provide a model for constructing a philosophy and psychology* of the phenomenon of civil wars worldwide throughout history?

From the Civil War Center's relationships with writers of all kinds and with over thirty publishers, many books were published and were in the works in a period of less than ten years. As part of its active participation in the education of the young, the center worked with publishers to create revolutionary interdisciplinary Civil War textbooks for courses on all levels.

The most effective way to study the war, to understand it and its legacy of good and ill in all its complexities, is to draw each individual, young and old, male and female, and of every ethnic origin, into the discourse in a multiplicity of forums. And one way to do that is to appeal to each person to bring the principles of his or her vocation to bear upon corresponding facets of the war.

While contributing to a multifaceted, myriad-minded approach to a complex subject, one gains a clearer and often rejuvenating perception of one's own discipline. For instance, at my suggestion, a psychologist created a profile of Robert E. Lee's life and personality to present to a routine conference of a state association of psychologists. Everyone, obviously stimulated to a degree that seemed to surprise themselves, joined in the discussion afterward. "This was the most invigorating interaction we have had with each other *ever*," declared the president. "It reminds us of what we got into the profession to do." I had a similar experience giving a talk on the role of engineers in the war at a convention of engineers. Looking at the Civil War from the perspective of your own profession will pitch you into another dimension of emotion, imagination, and intellect.

The Civil War is the ideal subject for such an extreme experiment with interdisciplinary studies as I am proposing and predicting here. Because every aspect of human experience in America was brought into play in that ordeal and because the consequences have affected every aspect since, to study the war is to study everything else; it is well suited to the formulation of strategies, principles, and techniques and to test the efficacy and reveal the possibilities and benefits of interdisciplinary studies itself.

The premise behind interdisciplinary studies is that just as no person is an island, no subject exists in isolation from all others, that a complex examination of a subject is rewarding, that several disciplines provide the milieu for that complexity, and that each discipline is enriched and made more powerful by interaction with other disciplines. The conscious effort to train and practice this process to achieve a multifaceted perspective on human experience can only yield positive results that even I in my overreaching enthusiasm and eagerness cannot yet conceive. What is learned from the United States Civil War Center's pursuit of its interdisciplinary mission may deepen our understanding of the nature, value, and dynamics of the realm of interdisciplinary studies itself.

Participation in interdisciplinary studies may be for some people an occasional exhilarating and rejuvenating excursion, while others may find a permanent home in interdisciplinary studies itself—a universe of possibilities. People have already embraced this approach with relief and even with fervor, in and outside of university settings. It is, of course, people young and old who come to it fresh, with no history of narrow focus, are most likely to follow where interdisciplinary studies may lead. The effect on education and, with the full participation of people in all professions and occupations, on society and ultimately on human consciousness can have revolutionary benefits that are yet to be enumerated.

(*Note:* With as much sweet reasonableness of which my nature is capable, I will one day write an account of "The Rise and Fall of the United States Civil War Center," the creation of which is one of the most important acts in my life and LSU's incremental dismantling of which is one of the saddest events in my life.)

Fletcher Pratt's *A Short History of the Civil War: Ordeal by Fire*

PREFACE TO THE DOVER EDITION

Although the evolution of the Great Depression may be traced back to the Civil War and the Reconstruction era, especially in the South, the thirties was not a great decade for nonfiction about the Civil War, while fiction did flourish in that decade. Even so, Fletcher Pratt's *Short History of the Civil War*, published as *Ordeal by Fire* in 1935, reached the kind of audience that one year later embraced *Gone With the Wind*, the twentieth century's best-selling Civil War novel. When a revised second edition of Pratt's book was published in 1948, the great era of Civil War book publishing that began with the onset of the centennial years had not yet begun. For almost three decades, then, Pratt's short history stood as this nation's most appealing introduction to what happened at what Shelby Foote called "the crossroads of our being."

Part of Pratt's appeal was that he rejected the pretensions of more scholarly writers. His original subtitle for the book was "An Informal History of the Civil War." The first edition's "Preface for the Nonmilitary Reader," a lucid explanation of military organization, put all other readers on notice that anyone looking for a footnote would, to mangle Mark Twain, be shot. Pratt's forceful prose style was forged in journalism and general nonfiction projects, always aimed at "the man in the street." Readers find in his book no academic apparatus, not even a bibliography. The narrative drive and the muscular style carry the reader along at a rapid pace through relevant facts and trenchant insights.

The absence of traditional academic trappings in *A Short History of the Civil War* is more than made up for by the author's enthusiasm for his subject, an enthusiasm he brought to all his projects. In only two decades Pratt, who called himself a "literary mechanic," published over fifty books on an impressive variety of subjects, from the Napoleonic wars to Japanese card games.

Naval history was his forte. His first book, *The Heroic Years*, a history of the Madison administration and the war of 1812, opened his great campaign of providing the American public with popular military histories. *Hail Caesar!* demonstrated his ability to write convincingly of military events in other times, other places. During the forties his books explained World War II to the American people; in the fifties he wrote several more Civil War books: *The Monitor and the Merrimack* (1952); *Stanton, Lincoln's Secretary of War* (1953); *The Civil War in Pictures* (1955), one of the first modern picture books about the war of which we now see a multitude; and *Civil War on Western Waters* (1956, the year of his death). He left a finished manuscript that was published in 1957, another attempt to give the average reader a sweeping, dramatic view of a vast subject in a short reading experience: *The Compact History of the United States Navy*. To the end, he maintained a style, stance, and follow-through technique that suggested his early days as a prizefighter.

Fletcher Pratt was born in Buffalo, New York, on April 25, 1897. He died at Long Branch, New Jersey, on June 10, 1956. In the years between, he was a college dropout who managed to become a public and a corporate librarian, a reporter, and a freelance writer for true-crime magazines and for various trade, naval, and military journals. In 1926, he married the artist Inga Stephens. In the late twenties he began writing fiction, helping to pioneer the science-fiction genre (*Double Jeopardy*, to name only one). He also translated many books into French and German.

Bearded, spouting pipe smoke, for almost twenty years the "Dean of Nonfiction" was a star attraction, along with Robert Frost, Bernard DeVoto, and Wallace Stegner, as a lecturer at Middlebury College's Bread Loaf Writers' Conference, where he was prone during the early forties to discuss the war then raging. (One of his students was Isaac Asimov, science and science-fiction writer, who was to write over four hundred books.) Pratt made time to become eccentric, collecting and raising monkeys. DeVoto spoke of him affectionately as "half genius, half rodent."

Considering the impressive academic credentials and affiliations of the vast army of Civil War historians who thrived before, during, and after his time, the question arises whether one should include Pratt as a member of that tribe. The Civil War was only one of his subjects. Although he was a war correspondent and an advisor on military affairs during World War II for *Time*, *Fortune*, and the *New York Post*, his contribution to Civil War studies had best be put into perspective. "Popularizer" is a somewhat odious term, until one looks closely at its implications. Historians and archivists attribute the recent upsurge of interest in the Civil War (not all of it, by any means, superficial) to the popularity of Ken Burns's controversial documentary of 1990, and especially to the segments that feature Shelby Foote, the author first of a

Civil War novel, *Shiloh*, and then of the ultimate popular history of the war, a three-volume work that is massive when compared with Pratt's 410 pages. The academic and the popular historian each has a place and function, and in each camp the quality and impact varies; I place Pratt at the top of the list of popular historians working in the shorter form. Responding to the appeal of the Civil War, many readers begin with something short; armed, they then step off to march the longer distance.

Pratt's was the first history of the war I ever read. On a plane to Omaha, Nebraska, February 27, 1979, I opened a paperback version and plunged into thirteen years of research on the Civil War for my novel *Sharpshooter*, research that also inspired the concept of the United States Civil War Center. Pratt's book remains one of the most stirring histories I have read. Not a single page of static prose impedes the pace. And reading his short history, I experienced a sense of Pratt's having read *many* histories of the war.

At first I thought that Pratt was very pro-North. On rereading, I experienced an evenhandedness. It occurred to me that when we read certain books for the first time, we are reading two simultaneously: the one we expect and the one the author wrote.

Perhaps I diminished whatever powers of persuasion I may have when I revealed that Pratt's was the first history of the Civil War I ever read. I was indeed impressionable. But since then I have read many histories and many topical books on the war; *A Short History* holds its own against them, and I certainly now have a basis for comparison. But what exactly am I comparing? Research ability, thorough documentation? No, Pratt calls his "An Informal History of the Civil War." What struck me, and perhaps DeVoto as well as Pratt's publishers Harrison Smith and William Sloane, was the man's conceptual power, his lunging style, his pugnacious sensibility. Those are all qualities that DeVoto, Sloane, Frost, Theodore Morrison, and other writers, editors, fellows, and students at the Bread Loaf Writers' Conference saw in action over two decades. "Command of word and language, mastery of a proper rhetoric or style. My impression," wrote Theodore Morrison in his history of the first thirty years of Bread Loaf, "is that Fletcher talked more about this topic than any other staff member." For reasons other than my own, then, Fletcher Pratt's colleagues, too, were impressionable.

But I offer an even more impressive authority, a young teacher from West Virginia who approached me twelve years ago, after I had given a lecture on hard-boiled novelist James M. Cain, to ask if I had read Fletcher Pratt's history of the Civil War. My affirmative nod set him off on a thirty-minute ramble through the book as he recited, in fine voice, his favorite passages, introducing each with the command "Listen to this!" I did, with a racing pulse.

> [General John C.] Fremont was a character out of a Victorian novel—soulful eyes and waving hair, a universal genius who stunned his contemporaries by learning Hungarian and marrying the fairest heiress of the west, the daughter of that formidable old Roman, Thomas Hart Benton . . . [he] turned up in St. Louis at the end of July, bareheaded in Arsenal Square with a drawn sword in one hand and an American flag in the other—ineffably poetic, ineffably patriotic.

We, he and I, are not alone in our devout belief. "This," said DeVoto, "is the best one-volume history of the Civil War I've ever read." My words exactly. Had enough people believed that over the past seven decades, I wouldn't have to back up that declaration now. Harrison Smith and Robert Haas believed it when they published Pratt's history in 1935, with sixteen illustrations by Merritt Cutler. Readers who kept it alive by word of mouth and made it a collector's item when it fell out of print believed it. William Sloane believed it when he published the revised edition in 1948, with fifty new maps by Rafael Palacios. Forget that DeVoto and Sloane taught with Pratt at Bread Loaf Writers' Conference during the time he wrote the book. Pocket Books believed it when in 1951 they published a paperback edition of the Sloane version as *A Short History of the Civil War*, with four printings in four years. The editors at Harpers and Bantam believed it when they picked up paperback rights in 1966 and 1968. I will go further now as one who admires several other short histories and declare that this work is the most powerful of all short histories of the Civil War published since the Depression. It is the book I chose to present as a rediscovery in a book in preparation of essays about neglected nonfiction masterworks.

Pratt's style is the main indication that he was speaking to the public of the Depression years, imagining his readers to be the same as those he'd had as a reporter and popular-magazine writer of both short stories and articles. His style is slam-bang staccato—as if the James Cagney of *Public Enemy* had taken the reader by the arm and said, "Okay, this is how it's going to be—I talk, you listen—got it?" Pratt's style sounds less like that of Pulitzer Prize–winning historian Douglas Southall Freeman and more like the first-person voices of James M. Cain's Frank Chambers, Dashiell Hammett's Sam Spade, or Raymond Chandler's Philip Marlowe. It is interesting to note that Pratt's contemporary, the Civil War novelist MacKinlay Kantor, wrote one of the first gangster novels, *Diversy* (1928).

Pratt talks tough directly to his reader. He says, "Lesson—never kick a man when he's down," and then tells how some Union soldiers, who were refused food when passing through Jackson as prisoners, returned and burned the town down. Pay attention, he seems to say with such lines as "What happened was this:" and, "Understand the picture; it was in the darkest hour . . ."

He gets his reader's attention with such chapter openers as this: "You shall not imagine, either, that all is abounding grace and united effort within the Confederacy. . . . Not even Robert Lee is immune . . . proving, if you will, how war acts on the intelligence like the curved mirrors of a hall of grotesques." Another chapter opens this way: "What to make of Ulysses Grant, behind the black cigar . . . his pockets blistered with the letters he never answered?" He quotes criticisms of Grant, then responds: "Wrong! . . . Also write down this about him; he was never jealous or envious of any man." Sometimes he taunts the characters in his narrative in that hard-boiled tone: "Be content, General Bragg, it was a Confederate victory. . . . A victory—that cost the victors 23,000 in killed and wounded, the heaviest butcher's bill of the war." Pratt delighted in paradox.

One could follow the passages on Abraham Lincoln, Ulysses S. Grant, Robert E. Lee, or any other major figure throughout Pratt's book and accumulate a vivid and memorable portrait. Pratt's admiration of Edwin M. Stanton, Lincoln's secretary of war, about whom he later wrote a book, is especially clear:

> So Stanton, the terrible Stanton, the man of iron, who solved all problems by rule of mathematics and a violent tongue, became Secretary of War. He feared neither God nor man nor devil, only Abraham Lincoln. . . . But he was one of the great war ministers of history. . . . On the Confederate side they had only Judah P. Benjamin, who spun endless iridescent cobwebs of theory and argument, brilliant as rainbows.

Pratt gives his reader images charged with emotion: "That night Stuart's horse rode into the rebel camp [at Gettysburg], eager but so fagged after their longest raid that men fell asleep while their horses were crossing a fence." He paints group portraits in lightning strokes: "Beyond the river the young Turks gathered round General Lee—Ewell with his piping krawk [*sic*], jovial Early booming like a cannon behind a fog of beard, gay Stuart, the heart-breaker, all stars and grace, a song on his lips." When his men cheered Thomas's promotion, "the new general of the Army of the Cumberland pulled his hat down on his nose to hide his school-girl blushes."

All the devices of rhetoric are at Pratt's command. Repetition carries the reader quickly through long paragraphs of analysis to a full grasp of the concept: "Admit freely that Lincoln botched his part in the Peninsular campaign. Admit he twice withheld McDowell's 40,000 when they might have struck to a decision; admit he tried to trip Jackson with an elaborately silly map maneuver which ignored not only time, distance and arithmetic but also the psychological element. . . . The onus for the failure, nevertheless, must rest upon the young Napoleon [General George B. McClellan]."

His metaphors enable Pratt to give the reader the facts, make the narrative stroke, and convey a feeling about the action: "Sherman dangled at Atlanta, a trapeze performer perilously suspended over nothing at the end of a single wire of railroad. Cut the line, he must perish." And Pratt was a master of succinct phrasing: "The Confederate government had been and was not . . . "

Pratt's ability to sustain a narrative pace that keeps the reader engaged is a major factor in the success of this short history of the war: "Grant rode through the press, straightening out the sagging lines, directing artillery here, reorganizing a company there, the calmest man on the field. His horse was killed under him; he got another. A bullet took his hat off; he fought bareheaded; another went through his coat." His style enables him to present a major action with brevity but impact: "A tall officer rode among them, the soul of their stand; some rebel sharpshooter drew a bead on him, and down he went, shot through the head. It was Reynolds." That tall officer was an early major loss at Gettysburg.

The pace of the narrative is quickened by Pratt's effective transitions. Pratt ends the Vicksburg chapter this way: "Lincoln proclaimed exultantly, 'The Father of Waters once more flows unvexed to the sea.'" Following that famous quotation Pratt begins the next chapter with a simple line: "There was a man named Bickley." Another technique ends one chapter with a general narrative setup: "So Grant went down into Virginia. . . . [William Sherman] was set free at last" to take Atlanta; he begins the next chapter with a general statement: "What followed was the greatest campaign in American history, one of the greatest in any history." (Readers may enhance their appreciation of Pratt's narrative thrust by comparing his key battle scenes with those in other short histories, written before, during, and after his time.)

Pratt knew his readers would enjoy trenchant comparisons and contrast: "Lee's one defect as a leader was that there was something unearthly about the man's best moments. . . . Lincoln, on the other hand, would have delighted Machiavelli"; "the North obtained its monarchial singleness of control by combination; the South essayed to obtain it through personality, but it moved too slowly."

Pratt knew just when and how to deploy a brief anecdote: "Curious symbolic note—as Sherman rode through a plantation yard he saw a book lying in the mud and dismounted to rescue it. It was a copy of 'The Constitution of the United States' and on the flyleaf was written 'My Property—Jefferson Davis.'" Another example is, "The lament of Van Dorn." Catching his wife in bed with the general, a doctor blew Van Dorn's brains out, "which was too bad for the Confederacy as the brains had been better than most in the Confederate west." He was adroit in the use of quotations, as when he reports that Fremont remarked on the suggestion that Grant be promoted, "I am not sure General Grant has the requisite force of character."

Having carried the reader along at a rapid narrative pace in a hard-boiled style, tough-guy Pratt would sometimes do what he must have been told not to do—he judged conduct: "Burnside, the personality expert, raging alternately at the 'thieving poltroons' who composed his army and the 'cowardly scalawags' who led it, was proposing to ride up Marye's Heights alone with his staff. They should have let him. It was not till night that he began to weep." Lee sent supplies to his starving army by train, but the politicians "changed the destination of the train to Richmond, threw the food off and loaded it with their archives. Archives! Lee's men had nothing to eat." Pratt expressed unaffected scorn there and here: "Let Longstreet take his corps on a flying march to Knoxville and capture the force Burnside had there as well, how Napoleonic! Psychology is a wonderful thing, but the two Napoleons erred by the calendar."

In his introduction to this edition, Pratt quotes one of the major German military leaders of the years before World War I, who urged the study of the campaigns of the American Civil War; the German military most likely carried those studies on into World War II. Pratt recognized the importance of studying that history, realizing that "the tactics and even the strategies developed in those campaigns in America controlled all subsequent wars down to the beginning of the atomic age." He was the man to write short histories of both World Wars. It is our loss that he did not.

Pratt's remains the best short history of the Civil War for beginners, even though an academic may cite mistakes and omissions. The Dover edition enables Pratt to capture such readers; let more academic scholars lead Pratt's readers into deeper territory. For those who have read every book on every aspect of the war, Pratt's value is that he is a source of pure enjoyment as one listens to his commanding voice. Sit still and listen and let the words carry you along, Pratt's veteran reader will tell you.

Fine-sounding words alone can not empower a book as Pratt's history is empowered. Pratt had the kind of conceptual and intellectual imagination that I craved in those early days before I had gathered unto myself four thousand other books on the war. On a Trailways bus from Jacksonville to Tallahassee, I read this passage: "What Lee attacked at Glendale was an armed mob; what he attacked at Second Bull Run was a group of quarrelsome old men; at Chancellorsville, he attacked a man; but at Gettysburg he came into collision with a system." A simple action is stated in such a way as to present a concept of Grant: "The bankrupt tanner left the room military dictator of a territory larger than Europe."

Describing an action of Lee's, Pratt slides into a conception of Grant and Sherman in relation to that general. "General Lee smiled and turned to give orders for the march. An impecunious leather-dealer named Grant sat at that moment in a street-car in St. Louis, gazing vacantly as the procession from Lindell's Meadows led through the hooting streets. The car belonged to a company-headed by a retired army officer named Sherman." At one stage of the war, a phrase conceptualizes the entire South. "The South limped toward independence on one leg. How to convince the world of national greatness."

Having spoken briefly for Pratt, I will now step back so that you can listen to his own voice relate the Civil War briefly.

On James McPherson's *For Cause and Comrades: Why Men Fought in the Civil War*

James McPherson does not begin to answer the question why Civil War soldiers risked their lives over and over again.

Each day, with civil wars raging all around the globe, newspaper readers, television viewers, and Internet surfers ask rhetorically (with little expectation of an answer), What in this world are they all fighting for? Because civil wars from the beginning of recorded history have many characteristics in common, we may turn for some enlightenment to McPherson, who asks that question of the combatants on both sides of the American Civil War in *For Cause and Comrades: Why Men Fought in the Civil War.*

The subtitle asks a familiar question: Why did men fight in the American Civil War? The main title states the two most important reasons: a cause moved each of them to enlist, but cohesiveness among comrades sustained them to the end. Turning the pages of the diaries and letters of 647 Union and 429 Confederate soldiers, McPherson follows a simple method: he categorizes the reasons and inserts four quotations from letters or diaries for each category. About each soldier, he provides basic information: whether he fought for the Union or the Confederacy, and when and to whom he wrote. His comments on each set of quotations are sparse. Here's a typical entry, early in the first chapter:

> "I am sick of war," wrote a Confederate officer to his wife in 1863, and of "the separation from the dearest objects of life"—his family. But "were the contest again just commenced I would willingly undergo it again for the sake of . . . our country's independence and [our children's] liberty." At about the same time a Pennsylvania officer wrote to his wife that he had to fight it out to the end because, "sick as I am of this war and bloodshed [and] as much oh how much I want to be home with my dear wife and children . . . every day I have a more religious feeling, that this war is a

> crusade for the good of mankind. . . . I [cannot] bear to think of what my children would be if we were to permit this hell-begotten conspiracy to destroy this country."

These convictions had caused the two men, and thousands of others, to volunteer and fight against each other in 1861. They remained more powerful than coercion and discipline as the glue that held the army together in 1864.

McPherson's research produced about fourteen key answers: martial enthusiasm, discipline, leadership, comradeship, character, religion, defense of homeland, preservation of the Union, liberty, slavery, vengeance, duty, glory, and honor. Rebels and Yankees give similar reasons, except, as one would expect, on the subject of slavery.

In his excellent topical index, McPherson provides other attitudes, motives, and types of experiences the soldiers recorded as they meditated upon their reasons for fighting: adventure, cowardice, the draft, coercion, desertion, skulking, combat stress, homesickness, rage, pursuit of promotion, and poor morale.

Borrowing from John Lynn, historian of the armies of the French Revolution, McPherson was guided by three categories of motivation: initial motivation, sustaining motivation, and combat motivation. As McPherson notes, "For Civil War soldiers the group cohesion and peer pressure that were powerful factors in combat motivation were not unrelated to the complex mixture of patriotism, ideology, concepts of duty, honor, manhood and community or peer pressure that prompted them to enlist in the first place." He argues "for a closer relationship among these three categories for Civil War soldiers than some scholarship on combat motivation posits for that and other wars."

A major appeal of this book is the purely interesting, sometimes astonishing, but always brief stories the soldiers tell to express their reasons for fighting. Studies that focus on speculative questions pose a risk to the reputation of academic historians who venture upon them. The risk is even greater for historians who appeal to a general audience. Assuming that readers want books on battles and leaders, publishers continue to fill the nation's bookstores with such volumes, but there are vigorous signs that Americans want to hear about the war from the men who fought it face-to-face and gave testimony of their experiences, emotions, and ideas in letters, diaries, and memoirs. McPherson states that it was Civil War soldiers who wrote this book.

Professor of history at Princeton, McPherson has a reputation as a risk taker. Although Shelby Foote's monumental three-volume Civil War history remains the longtime favorite of the American people and Ken Burns's documentary has made Foote even more welcome in millions of homes, McPherson's best-selling, Pulitzer Prize–winning *Battle Cry of Freedom* has made him the Civil War historian of the hour. His distinguished career began taking shape and definition in the final years of the centennial, with the publication of several works that focused on abolitionism and the Negro in the Civil War and Reconstruction. How did American Negroes feel and act during the war for the Union? He has asked and given answers to similar essential questions ever since.

In several books, McPherson has used the method he employs in his latest. He also has a tendency to approach a subject in two books, the first exploratory, the second more detailed. The three Fleming lectures he delivered at Louisiana State University in 1993 and published as *What They Fought For, 1861—1865* "focused on the political ideological issues" that soldiers on both sides "perceived to be at stake in the war." Those themes have been absorbed into *For Cause and Comrades*. In 1996, more than thirty years after his first book appeared, McPherson felt ready to look back and reassess his interests and preoccupations in *Drawn with the Sword: Reflections on the American Civil War*. Readers may be expected to pay serious attention to the questions this experienced historian poses in his latest work.

Because what a person writes is in many ways even more suspect than what a person says, we can only hope or wish that men (and now women) in all wars fight for the reasons they say, in letters, journals, and memoirs, and on tape recorders or videotape. McPherson's own caution is that the historian must be careful not to read too much between the lines of soldier's letters. We cannot know whether those who spoke of duty, honor, country, and liberty were merely "masking" other motives. For that matter, the motives of many volunteers were mixed in ways that were impossible to disentangle in their own minds.

McPherson tries to unmix mixed motives and takes up each in separate chapters: conviction and lack of it, cowardice and courage, and so forth. But for the most meaningful results, motives must be examined in their *mixed* state. McPherson is, on the whole, inclined to believe that "these volunteers really meant what they said about a willingness to die for the cause." Should a statement be taken literally simply because a soldier writes it? Has McPherson asked a question that is doomed to produce unreliable and not really useful answers? Might a more apt title for his book be "What Men *Say* They Fought For"?

McPherson notes the irrational, almost perverse—at the very least, odd—basis for praise of the Civil War soldier's heroism expressed in 1992 by the commander of the New York chapter of the Sons of Union Veterans; he claimed that "our fathers . . . didn't know what they were fighting for exactly, and they fought on anyway. . . . That's what made them heroes." But McPherson's own claim may not survive close scrutiny either. "Research in the letters and diaries of Civil War soldiers will soon lead the attentive historian to a contrary conclusion," he ventures. Perhaps. But the attentive linguist, psychologist, or student of rhetoric may examine the same samples and give a set of answers that interact and interrelate in more complex ways. Even so, is it possible to achieve anything more than a speculative answer to this question?

McPherson's achievement is that he has found these letters and categorized what is in them. Let us turn now to the twenty or so other tantalizing questions that beg for our attention. None of the motives McPherson catalogs can ever be proved to be actual, certainly not by testimony in letters or diaries, and perhaps not even by a quantitative statistical analysis of all the letters ever written, with linguistic, psychological, sociological, and cultural scrutiny. Motives alone, by their very nature, have few of the necessary properties of fact, or the kind of transcendent truth McPherson has reached for.

In the end, we are left only with speculation but speculation that may be sometimes and in certain ways useful. As we read the testimony of soldiers on their motives for fighting, it is interesting to *speculate* as to what conscious or subconscious motive they may have had for saying what they say. Sometimes the writer's conscious motive is, for example, to reassure, while his subconscious motive is self-delusion. The soldier asks himself, Why do I fight? He answers "religion." But what matters is not so much *what* he answers as *why*. "I believe in God" (because I wish I could). In the chapter called "Religion Is What Makes Brave Soldiers," McPherson quotes a Confederate naval lieutenant, writing to his fiancée before going into action. "Do you not know that the path of every ball is directed by our kind father, and that no harm can come near me except by His special permission?" The choice of rhetorical phrases strongly suggests that this man *is* trying to reassure his fiancée and possibly trying to convince himself. No definite conclusion lies hidden in the nest of rhetorical phrases.

McPherson's latest study is an achievement that provides a rich and valuable basis for further exploration and speculation. He has taken a necessary first step. Although none of the reasons he gives are new, he has brought together many vivid testimonials. He has not given a transcendent *why*, only the soldier's own stated *why*. What he set out to do, he has done, thoroughly, in good order, and in a readable style. But his approach, if taken as having provided even near-final answers, simplifies what is an inherently complex dynamic. Experts in other disciplines may take several steps further.

As I listened several years ago to Professor McPherson, in his Fleming lectures, articulate his answers to the questions he posed, a battery of related questions came rushing to the forefront of my mind.

Who is the person being quoted? Is he an officer, A noncommissioned officer, or common soldier? Which part of the North or the South is he from? (An appendix gives the reader some statistics.)

Out of what cultural matrix, rich in rhetoric, did the letter writer come to war? Our deepest understanding of the answers to all questions depends upon a full rendering of the Southern or the Northern context.

At what point in the war and in what month of the year does he write? In later years, does he reassess, as Sam Watkins does in one of the most famous and most complex memoirs: *"Co. Aytch"*?

Where is the soldier when he writes? At the front or in winter quarters? In his home state or far away? In a hospital or a prison? On a ship?

Why does he write? To reassure? To reproach? To brag? To justify?

How does he write? In a letter, a diary, or a memoir? Each is different from the other.

Perhaps more important than who the writer is, to whom does he write? To mother, grandmother, father, grandfather, brother, sister, uncle, aunt, cousin, friend, priest, sweetheart, wife, little child, politician, teacher, or fellow soldier? Or does he write to and for himself in a diary? A different rhetoric is aimed at each person in this array of types.

Each letter is written out of and into a set of circumstances that is always changing, letter by letter, over time and space. And every writer anticipates the response of his audience. Thus, the sentiment and the choice of words to express it have been chosen for him, in effect, by his own awareness of the expectations of his recipient. Regardless of the audience, a relevant question is, Who is the writer trying to persuade with such rhetoric, himself, the other person, or both? Context is everything.

Answers to the many questions I pose above would provide a complex setting for answers to the question McPherson poses. He does not pose these related questions because his stated purpose is to name a subject that deserves research, uncover what is in the record, and then give a report of the matter. Certain analytical questions can be answered most effectively by experts in disciplines other than history. Most questions about the Civil War are posed in isolation from all or most other disciplines and asked from the perspective of a single discipline. The Civil War in most of its aspects defies single-perspective explanations. Answers to McPherson's question are most useful after the various perspectives have been brought to bear. This is a task of interdisciplinary study, including innumerable areas: psychology, linguistic anthropology, statistical analysis, cultural geography, religion, political science, social science, literary criticism, and military science. No one discipline serves well enough.

If the questions I have posed are relevant and rich in implications, perhaps we ought then to consider the possibilities for multidisciplinary approaches to such complex issues. The appendixes to McPherson's book point the way to the larger, more complex job to be done. More direct interpretation of McPherson's quotations in light of such information is needed. The appendixes provide the geographical distribution of white Confederate and white Union soldiers and their occupations.

In his preface, McPherson cites statistics to explain biases in his sample toward native-born officers from the middle and upper classes overall. The Civil War, it has been argued, was a class war—a rich man's war but a poor man's fight. A major question remains: why did the poor and illiterate, white, black, and foreign born fight? It is with this question that application of interdisciplinary study (including fields such as anthropology, cultural geography, and linguistics) would be most illuminating. The lower level of education among those underrepresented—blacks, immigrants, and non-slave-owning families—is a factor that hovers over the answers McPherson is able to derive from his educated samples.

Incompleteness is another reason no reliable answer can be given to the question McPherson poses. For instance, given that African Americans constitute only 1 percent of McPherson's sample, why include them at all? His answers would have been more forceful had he limited himself to telling why officers, the educated, and property owners fought, without trying to fit in quotations from the soldiers who are underrepresented in the sample but who, in the case of whites, fought in much greater numbers. Their inclusion limits the usefulness and meaning of his conclusions.

From what sources did soldiers derive reasons and the rhetoric they stated in letters and diaries? What they say lacks meaning to the extent that folks at home are not part of the sample. McPherson refers to the same soldier more than twice in some cases, but we need analysis of groups of letters by a few soldiers as they express several of these reasons, over a span of time and space and to a variety of recipients. The kind of further study that is implicit in McPherson's book would, perhaps, compare one politician, one woman, one white, and one black soldier on each side with each other.

Among the disciplines that can illuminate McPherson's sample is rhetoric. An analysis of the rhetoric of the quotations, in the context of the complex of questions I suggested earlier, would show what Ralph Waldo Emerson meant when he said, "Words are actions." Rhetoric was the fuel for the war in the first place, especially the Northern abolitionist and Southern political "fire-eating" rhetoric of politicians and religious leaders. Expressions of feelings and convictions in letters draw on a matrix of available rhetoric, spoken and written before and during the war—from novels, poetry, exemplary biographies of great men, and from religion, politics, and the military.

McPherson's excellent essay on "How Lincoln Won the War with Metaphors" shows that McPherson himself has a feel for that discipline. What is called for here is much more of what he only touches upon: "Sometimes the Victorian idioms in which soldiers expressed their patriotism became almost cloying." He goes on to give an excellent example but refrains from analyzing it in the many ways I am proposing here.

Another example comes at the end of the book. A Union captain wrote to his ten-year-old son congratulating him on a neatly written birthday letter to the daddy he had scarcely seen during the past three years.

> It tells me that while I am absent from home, fighting the battels [*sic*] of our country, trying to restore law and order, to our once peaceful and prosperous nation, and endeavoring to secure for each and every American citizen of every race, the rights guaranteed us in the Declaration of Independence . . . I have children growing up that will be worthy of the rights that I trust will be left for them.

Absent from this passage is any sense of a real father writing to an actual child. Overwhelmingly present is a sense of the power of rhetoric to convince writer and perhaps reader that a lucid experience, in some rich context, has been shared. Answers to questions as to where, when, and why must be given, and answers to questions about the father-son relationship, actual and in correspondence, in times and places before this one, must be supplied if the quotation is to have any value as part of a complex speculative venture. Rhetoric is by its nature unreliable, and the status of fact can never be conferred upon it, as McPherson, explicitly or implicitly, seems often to do.

McPherson has provided us with the means to begin to ask major questions. What do his answers mean when applied to later years, the Reconstruction era, for instance? How do answers to McPherson's question illuminate our understanding of the evolution of the American character from 1865 to the current chapter in our history? What do his answers mean as we deal now with the legacy of violence, racism, distrust of government, and economic instability? How does that understanding of ourselves help us to understand others who are enduring or surviving the crucible of civil war around the globe?

We entered the new millennium in the midst of civil wars, some already raging, many about to explode. We can deal with those wars from within and from without more effectively if we understand why men and women fight them. The American Civil War provides a complex model for a complex phenomenon. To that effort to understand, James McPherson has contributed a simple and clear foundation upon which to build a more complex model.

Classics of Civil War Fiction

In 1987, Peggy Bach, an independent scholar working on a biography of Evelyn Scott, and I discussed creating a collection of original essays by novelists and critics to make a deliberate and, we thought, positive contribution to a debate that got under way only two years after the end of the Civil War. In 1991, that volume appeared as *Classics of Civil War Fiction* and has remained in print—a testament to its enduring relevance.

In 1867, the year in which one of the finest Civil War novels, *Miss Ravenel's Conversion from Secession to Loyalty*, written by a veteran of the war, John William De Forest, was published, William Dean Howells, editor of the *Atlantic Monthly* and father of realism in American fiction, lamented that "our war has laid upon our literature a charge under which it has hitherto staggered very lamely."

Almost fifty years later, in *The Spirit of American Literature* (1911), literary historian John Macy echoed Howells: "Thousands of books were written by people who knew the war at first hand and who had literary ambition and some skill, and from all of these books, none rises to distinction" (12–15).

The debate is usually posed in the negative with this question: Given the central importance of the Civil War in the history of the United States, why has no novel embodied, to the satisfaction of a majority of critics, the profound essence of that event? Most critics who touch on this debate agree that the great Civil War novel warranted by the magnitude and the central importance of the war remains unwritten. They give various reasons it has not and describe what it should be when it comes to be written.

But claims, pro and con, are argued more incidentally than in sustained works of criticism. Given the tremendous interest in Civil War history, it is strange that very little literary criticism has been devoted to fiction about the war. *Classics of Civil War Fiction* is only the second book to be devoted exclusively to Civil War fiction.

The first, *Fiction Fights the Civil War* (1957), a title adopted from an article by Bernard DeVoto, is an indispensable descriptive and critical survey of over five hundred Civil War novels, with a subtitle that continues to be excruciatingly appropriate: "An Unfinished Chapter in the Literary History of the American People." It was written by Robert A. Lively, a historian with more than sufficient literary acumen who dared to venture his "Selection of the Best Civil War Novels."

We too committed ourselves to quality choices. All but one (Lively represented William Faulkner with *The Unvanquished*) of the novels discussed in *Classics of Civil War Fiction* (1950 being our limitation date) appear on Lively's list of fifteen. From the five hundred he studied, he chose thirty "Other Representative Civil War Novels." Plus or minus a few titles, we agree—although not necessarily with the concurrence of our contributors—with Lively's list. Lively includes a bibliography of all five hundred novels, along with a fairly complete list of critical articles and books. Lively's collection resides now in the Wilson Library at Chapel Hill.

Earlier, in 1950, Ernest E. Leisey provided a selective, annotated list in his more general study *The American Historical Novel.* Also useful is Arthur Taylor Dickinson's substantial, annotated list of novels in his even broader study *Historical Fiction* (1958). As late as 1969, only two and a half pages are devoted to criticism of Southern Civil War literature in Louis D. Rubin Jr.'s *A Bibliographical Guide to the Study of Southern Literature.*

Several notable articles joined the debate just before and after Lively's book appeared. In "Southern Novelists and the Civil War," published in 1953 and reprinted in *Death by Melancholy* (1972), Southern critic Walter Sullivan did not declare a position on the question of quality; rather, having stated the importance of the war in the history of the South, he commented on *The Fathers*, *The Long Night*, *Absalom, Absalom!* and several other Southern novels on the implicit assumption that they were achievements of a very high order. "To the Southern writer who would deal with the past, the Civil War is the most significant image of all. For it is the pregnant moment in Southern history, that instant which contains within its limits a summation of all that has gone before, an adumbration of the future" (69).

One of the most famous books dealing with the literature of the Civil War is Edmund Wilson's *Patriotic Gore: Studies in the Literature of the American Civil War*, which appeared in 1962 during the period of what he called "this absurd centennial." (Interestingly, the only notable Civil War novel to appear within the four-year celebration was Robert Penn Warren's *Wilderness*, 1961.) But Wilson limited himself to describing "some thirty men and women who lived through the Civil War, either playing some special role in connection with it or experiencing its impact in some interesting way, and who have left their personal records of some angle or aspect of it" (x). Of the works discussed in *Classics of Civil War Fiction*, he discusses only De Forest's novel and Ambrose Bierce's *Tales of Soldiers and Civilians* (1891). His excellent discussion of the nonfiction of the period provides a background for any study of the fiction published in the same period and later.

Another source of nonfiction recommendations is "A Confederate Book Shelf" in *South to Posterity* (1936) by Douglas Southall Freeman, a major biographer of Robert E. Lee. A more recent, nonpartisan list, based on solicited recommendations, appeared in *Civil War Times Illustrated* (August 1981, pp. 46–47); *The Red Badge of Courage* is the only novel listed, a stark indication of its pride of place but a novel I feel is overrated.

Some of the finest Civil War novelists, several of whom are represented in this volume, also wrote some of the most intellectually vigorous nonfiction on the subject: De Forest's *Volunteer's Adventures: A Union Captain's Record of the Civil War* (not published until 1946); Allen Tate's *Stonewall Jackson, the Good Soldier: A Narrative* (1928) and *Jefferson Davis* (1929); Robert Penn Warren's *John Brown: The Making of a Martyr* (1929); Andrew Lytle's *Bedford Forrest and His Critter Company* (1931); and Evelyn Scott's *Background in Tennessee* (1937). The Warren, Lytle, and Tate books, written in their agrarian period, will surely be reissued by a university press; University of Tennessee Press reprinted Scott's in 1980. A major recent nonfiction achievement by a novelist is, of course, Shelby Foote's monumental *Civil War: A Narrative* (1958–1974); his *Shiloh* (1952), unusually short for a Civil War novel (as is *The Red Badge of Courage* and my own *Sharpshooter*), appeared during the Korean conflict era.

One of the most prolific and astute Southern critics, Louis D. Rubin Jr., has written almost exclusively on Southern literature, but "The Image of an Army, Southern Novelists and the Civil War" (reprinted in his *Curious Death of the Novel*, 1967) is one of the few pieces in which he has focused on Civil War fiction. Unlike Sullivan, he takes a clear position on the question of quality. Having observed that "more than a thousand novels have been written about the war by Southerners alone," he concludes that "most of the South's Civil War fiction . . . is wretched stuff. . . . No single Confederate war novel exists which we can read and then say with satisfaction and admiration *that* was the *Lost Cause*; *that* was Lee's army. . . . There is no *War and Peace* about the South and its army. . . . All we have is *Gone With the Wind*" (which, in the popular imagination for eighty years, has been more than enough; 184, 185, 186).

In light of those observations, Rubin discusses fifteen or so novels, including a few discussed in *Classics of Civil War Fiction*, that come close in various ways to achieving his definition of the great Confederate novel, a definition he makes clearest in the final paragraph: "What the Southern novelist who would create a great Civil War novel can do is not to forsake his sense of society and history, but add to it the ability of a Crane to see the lonely individual soul as well. . . . Through the perceptions of such a protagonist, the full tragedy of the Civil War might be captured in fiction" (206). One can imagine Rubin reading Lewis Simpson's essay on *Absalom, Absalom!* in *Classics of Civil War Fiction* with particular interest.

In 1973, a Midwesterner offered a critical survey of the contributions of both Southern and Northern writers to the literature. While it did not focus primarily on fiction, Daniel Aaron's *Unwritten War: American Writers and the Civil War* (1973) encompassed far more fiction than Wilson's book, including examinations, however, of only six of the works of fiction discussed in *Classics of Civil War Fiction*. He quotes Howells, almost a century after the war, and, as his title declares, agrees with him: "As yet no novel or poem has disclosed the common soldier so vividly as the historian Bell Wily does in his collective portraits of Johnny Reb and Billy Yank." Aaron argues that most fiction has failed to reveal "the meaning . . . of the War." "Some, like the majority of their fellow Americans (I paraphrase Oscar Handlin), draped the War in myth, transmuted its actuality into symbol, and interpreted the Republic's greatest failure as a sinful interlude in a grand evolutionary process" (xviii). (*Note:* The United States Civil War Center facilitated the republication of Aaron's book at the University of Alabama Press in 2003.)

Aaron goes on to say that the lack of "'masterpieces' is no index of the impact of the War on American writers. . . . . The War more than casually touched and engaged a number of writers, and its literary reverberations are felt to this day" (xviii–xix). At the end, Daniel Aaron quotes the judgment in 1916 of Sherwood Anderson: "No real sense of it has yet crept into the pages of a printed book" (*Windy McPherson's Son*, 21–22).

Aaron's own last line, "Our untidy and unkempt War still confounds interpreters," sounds the same negative note on which the debate began. Even so, almost twenty years later, he joins other critics and novelists in a continuation of the debate in *Classics of Civil War Fiction*. He focuses on Ross Lockridge Jr.'s *Raintree County*, a novel he did not mention in his book, about the quality of which there is much controversy; he praises it but with reservations. In recent years, in conversation, he told me that he wished he had included Evelyn Scott's *Wave* in his study.

Some of the essays in *Classics of Civil War Fiction* imply that the great Civil War novel may just not have gone unwritten, but readers of the recommended novels will have their own say about that.

Some general questions and observations may provide a setting for reading those novels.

The question has often been posed, What criteria might one use to choose the best novels about the War between the States by Southerners?

What different criteria might apply in evaluating the work of Northern novelists?

If distinctions between Northern and Southern are relevant, how are we to determine what characteristics and qualities the great nonpartisan American Civil War novel should have?

While contributors to *Classics of Civil War Fiction* did not explicitly pose any such criteria, implicit in some of the essays is an awareness that such questions have been raised. From the scant literary criticism on the subject, one may derive a few general criteria; whether one feels it is or is not relevant to apply them, they do constitute characteristics of the better novels that have been written.

The Great American Civil War novel would perhaps dramatize an important or noble theme; authentically depict family life on the plantation; encompass the antebellum era, major battles, and the Reconstruction era; demonstrate exhaustive factual research; reveal the war through the microcosm of a battle; present the common soldier's view; re-create events "as they really happened"; and "bring the war alive" for modern readers.

And, of course, it would exemplify the criteria usually applied to determine artistic excellence. It would be written out of a coherent philosophy of the Civil War, controlled by a complex artistic conception. The author should imagine new techniques for illuminating ways through which the war may become and stay part of the living essence of the character's and the reader's everyday consciousness.

In the ideal Civil War novel, the author's vision and purpose emerge out of the complexities of the war experience but transcend them. The novel succeeds in stimulating and engaging the emotions, the imagination, and the intellect to make the war agonizingly alive in the reader. Its point of view, style, and other techniques make the reader a collaborator with the author in creating a conception of the Civil War that will enable the reader, long after the fiction ends, to illuminate his or her experiences. It would be the novel Americans need to stimulate a revolution in our way of feeling, imagining, and meditating on an event that has determined the development of this nation and that continues to affect our behavior in ways we do well to see and understand.

Some would question whether the value of a particular Civil War novel need rely at all on all-encompassing criteria. It is, even so, a fact of American literary history that major differences between Civil War novels by Southerners and those by Northerners determine the criteria by which they have been evaluated over the years. For instance, it has been argued that it was industrialism that shaped the consciousness of Northerners and that the Civil War was only a dramatic episode; but, it has often been argued, it was the War between the States itself that shaped the consciousness of Southerners.

If the war is the central experience in the lives of Southerners, in some sense every work of fiction by a Southerner is an expression of the long-developing cause, the bloody agony, and the lingering effect of the war. The aim then of most Southern novels about the war has been to defend, explain, or criticize—sometimes to extol or preserve—the Southern way of life.

The Northern writer's aim is totally divorced from such an attitude. For the Northerner, the North as a coherent region with a history and an identity, and his or her place in it as a Northerner, has very little reality. The Northern writer's perspective is, the Civil War was interesting as a human drama and it ended with an important moral victory. De Forest was moved to write out of the urgency of a participant who could imagine the Southern young lady's point of view. *The Red Badge of Courage* (1895) is based on facts (and on Stephen Crane's reading of De Forest more than any other novelist)—but facts processed by his imagination. By contrast, Joseph Stanley Pennell had actual divided loyalties, with grandparents on both sides, and like Faulkner's Quentin Compson, his autobiographical hero was obsessed generations after the war with that combined legacy.

Given these contrasting visions, or attitudes, and purposes, it is not surprising that most Southern writers concentrate on the war's effect on the traditional Southern aristocratic family on a plantation (Allen Tate's *The Fathers*, 1938; Ellen Glasgow's *Battle-Ground*, 1902; and Stark Young's *So Red the Rose*, 1934). Relationships in the family unit are dramatized; that unity is disrupted by the intrusion of the war or by members of the family having to go to it; involvement in a major battle or in the eastern or western campaign is depicted; they return to the shattered family and all it signifies in the Southern way of life. Ironically, one of the best works with this plot structure was one of the first and finest of novels written by a Northerner, De Forest's *Miss Ravenel's Conversion from Secession to Loyalty*. By sharp contrast, examination of the Northern novels reveals a concentration on the common soldier in a specific battle, Crane's *Red Badge of Courage* being the most famous example.

Whether the author is male or female, the focus, in serious novels, as opposed to *Gone With the Wind* (1936) and other historical romances, is on male characters. A notable exception is Robert Penn Warren's *Band of Angels* (1955), narrated by a mulatto woman.

Southern novelists devote a great deal of space to the antebellum era (DuBose Heyward's *Peter Ashley*, 1932; and Allen Tate's *The Fathers*), while Northerners usually plunge into battle as quickly as possible, intent upon destroying the plantation family, with its slave economy as a major cause of the conflict.

Although we have used the term Civil War fiction, we include the era of causes before and the era of effects afterward. The Civil War novel's time span then is from the events depicted in Harriet Beecher Stowe's prophetic *Uncle Tom's Cabin* (1852), published a decade before the war, to the World War II era of Joseph Stanley Pennell's *The History of Rome Hanks and Kindred Matters* (1944).

In some of the novels, the war is mostly in the background, as in John Peale Bishop's *Many Thousands Gone* (1951) and MacKinlay Kantor's *Long Remember* (1934). In others, the war is an episode in a larger story, as in *Raintree County* (1948). Or, by contrast, it is not directly depicted, but memories of its causes and effects on into the present moment are dramatized, out of a rage to tell or explain, as in Faulkner's *Absalom, Absalom!* (1936), Pennell's *The History of Rome Hanks* (1944), and Warren's *All the King's Men* (1946, chapter 4).

That way of expanding the body of Civil War novels is anticipated by the fact that some novels we already think of as Civil War novels take up the war only at the end (*Peter Ashley* and *The Fathers*) to focus on causes; some start with Reconstruction (Colonel William C. Falkner's *White Rose of Memphis*, 1881; Josephine Herbst's *Pity Is Not Enough*, 1933; and Richard Marius's *Coming of Rain*, 1969) to focus on effects. Some of those novels are more effective conceptually (*The Fathers* from the South and Francis Grierson's *Valley of Shadows*, 1909, from the North) than many novels that are mostly about the war itself. Knowing what they know and still feel about the Civil War, the imaginations of Southern readers especially are stimulated, within a provocative conception, by reading novels about the antebellum and Reconstruction eras.

In that broad perspective, *Huckleberry Finn* should be considered one of the great Civil War novels. In his essay on *Absalom, Absalom!* in *Classics of Civil War Fiction*, Lewis Simpson claims that *Huckleberry Finn* is "basically an exploration of the Southern society that fought the Civil War." Some may consider it perverse to call Mark Twain's *Huckleberry Finn* a Civil War novel. But what if those who call it the Great American Novel are at least close to being right? They claim that it is the fullest expression of the American character and land, the American Dream and its nightmare obverse, not by the author's conscious intention, nor by any superabundance of diverse raw material, but by what it embodies and simultaneously implies about America then and America to come. What it most prophetically suggests, as Simpson declares, is the Civil War. If each American reads it with all she or he knows about the war conceptually and imaginatively in mind, it may shed a kind of light no conventional Civil War novel can. At the very least, reading this novel as a Civil War novel may alter the way one perceives all those novels more confidently called Civil War novels.

Another indirect illumination of the war is *Raintree County*, set in 1892 on July 4, with flashbacks to the past, especially the war. And Joseph Stanley Pennell in *The History of Rome Hanks and Kindred Matters* features a protagonist like Faulkner's Quentin Compson who strives to make sense of his private present in the 1930s in terms of the historical past. In chapter 4 of Robert Penn Warren's *All the King's Men*, Jack Burden tells us about his historical research into the tragic Civil War–era story of his supposed distant relative Cass Mastern. Jack tried to escape from the present into his research only to discover that "the world is all of one piece," that to touch even the remotest strand of the web alerts the spider—and our past, present, and future merge in alarm.

The Civil War shattered the Southern institutions, and time has finished the process of destruction. Perhaps that is why fewer Southern writers now write Civil War novels and those that have appeared recently are more likely to resemble Northern novels with their concentration on battles—Shelby Foote's *Shiloh* (1952), Douglas C. Jones's *Elkhorn Tavern* (1980), and Tom Wicker's *Unto This Hour* (1984)—rather than the traditional family-centered Southern novel. Ironically, it is the popular historical romance novel that continues to focus on the plantation and the family, the vein most effectively worked by William Faulkner's great-grandfather Colonel William C. Falkner in *The White Rose of Memphis*, Stark Young in *So Red the Rose*, and Margaret Mitchell in *Gone With the Wind.*

The central question of the Civil War novel raises other questions. Why is it that no major Civil War novel was written by a Northern woman? Many would agree that of the better Civil War novels, several were written by Southern women: Tennessee writers Mary Noailles Murfree (*Where the Battle Was Fought* (1884) and *The Storm Centre* (1905)), Evelyn Scott (*The Wave* (1929)), and Caroline Gordon (*None Shall Look Back* (1957)); Virginia writers Mary Johnston (her epic *The Long Roll* (1911) and *Cease Firing* (1912)) and Ellen Glasgow (*The Battle-Ground*). These Southern women writers also wrote many non–Civil War novels.

For almost a century and a half, the Civil War genre of fiction has instilled certain expectations in readers as they pick up a new one. A goodly company of readers want an end to, or a curtailment of, repackaging in both fiction and nonfiction about the Civil War. With each repackaging of readily available facts and fictive elements, one gets the feeling that a time of acute critical reassessment is long overdue. The mania for the facts that the historian and too many novelists share has outlived its necessity. For the facts, we may consult *War of the Rebellion: Official Records of the Union and Confederate Armies*, in 128 volumes, with atlas, published in Washington from 1880 to 1901.

The obsession with authenticity produces some novels that are a kind of semidocumentary, a re-creation, like historical reenactments of famous battles on their actual sites or a parade of well-researched details in uniforms and armament "brought back to life" by pretenders of our own day. Recent novels give us authenticity laced with imagination or imagination laced with authenticity—the effect is similar: an aura of artificiality. The reader may have the uneasy sense that the novelist, primarily committed to either the power of imagination or the force of fact, is straining to appease the neglected of the two masters.

A good many recent novelists and historians as well justify their notions for yet another Civil War book on the misconceived distinction between the military or political as opposed to the so-called human side of the story. Some reviewers of Civil War novels offer as criteria for excellence or distinction for a novel the fact that it "dares" to present "the human side." As opposed to what? The common soldier, it is presumed, is a creature somehow more authentic than the generals. It is a vapid distinction. The "human" eyewitness turns out to be someone who saw or remembered little more of the battle than the general who sat it out on the other side of a mountain or the civilian who cowered from it in a basement.

No eyewitness could ever produce a coherent view of any aspect of any major battle. Ironically, paradoxically, or just plain logically, the modern novelist or historian, possessed of millions of fragments of his or her own sensibility, of a conceptual imagination, stylistic taste, and an intellect commensurate to the task, is far better equipped to give us a coherent view than a multitude of eyewitnesses.

It may be argued that the leaden blow of fact after fact blunts the writer's sensibility, inhibits the imagination. Once the formula takes effect, it is the formula itself one experiences page after page. Clearly, there are those who long to consume large doses of this formula. But those with a low tolerance for it may wonder repeatedly, Is this detail here because it is essential and illuminating to a conception derived from the author's vision of the war, or because the obeisance to fact dictates the use of it at this particular moment?

From the beginning, fiction has offered a wide variety of fresh perspectives. De Forest gave us a Northerner's perspective on the Southern plantation owner and insight into a so-called minor battle, at Port Hudson, Louisiana, a battle or siege that we now know had major consequences. In his stories of soldiers and civilians, Bierce gave us a bitterly ironic vision of the universal nature of things that shape our individual fates. Crane gave us the perspective of the ordinary soldier. Kantor showed the battle of Gettysburg from the point of view of the townspeople. Evelyn Scott's novel gave us a multifaceted omniscient view of the entire war. Hers, along with Pennell's and Lockridge's, offered epic dimensions to the war. Faulkner showed how several oral perspectives affected the lives of survivors and descendants, both military and civilian.

Nonfiction has offered more than general histories and biographies and autobiographies; it has also taken up very special and specific subjects. It has dealt with some aspects that fiction has not approached, while fiction has done what nonfiction has not.

The success of the work of rediscovering and reassessing depends upon the simultaneous revitalization of Civil War fiction. Talk of the unwritten war might also include aspects that neither fiction nor nonfiction have explored sufficiently.

As they attempt to envision what might yet be done, future Civil War novelists would do well to survey the scope of the nonfiction that has already been written to determine what remains to be done. Fiction has not dealt sufficiently with African Americans, Native Americans, and other minorities, and with women in the war; with combat artists and photographers; with lesser-known historical figures such as Parson Brownlow, Edmund Ruffin, Oliver Wendell Holmes as a young officer, and his famous father as a parent who searched for his son on the battlefield; and with bridges, railroads, churches, and other structures as focus settings for key experiences.

There has been no comic Civil War novel remotely like *The Story of Don Miff, as Told by His Friend John Bouche Whacker: A Symphony of Life* (1886) "edited" by Virginius Dabney. Dabney was the Walker Percy of his day. His satirical vision, witty style, and comic innovative devices, reminiscent of Laurence Sterne's, shift our perspectives as if we were riding in a square-wheeled carriage over a backwoods, washboard road.

No book, fiction or nonfiction, has yet been written out of a coherent philosophy of the Civil War, controlled by a complex conception. Most Civil War books these days—nonfiction as well as fiction—are inspired less by conceptions than by mere notions, such as, How about looking at the Civil War through a microcosm of the battle of the Crater, through Andersonville prison, and from a science fiction angle?

Some of the most intriguing mysteries, paradoxes, questions, and curiosities of American literature have to do with Civil War novels. For instance, it is strange that although most Civil War novels are by Southerners, no Southern writer of major importance, except Evelyn Scott and William Faulkner, has produced as his or her best work a Civil War novel. That is even more incomprehensible if you agree with the statement made earlier that many or most novels by Southerners are in some sense expressions of the cause and effect of the Civil War.

The best Southern novels do not generally compare well on artistic grounds with Northern fiction about the war. Out of the North have come several classics, the best work of their authors: John William De Forest's *Miss Ravenel's Conversion from Secession to Loyalty*, Ambrose Bierce's *Tales of Soldiers and Civilians*, Stephen Crane's *The Red Badge of Courage*, MacKinlay Kantor's *Long Remember*, Joseph Stanley Pennell's *The History of Rome Hanks and Kindred Matters* (he wrote only one other, second in an unfinished trilogy), and Ross Lockridge Jr.'s *Raintree County* (his only novel).

Most critics discuss Civil War novels or argue their relative excellence almost exclusively in terms of theme, while describing the raw material and the social and historical considerations, as if development of one theme more than another accounts for excellence. It is all the more curious then that the more intellectually conceived novels, *The Wave, Absalom, Absalom!* and *Rome Hanks*, have not endeared themselves to critics who lament the lack of a masterpiece—they usually don't even mention Scott or Pennell. Readers have been on their own then in their considerations of the aesthetic qualities of these and other novels. In the final analysis, of course, it is the aesthetic power of any work of fiction that enables it to continue generation after generation to have all its other elements affect readers forcibly. In their use of innovative techniques, *The Wave, Absalom, Absalom! Rome Hanks*, and *Raintree County* are rare among Civil War novels.

The author's choice of point of view and the kind of style produced by point of view are of major importance in evaluating the achievement of Civil War novels and stories. The first-person, eyewitness account, usually in the spirit of the many collections of letters, journals, and memoirs kept by men and women, is employed mostly by Southerners, as in *The Fathers*, *The Long Night*, and *The Unvanquished*. The style of the first two is literary; the third, vernacular.

Very seldom is the point of view third-person omniscient but limited to the perceptions of a single character. Stephen Becker's *When the War Is Over* (1969) stands almost alone. The prevalence of the omniscient point of view may explain to some extent the general impression that the Civil War novel is inevitably a very long novel. Artistic compression produced *The Red Badge of Courage* and *Shiloh*, but that most Civil War novels are over four hundred pages is inherent in the massiveness of raw material and in the intent of the author to capture the war and is encouraged by the omniscient point of view. Northern novels tend to run a little longer.

Whether the writer depicts the impact of battles on the members of a family or on soldiers in an army in a single major battle, the point of view that is most appropriate is obviously the godlike omniscient, and both Southern and Northern writers employ it most frequently. It promotes a chronological plot structure and a complex, rich, and sometimes ornate literary style.

Howells's question, taken up by others over the past century and longer, remains unanswered. We wonder whether Howells's question did not derive from a larger question in the popular imagination: Why has the Great American Civil War failed to produce the Great American Novel?

Americans seem to need to keep unanswered those two major, perhaps inseparable, questions about American fiction: Why is there no Great American Novel? Why is there no great Civil War novel? For Americans, the Civil War provides the single richest and most meaningful perspective on the entire American experiment. Wouldn't the Great American Novel then have to be simultaneously the Great Civil War Novel?

Some readers are satisfied that *Huckleberry Finn* has been the answer to the first question since 1885, but for most readers, the first question remains unanswered. Most serious readers, North and South, agree that Stephen Crane's *The Red Badge of Courage* is the answer to the second question. But I am not alone in arguing that Crane's novel is more about war in general than it is about the American Civil War. In the consciousness of most of the public, North and South, Margaret Mitchell's *Gone With the Wind* is not only the greatest novel about the war by a Southerner but also the greatest by anybody. *Gone With the Wind* is granted by most critics a kind of grudging admiration: strong narrative pace offset by shallow characterization, except for Scarlett perhaps, and so on. The phenomenal popular success of the novel and the movie make *Gone With the Wind* a monumental distraction from the serious debate, unless one sides in the current debate over the canon with those who argue that fiction should both reflect and affect society, in which case the general public would be right about Mitchell's novel, the effect of which is wide ranging and complex.

Here is a list of the essays we offered in *Classics of Civil War Fiction*. They lent new substance to the debate—and perhaps some help in the individual reader's own attempts to achieve an answer.

John William De Forest's *Miss Ravenel's Conversion from Secession to Loyalty*, Stephen Becker
Ambrose Bierce's *Tales of Soldiers and Civilians*, Ishmael Reed
Stephen Crane's *Red Badge of Courage*, James Cox
Ellen Glasgow's *The Battle-Ground*, R. H. W. Dillard
Mary Johnston's *Long Roll* and *Cease Firing*, George Garrett
Evelyn Scott's *The Wave*, Peggy Bach
John Peale Bishop's *Many Thousands Gone*, Mary Lee Settle
DuBose Heyward's *Peter Ashley*, Rose Ellen Brown
MacKinlay Kantor's *Long Remember*, Robie Macauley
Andrew Lytle's *The Long Night*, Robert Penn Warren
William Faulkner's *Absalom, Absalom!* Lewis P. Simpson

Allen Tate's *The Fathers*, Tom Wicker
Joseph Stanley Pennell's *The History of Rome Hanks and Kindred Matters*, David Madden
Ross Lockridge Jr.'s *Raintree County*, Daniel Aaron

For my choices in my regular column, google "Rediscovering Civil War Classics" in *Civil War Book Review*, which I created as founding director of the United States Civil War Center.

William Faulkner's *Absalom, Absalom!* Quentin! Listen!

Ernest Hemingway once declared that "all modern American literature comes from Huckleberry Finn," and there is some truth in that pompous pronouncement.[1]

Risking pomposity, I wish to make not one but several declarations: that all Southern literature *comes out* of the Civil War and Reconstruction; that all Southern novels are *about* the Civil War and Reconstruction; that *Absalom, Absalom!* is the best example of that phenomenon, not only in the Faulkner canon, but also in all Southern literature; that *Absalom, Absalom!* is my choice as the greatest Civil War novel; that Colonel Thomas Sutpen, man of action in the antebellum, Civil War, and Reconstruction eras, is not, as he is often held up to be, the protagonist of *Absalom, Absalom!*; that Quentin Compson, the most passive of Sutpen's vicarious witnesses, *is* the protagonist; that the most pertinent way to show that Quentin is the protagonist is to examine the techniques of the art of fiction that William Faulkner employs in this novel; and that Quentin Compson's consciousness is the most trenchant expression of the legacy of the Civil War at the deepest existential level.

How is it that all Southern literature *comes out* of the Civil War and Reconstruction and that all Southern novels are *about* the Civil War and Reconstruction? The effect of the war and Reconstruction has so permeated Southern history and consciousness that anything a Southerner writes derives from that prolonged effect process, and that process itself is delineated in *Absalom, Absalom!* more deliberately and clearly than in any other Southern novel. By contrast, there is no such thing as a Northern novel, nor a true Civil War novel by a Northerner—*The Red Badge of Courage*, for instance, is about war per se—because there is no such thing as a Northerner, except in the minds of Southerners, who are however both very real and very surreal to Northerners.

A catalytic experience for civilizations throughout history, *war*—especially the Civil War—is a catalyst for Faulkner personally and for his characters, especially Quentin Compson, whose consciousness is at the center of Faulkner's creative consciousness. Every force seeks a form. I use "Civil War" as an all-embracive term for antebellum, Civil War, Reconstruction force and legacy eras because the Civil War is a catalyst for all lines of trajectory. The lines of trajectory of antebellum forces converge and explode in the Civil War, the lines of trajectory in the Civil War are tangled, the lines of trajectory in Reconstruction spread out and hang like a web until Quentin's last year, 1910, four years before the start of World War I; the web was reshaped by Jim Crow, World War I, the Depression, and the civil rights movement, and it hangs still over us all, North and South. Obsessive talk of the myriad trajectories of those external forces ignites forces of emotion, imagination, and intellect in Quentin's consciousness and unconsciousness.

Absalom, Absalom! is my choice as the greatest Civil War novel, not *even though* it does not directly depict war, but *because* of the ways in which the war is more alluded to and its effects implied than dramatized. Faulkner implies ways in which life in the South led up to the war, was profoundly traumatized by it and, more emphatically, by Reconstruction; we may infer that it permeated, in myriad ways, Faulkner's own life. In *not* dealing directly with battles, Faulkner evokes, in his pervasive use of the technique of context and implication, what is more important: the war's effect on Americans, especially Southerners, right on up to you and me today.

In the works in which he figures, Quentin so seldom acts upon or interacts with other characters that readers are enabled to respond only to his consciousness as he passively reacts to and reluctantly but in anguish meditates upon the actions of others. Quentin is Faulkner's expressionistic embodiment of the process that makes all Southern literature about the Civil War. There is no character quite like Quentin in Southern fiction—not in Carson McCullers's *The Heart Is a Lonely Hunter*, all of whose four major characters are locked in the isolation of their own psyches but do at least tell their personal stories, even if only to a mute, who is himself somewhat like Quentin; not in William Styron's *Lie Down in Darkness*, although that novel resembles *The Sound and the Fury*; not in Thomas Wolfe's four epic novels, even though they feature the same hero; and not in any Civil War novels by Southerners, although the hero of *The History of Rome Hanks and Kindred Matters*, by Northerner Joseph Pennell, faintly resembles Quentin-as-listener. Having found nothing in all fiction as fascinatingly complex as Quentin's shifting role in the works of Faulkner, I would claim for Quentin a significant uniqueness in all world literature, while lamenting that he is one of its most neglected characters, even though several critics, especially John Irwin in *Doubling and Incest, Repetition and Revenge*

(1975), Estella Schoenberg in *Old Tales and Talking* (1977), and Noel Polk in *Children of the Dark House* (1996), have made us more aware of him.

That compared with his other characters, Quentin was always a vital, sharply focused presence in Faulkner's consciousness is demonstrated by the fact that when he discussed his characters in public; he referred to the males as "the boy" and often had lapses of memory about them, but he almost always called Quentin by name, and about *him*, his memory was always clear. Several major and numerous minor characters reappear in Faulkner's work, but Quentin has the distinction of being a major character in two of Faulkner's major works and in four short stories: "That Evening Sun," "A Justice," "A Bear Hunt," and "Lion." That Horace Benbow resembles Quentin, especially in the early versions of *Sartoris* and *Sanctuary*, that Faulkner "rehearsed" Quentin and Sutpen in the short story "Evangeline," and that one *might* imagine Quentin as the anonymous "we" narrator of "A Rose for Emily" adds emphasis to Quentin's centrality in the Faulkner canon.

The other three narrators of *The Sound and the Fury*, Benjy, Jason, and Faulkner himself, seldom refer to Quentin. Benjy's stream of consciousness expresses pure being in timelessness. Had Faulkner allowed Caddy (his "heart's darling"), to whom all the narrators relentlessly refer, to speak, would she have spoken of Quentin? I think not. Caddy's naming her daughter Quentin seems an ironic dismissal of Quentin and his incestuous longing for her.[2] Quentin's obsession with Caddy is so strong that his confession is that of a man whose life flashes before him as he drowns. Jason's tough-guy narration is realistic self-justification. But to whom do these brothers speak? Isolated within their very different egos, none of the three brothers have listeners. Faulkner presents their narrations as pure literary artifice. But Faulkner narrates the fourth section of *The Sound and the Fury* in full awareness that he has what his characters, especially Quentin, his alter ego, *lack* but do not crave: a community of readers, of listeners.

I am now proposing to publishers that the two novels and four short stories in which Quentin is either the protagonist or a major character be brought together in a single volume of about six hundred pages. Faulkner thought of something like that himself. My study of those works and their effect on me personally and as a fiction writer have led me to the conviction that if they are gathered into a single volume, with an introduction explaining why, the average Faulkner reader will grasp the essence of this elusive character.

Colonel Thomas Sutpen, man of action in the antebellum, Civil War, and Reconstruction eras, is not the protagonist of *Absalom, Absalom!*[3] I am convinced that the repeated focus on Sutpen by many readers and critics distorts the novel and turns Quentin into a mere narrative device at best and makes him gratuitous at worst.[4]

On the surface, *Absalom, Absalom!* is a dramatic rendering of the ways in which Thomas Sutpen the legend becomes the creation of the Southern oral storytelling tradition, a tradition nurtured in antebellum wilderness, magnified in Civil War defeat, and transmuted in humiliation, resentment, and self-loathing through Reconstruction on into 1910, Quentin's twentieth year.

As a little boy, Sutpen, who sprang from poor white trash, was commanded by a black servant to enter a mansion by the back door. This wound to Sutpen's very identity inspired his dream of becoming the owner of a mansion and slaves. He obsessively and savagely pursued a grand design to force that dream into reality, a dream that became a nightmare for everyone around him, especially his wives, white and black; his sons and daughters, white and black; his sister-in-law, Miss Rosa; the children of his black son; the poor white trash man who worshipfully served him; and that man's granddaughter and great granddaughter. Sutpen himself was satisfied only with the image of himself that the design was created to produce, the image of a man above all other men, who were to be merely witnesses to his rise and to the perpetuation of his blood, while he seemed to take little pleasure in the land, the mansion, the women, the children, or in the many other men and women who figured in his operatic design.

From the moment the townspeople set eyes upon the wild stranger who would become known as Thomas Sutpen, the demon, the ogre, leading his gang of wild slaves through the town, the exaggerated and conflicting stories began, stories that told how he bought a hundred acres of wilderness, tamed the wilderness, built a mansion, amassed a fortune, married the daughter of a prominent citizen, on whom he begat a son and daughter, Henry and Judith, how he went off to war to protect those products of that design, how during Reconstruction, his fortunes so declined that he became the keeper of a store, and how Wash Jones, his poor white trash Sancho Panza in this Quixotic epic, slew Sutpen with the scythe he had borrowed from Sutpen.

That is far more than enough for storytellers—that is, *everybody*—in any impoverished Deep South small town to thrive on. Faulkner thrived on such stories until he could become a writer and reimagine and expand upon them, until he could imagine what is missing, the answers to the many mysteries and secrets that always germinate behind the facade of such legends. So Faulkner creates the keepers of the secret answers to the mysteries that seem to constitute the very identities of the later storytellers and their children. They are motivated in that later era, a time of no grand actions such as the Civil War, in that long, trancelike era of "old tales and talking" (243), to bring the dark mysteries out into the daylight. They discover finally that Charles Bon, Henry Sutpen's roommate, at the University of Mississippi, who followed a design of his own, schemed to go with Henry to Sutpen's Hundred to confront Sutpen for abandoning his mother and to reveal that he is Sutpen's son, but that he meets Judith, who falls in love with him; that the confrontation with Sutpen was delayed by the war; that when his father revealed to him that Bon was his half brother and part Negro, Henry shot Bon to defend his sister's honor and then fled; that when Sutpen's wife Ellen died, he proposed that her sister, Rosa, become a mere body out of which he could produce a male heir and that he was refused; that the Negro house servant Clytie was also Sutpen's daughter and that Sutpen had not only begotten children of his slaves but had turned at last to a poor white trash girl and begot a child by her, all three of whom the grandfather, Wash Jones, slaughtered; that Bon's child too came to Sutpen's mansion and was taken in by Judith and Clytie; and finally that Henry returned from exile almost forty years later and hid in the now-derelict "dark house," until discovered by his Aunt Rosa and Quentin, and that it was Clytie the slave daughter who applied a scorched-earth climax to the Sutpen epic by setting the mansion on fire that very day of discovery, perishing with her white brother Henry.

Although the long postwar era of the Lost Cause produced few men of action like Colonel Sutpen, it produced a legion of storytellers and multitudes of listeners, and this backward-marching, backward-looking parade of storytellers and listeners comes finally to a dead end in Quentin Compson.

Given the obvious fact that lives like Colonel Thomas Sutpen's have been the stuff of fiction, both very good and very bad, from Homer and Sophocles to the present, why do I feel compelled, almost messianically, to urge, along with too few other scholars, that greater attention must be paid to Quentin, whose affinities are all with the palest of postmodern antiheroes?

Sutpen's story expresses the desire of Southerners to be both civilized, as in Jefferson County, and wild, as in the Civil War. Quentin can be neither, nor does he even aspire to be either. Both the South and Quentin are transfixed between the nightmare of the past and its legacy in the present. Jason gives his son the same name Sir Walter Scott gave his man of action Quentin Durward, the young Scot who fought for a foreign king in 1468, an ironic contrast to Quentin Compson. Quentin's grandfather's storytelling does not inspire Quentin's father, Jason, to a life of action, and Jason's storytelling fails to inspire Quentin to a life of action; Jason's only act is to pass on the story, imbued with his own intellectual character and personality. Quentin's only acts are the passive ones of reluctant listening, of anguished retelling, of going along with his father to the Sutpen cemetery and going along with Miss Rosa into Sutpen's house, and of staring at his father's letter in his room at Harvard.

Unlike his father, Jason, Quentin does not want to know, understand, become involved in the story of Sutpen and others, and tell it to future kin, to a community of listeners. Part of Quentin's problem is that he knows that, like people, like Sutpen himself, civilizations such as Greece and Rome come and go, so why not the South and its Sutpens? Quentin knows that he cannot forge an identity out of a heroic past as precarious as common everyday life, even if he could or desired to do it.

Quentin's negativity, both stated and implied, pervades the novel. In early chapters, Quentin responds to questions with a yes that conceals a diffident no and later with a no that conceals a panicked yes. "Better that he were dead," Grandfather said of Charles Bon's son, "better that he had never lived."[5] Quentin, Faulkner implies, would apply that comment to himself, the Quentin who says of himself, "I am older than many people who have died" (301). Miss Rosa will not "reconcile herself to letting him [Sutpen's son] lie dead in peace" (289), Shreve says to Quentin, who, the reader may infer, has already "become" Henry, wanting to lie dead in peace himself. "So now I shall have to go in" (294), thinks Quentin, invading Henry Sutpen's hiding place to satisfy Miss Rosa's craving for an answer to the mystery of "a ghost" in the old mansion. Miss Rosa has refused to remain a ghost herself, and so Quentin moves out of the storytelling into reality, to witness the suicide by fire of Clytie and Henry (and to commit his own suicide by river water in *The Sound and the Fury*). The reader might wonder whether Charles Bon, recently revealed to be Thomas Sutpen's mixed-blood son, forced Henry to kill him to avoid marrying their sister and fathering another mixed-breed child, but the context of Quentin's listening might well imply that Quentin would conclude he did, because, unable to respond to any positives intended by the storytellers, Quentin is deeply affected by all the suicides and suicidal behavior.

Faulkner implies that as each storyteller tells a story, earlier storytellers are remembered, so that Quentin's grandfather is a dominant figure hovering over Jason's telling about how his father helped Judith, and the reader feels his presence also, and so does Quentin, even more intensely. The reader must imagine, then, that as he listens specifically to Rosa, then to his father, and then to Shreve, Quentin feels the urgent speaking presence of many other storytellers. Quentin is never of one mind. As early as the first few pages, Faulkner tells the reader that there are "two separate Quentins now talking to one another in the long silence of notpeople in notlanguage" (4–5) and that a third Quentin is listening to those two voices. "The eagerness of the listener," says Jane Eyre, in Charlotte Brontë's novel, "quickens the tongue of a narrator," but unlike his father and Shreve, Quentin is not an eager listener, so the storytellers strive harder to capture and keep his attention and stimulate his interest, with the effect that he is all the more tormented, giving rise to the relentlessly implied questions: Why me? What do you want me to do? Early in the novel and then again halfway through, Quentin thinks, "Yes, I have had to listen too long" (102, 157). To what? To the implied pleas that he forge his identity out of these stories but even more to the implications of the stories as they apply to who he really is, a potential suicide. Near the end, when Shreve's telling the story back to Quentin reaches a high pitch of intensity, Quentin yells, "Wait!" thinks, "I am going to have to hear it all over again. . . . I shall have to never listen to anything else but this again forever" (222). Influenced by the vigor and pace of Shreve's own enthralled retelling, Quentin takes up parts of the tale yet again, compulsive, obsessed, manic (225).

Sutpen's saga is unimaginative, in itself uninteresting; it is simple, operatic melodrama (not tragedy, as some have argued, not even near tragedy), and as such, it is *one* major expression of the South's and the world's conception of life in the South before, during, and after the Civil War. Sutpen's motive for telling his story to Grandfather Compson is self-justification and self-aggrandizement, a simple continuation of all his other actions. The men, women, and children, white and slave, who, caught in his web, witness Sutpen's life, create his legend by telling his story in fragments that promote mystery and suspense, fragments embellished by imagination and repeated from generation to generation until they torment Quentin's ears. Exhorted to listen, Quentin is the principal listener in the novel. As Nick Carroway, not Gatsby, is the protagonist of *The Great Gatsby*; as Jack Burden, not Willie Stark, is the protagonist of *All the King's Men*; and as the narrator, not Roderick Usher, is the protagonist of "The Fall of the House of Usher," an even more apt example—because the true protagonist of all first-person narratives is the narrator—so Quentin, not Sutpen, is the protagonist of *Absalom*. The major difference is that Quentin the listener is not the sole storyteller in the novel. That some critics mistakenly identify Quentin as the sole narrator of the novel testifies to the strength of the impression one gets of the pervasiveness of his consciousness, an effect toward which all Faulkner's techniques are deliberately working.[6]

Had he intended Sutpen to be the protagonist, Faulkner was in command of an array of techniques that he could have adroitly employed to tell Sutpen's simple, melodramatic story, to delineate its complex implications about the South, much more effectively. For instance, he could have used the omniscient point of view, getting into the perspectives of all the major characters; or he could have used the third-person, central-intelligence point-of-view technique from Judith's or Henry's perspective; or he could have imagined a first-person narration, with Judith or Henry as narrator, with one of Bon's descendants as listener.

Who *does* tell the story and to whom? Faulkner uses the omniscient point of view, from which he tells the reader that Miss Rosa and Quentin's father told Sutpen's story to Quentin, who tells it to Shreve, who tells it back to Quentin. Why does Faulkner create Rosa and Quentin's father as storytellers, since neither knows enough to tell the whole story? And why is Quentin necessary as a listener-storyteller since he knows only what they tell him and especially since his verbal responses seldom exceed yes and no and his mental responses do not directly express the intended effects of their storytelling upon his consciousness? The blunt question Faulkner deliberately poses for readers is this: *What is Quentin doing in this novel?*

We know that Faulkner had already told Sutpen's story with two narrators like Quentin and Shreve in the short story "Evangeline," written five years before *Absalom*. In that story, both the basic "I" narrator and his friend who tells him parts of the story are keenly interested listeners who are motivated to seek answers to mysteries. By contrast, in the novel very little narrative evidence but all of the fiction techniques point to Quentin as Faulkner's primary interest. There are two Faulkners in this novel, one the artist at work, the other Faulkner's alter ego, given the name "Quentin."

Faulkner implies that before chapter 2 begins, Quentin has told his father the story Miss Rosa told him, and he implies that before chapter 6, Quentin has told Shreve the story of Miss Rosa. Faulkner directly renders Quentin's telling a story only once, when he and Shreve are retelling Sutpen's story together. The effect of this use of the technique of context and implication is only to *suggest* that of all the storytellers Quentin has been the major storyteller, while providing the reader's basic actual experience with Quentin as the Quentin who is listening to stories, not telling them.

The most pertinent way to show not only *that* Quentin is the protagonist but also *how* he is the protagonist is to examine the techniques of the art of fiction that Faulkner employs in this novel and their effect on the reader. The techniques fiction writers use are in themselves expressions of meaning and conveyors to the reader of experience; that is true especially of innovative writers and truest of Faulkner the innovator in this novel. One may see in an examination of Faulkner's careful and full revisions the stress he placed on the use of innovative techniques that in themselves would express the emotional, imaginative, and intellectual meaning of the novel.[7] This novel is a veritable encyclopedia of innovative techniques and innovative use of conventional techniques. Gathering all the Quentin fiction around *Absalom, Absalom!* will enable readers not only to understand Quentin and the works in which he figures but to understand Faulkner's innovative techniques as well, and that understanding would most probably make all his works far more accessible.

Faulkner's overall technique in this novel is to combine innovative literary techniques with the dynamics of oral storytelling techniques to achieve the overall effect of a complex meditation, which the reader responding to implication must attribute to Quentin. The unique passiveness in Quentin's character enables, perhaps forces, Faulkner to achieve technical effects not otherwise possible, effects that constitute much of his greatness as an innovative literary artist.

The ideal reader for this novel will examine Faulkner's use of the techniques of fiction to express his intentions. Just as readers may be aware of Faulkner's literary techniques, even Quentin and the storytellers themselves are conscious of the techniques of storytelling that they use to affect their listeners. Quentin tells Shreve, "I reckon Grandfather was saying [to Sutpen] 'Wait wait for God's sake wait' about like you are until he [Sutpen] finally did stop and back up and start over again with at least some regard for cause and effect even if none for logical sequence and continuity . . . telling it all over and still it was not absolutely clear" (199).

By his use of techniques, such as metaphor, Faulkner teaches the reader how to read *Absalom*. "Maybe nothing ever happens once and is finished," meditates Quentin. "Maybe happen is never once but like ripples maybe on water after the pebble sinks, the ripples moving on, spreading" (210). Quentin's metaphor alerts the reader to expect that the narrative events and other elements in this novel will not happen only once but will be repeated in various other forms, enhanced by Faulkner's patterned and controlled repetition of motifs, metaphors, and phrases.

Only through an awareness of Faulkner's artistry can the general reader feel the full impact and respond to the myriad implications of Quentin's drama of consciousness. Faulkner's ideal reader for this novel will become aware of not just his narrative strategy but also his use of the technique of point of view, a complicated mixture of omniscient, third-person central intelligence, to use Henry James's term, interior monologue, and *four* quoted first-person narrations, with variations in style; his manipulation of shifting contexts to make simultaneous implications about Sutpen's story and Quentin's responses; his use of allusions to enrich the contexts; his use of transitions and lack of transitions in time and space, to disorient and then reorient the reader and Quentin; his deliberately ambiguous and tormenting use of pronouns, especially "he," "they," and "it"; his use of the devices of incremental repetition, questions, digressions, interruptions, odd punctuation, long, complex parentheticals, long convoluted sentences, paragraphs as long as eight pages, juxtapositions, expressionistic effects, irony, parallels, symbolism, and startling imagery.

All those techniques achieve a sense of simultaneity and inevitability that result in a unity so complex many readers and some critics do not fully comprehend it, partly because the techniques I have listed cause disorientation and dismay, as his first vital reader, his editor, lamented to Faulkner.[8] While all of his techniques serve the Sutpen story, they simultaneously serve the more important characterization, created mostly by context and implication, of Quentin, whose responses are often similar to the frustrated, irritated, gasping reader's.

Readers have asked, Why does Faulkner use such a vast array of techniques? Faulkner strives to create shifting, complex contexts within which to stimulate the reader's mind with implications that express what cannot be directly expressed—as he knew from the limited effect of Quentin's first-person testimony in *The Sound and the Fury* and in "That Evening Sun," published two years later—and simultaneously to explore, perhaps subconsciously, his own (Faulkner's) psyche indirectly through Quentin's implied psyche.

The ostensible antebellum, Civil War, Reconstruction generic narrative of the stock character Sutpen becomes meaningful as a paradigm of the decline of the South, not in itself, but mainly as fragmented and embedded in the neurotic, probably psychotic consciousness of Quentin. Sutpen's story is an objective correlative of Quentin's ineffable state of consciousness.

Faulkner's achievement in this novel, as in all his best work, lies not in his having imagined the story of Thomas Sutpen but in his having imagined the techniques that innovatively render that story and its implications; and a unique achievement of this novel alone is that it is not mainly Faulkner's character-narrative-based imagination but his techniques that create Quentin Compson. The medium is the message.

Faulkner is interested in each of the characters, especially in listeners who become storytellers, but his identification with Quentin was essential to his being. Faulkner is Quentin, but he takes a major step further than focus on Quentin by delineating each of three other character's immersion in Sutpen's story, with the effect that the novel is more about each of the characters and about the process of their storytelling than it is about Sutpen himself.[9] But when we compare the centrality of Quentin as listener and storyteller with the other characters, we find that no potential for further development is active at the heart of Rosa's story, because it is static and always was. Mr. Compson's narrative is impersonal—he has no motive beyond a pure compulsion to tell stories, except for the weak inference that he aims to affect and teach Quentin; Shreve's involvement is transitory. Southerners tell stories to teach and to create and sustain identity, especially as a postwar, Lost Cause ritual. Rosa and Quentin's father say, in effect, Quentin! Listen! So you can transmit it to our own kind, to your children! But Quentin will have no children. Staring at his father's letter about Rosa's death, as if in a trance, he tells the story to a sardonic, Northern foreigner, Shreve, as if to be overheard telling it to himself, a dramatic monologue that is simultaneously a soliloquy. He tells it to take possession of the story, to give himself a sense that he exists, that he is not himself a ghost engendered by the ghosts of the past; but finally, he tells it to rid himself of the burden of Southern history, which as one of the last of the Compson line, he feels but by mere torpor does not accept. Nor does he accept the implied obligation to pass it on through the representative story of Sutpen. Quentin starts with no ostensible motive to tell, and ends with none, but the reader must infer his existential dilemma from the innovative techniques Faulkner employs.

As omniscient narrator unusual in the infrequency of his speaking, Faulkner meshes his own narration with each of the storytellers, who also have a kind of omniscience through overreaching imaginations, and Faulkner's complex consciousness finally meshes with Quentin's. Faulkner, a master of point-of-view technique, creates his most complex pattern in this novel. There are three elements: Faulkner's omniscient voice, voices telling "old tales and talking" (243), and Quentin's meditation voice. Within Faulkner's omniscient point of view, the various storytellers tell their stories. As Faulkner moves from one to another, sometimes within only a few sentences, the very juxtaposition of one storyteller to another expresses some aspect of Quentin's consciousness of storytellers and of times and places. Near the end of chapter 8, for instance, three storytellers intersect and interact on a single page: Clytie, like a messenger in a Greek tragedy, describing Wash Jones's slaughter of his granddaughter and his great granddaughter; and Sutpen, as retold by Quentin's father, who imagines the missing parts, retold again by Quentin to Shreve, and who interrupts, as told by Faulkner (233–34). Faulkner's own infrequent narration almost always relates to Quentin, with the effect that the reader is always aware of the presence of the Faulkner-Quentin consciousness even as Miss Rosa, Jason, or Shreve are telling the Sutpen narrative. The precept that the protagonist of every first-person narrative is the narrator applies to each storyteller in this novel. Faulkner modifies that aesthetic so that the novel becomes essentially more about Quentin as the major listener than as storyteller.

"So they will have told you doubtless already" (107) is one of the phrases repeated to Quentin often. Subconsciously, Quentin is acutely aware of not just the listener-tellers Faulkner quotes but of also those people who are listeners only and even of tellers and listeners who are only implied in the novel: Charles Bon has told stories to his roommate Henry, Clytie has told Grandfather Compson a story, Grandfather Compson has told his son Jason a story—all those tellings are paraphrased by Miss Rosa and Jason, who tell the stories to Quentin, the all-encompassing listener. The reader must pay attention to Quentin and imagine the conscious and subconscious effects on Quentin of Shreve's sardonic retelling of the Sutpen story. As these listener-storytellers talk, readers should be ever mindful, as Quentin is, of the always-hovering presence of those characters to whom Faulkner does not give a storytelling voice: Sutpen's children, Judith and Henry, those with black blood, Clytie and Bon, and that ever-present representative of the poor white trash from which Sutpen also sprang—Wash Jones. Faulkner does not directly give them storytelling voices because the technique of context and implication enables him to evoke their voices without quoting them—and isn't indirection a powerful technique?

Faulkner stresses the fact that each of the tellers of the Sutpen tale dwells upon fragments that reflect needs in their own lives: Rosa's love for Sutpen; Quentin's grandfather's friendship with Sutpen; Sutpen's own egocentric story of himself as told to Grandfather Compson; Jason Compson's desire to exhibit to his son Quentin his intellectual analysis of the Sutpen-Rosa story; and even the wisecracking Northerner Shreve's escalating exhilaration in retelling to Quentin the saga Quentin has just told him. The narrative logic of the Sutpen story as told by Rosa and Quentin's father calls for a listener who can and does respond fully, interactively, and meaningfully as the telling progresses. But Quentin is as far from being that kind of listener as any Southern twenty-year-old could be. Through Quentin's responses, and lack of responses, to the telling and the tale, Faulkner suggests to the reader the negative nature of the values of the world Sutpen and his witnesses represent. At no time does Quentin even hint that he derives any value on an exemplary level from what is being transmitted to him; he responds on a personal, subjective level to the stories he is told, affected most by parallels in his own life, mainly the relationship between himself and his sister Caddy, as seen in the brother-sister relationship of Henry Sutpen and Judith Sutpen, and, far less important, by parallels between the friendship of Henry and Charles Bon and the roommate relationship of Quentin and Shreve. Faulkner was once asked, "How much can a reader feel that this is the Quentin, the same Quentin, who appeared in *The Sound and the Fury*—that is, a man thinking about his own Compson family, his own sister?" Faulkner replied, "To me he's consistent. That he approached the Sutpen family with the same ophthalmia that he appreciated his own troubles."[10] Is that so? Yes, but also not quite so, Caddy being far more important to Quentin than family-region history.

The legacy of the Civil War and Reconstruction in the South today is expressed in the varied responses of individuals. Quentin Compson, the most passive of Sutpen's vicarious witnesses, is the protagonist. The vigor of the transmission of the values of the Southern way of life, symbolized in Faulkner by high-potency sexuality, mostly perverse in various ways, from generation to generation ends in Quentin's implied impotence, which is not only sexual but also intellectual. Faulkner dramatizes the fact that while the conventional Southern values, which coalesced in the issues and the warrior mentality of the Civil War, fail to produce creative acts in the lives of individual descendants, the legends do stimulate each individual listener's imaginative participation, a value that transcends the ritual teaching function of the South's past. For them the unvicarious life is not worth living; at least they have *that* much of a life.

Storytelling inflames the imagination of the listener. Jason demonstrates that effect, saying often, "I imagine" (82, 85–87). But Quentin goes further and *imaginatively becomes* one of the characters with whom he most unconsciously identifies: Henry, Sutpen's son. The image of Henry and Charles Bon "facing one another at the gate" triggers Quentin's own vicarious response: "It seemed to Quentin that he could actually see them" (105). A paradox in the power of the imagination is suggested when Faulkner as author says that Quentin "could see it; he might even have been there," as Henry kissed his sister Judith before returning to war, but Quentin contradicts his creator, thinking, "*If I had been there I could not have seen it this plain*" (155). He knows he has listened too long and too much, until he is not listening anymore, and has no desire to be a storyteller (280). Quentin responds to his Canadian roommate, Shreve, when he exhorts him to "tell about the South" (142). Quentin infects Shreve with "the virus of suggestion" (Henry James's phrase). Shreve's imagination is so activated that he reimagines the story of Henry and Charles Bon, exploring possibilities, rendering the story even more ironic so that, for instance, Charles Bon saves the life of his brother Henry who later kills Charles Bon *because* he is his and Judith's brother (237–38, 254, 275). Quentin tells the story to Shreve only to get rid of it by telling it as an act of betrayal to a cynical listener, who tells it back to him, ironically, in an empathy that is finally so profound, Quentin and Shreve together not only retell it in two voices as one voice but also imagine their counterparts, Henry Sutpen and Charles Bon, so vividly that Quentin and Shreve feel they have become one; then they become Henry and Bon, "in the cold room . . . there was now not two of them but four," so that Quentin and Shreve and Henry and his roommate Bon are "riding the two horses through the iron darkness" (236–37).

The inflamed imagination leaps into vicarious experience. Sutpen, Bon, and Henry enact a story—and Wash Jones violently ends it. Rosa, Jason, Quentin, Shreve, and Faulkner do not act—they listen to the story and retell it. Faulkner sustains vicarious experience as a major motif. All the storytellers to whom Quentin listens are people whose lives are intensely vicarious, so that he the listener is a captive of the vicariousness of others. The South that Quentin knows through storytellers has, ever since defeat in the Civil War, been living vicariously at a level that threatens sanity, and Quentin symbolizes the product of that quality in the South—the inflamed imagination in an action vacuum. "But you were not listening," Quentin tells himself, in one of his meditation passages, "because you knew it all already, had . . . absorbed it already without the medium of speech somehow from having been born and living beside it, with it" (172). But in the telling, the lives of others seem, compared with his own, very compelling: the lives of Henry and Judith, especially, but even Miss Rosa's and his father's. Jason tells Quentin that Judith and

Henry were a "single personality with two bodies both of which had been seduced almost simultaneously by a man [Charles Bon] whom at the time Judith had never even seen" (73), knew only through her brother's stories. Judith communes with her dead lover Bon through his son by another, alien woman, taking care of him, and when Judith dies Clytie lives vicariously through the same boy, raising him. From the same class as Sutpen, Wash Jones vicariously lives the dream of wealth through Sutpen. After the war, Wash meets the returning hero at the gate: "Well, Kernel, they kilt us but they aint whupped us yit, air they?" (150). Unlike Quentin and the others, Wash Jones, who has lived vicariously through his hero Sutpen, finally commits a real act, but out of the kind of past he has vicariously lived, he can act only in violence.

Every nonreality quality in the other nonactive characters is paralleled in Quentin, usually to a greater degree: meditation, imagination, passivity, and accede (torpor or inaction). As he listens to stories about Sutpen and other men of action all his life told by numerous people, Quentin becomes aware that he has no life of action. Unlike Jack Burden in *All the King's Men*, he does not touch the web in such ways as to cause others to touch it. The kind of storytelling and listening process Faulkner presents is a form of meditation, but the only literal meditation to which he gives the reader access is Quentin's.[11] Faulkner is interested less in the drama of action than in the drama of human consciousness. By the end, Quentin has turned even more inward (and will finally turn against himself in suicide). Even his imagination and his meditations are limited, narrow in scope, and fail to result in a compulsion to tell stories as a means of perpetuating the past and maintaining a sense of community.

Myriad voices speak obsessively to Quentin about his legacy, the epic story of the settling of his home region, and the lingering effects of the war fought to preserve that way of life. But Quentin brings to his reluctant listening to those voices his own private sexual feelings about his younger sister, Caddy, delineated in *The Sound and the Fury* and, as a submerged psychological process, in "That Evening Sun," in which again Quentin, not Nancy, is the protagonist. Joseph Blotner quotes Faulkner as saying that Quentin in *Absalom, Absalom!* listens to the story of the brother and sister, Henry and Judith Sutpen, as a bitter parallel to his own incestuous longings for his sister Caddy and his own bitter failure to protect his sister's honor.[12] Similarly, in "That Evening Sun," Quentin, who does not act, who only listens, is listening most attentively to Caddy's questions that relate to sex. The effect of Faulkner's technique of implication from shifting contexts in the various works featuring Quentin may culminate in the general implication that Quentin kills himself (which he does, in *The Sound and the Fury*) not so much out of guilt for merely desiring his own sister as out of a profound apprehending of the fact that he exists intensely only when he responds in amazement and bewilderment to the tales people tell him about people who are, compared with himself, very much alive. His is a purely existential dilemma, as posed by Søren Kierkegaard in *The Sickness unto Death*, Martin Heidegger in *Existence and Being*, Rollo May in *The Meaning of Anxiety*, Jean-Paul Sartre in *Being and Nothingness* and *Nausea*, Albert Camus in *The Stranger*, and Katherine Anne Porter in "Flowering Judas." Quentin is far less active, less questing than even the narrators in the Sartre and Camus novels, and his accede, a mortal sin in the Catholic Church, is more severe than Laura's in Katherine Anne Porter's "Flowering Judas."

We know that the storyteller's need to identify a personal parallel among the characters in the stories is most acute in Quentin (who "becomes" Henry) because Faulkner *implies* the need, rather than letting Quentin directly state it, but his need is so great that the active, vicarious imagination cannot save him. Quentin's need is the basic need to *be*; and his basic dilemma, the anxiety that emanates from the inability to be. If existence precedes essence, Quentin's sense of his own existence is such that essence can hardly flow from it. Existential psychologist Rollo May defines anxiety as

> the experience of the threat of imminent non-being. Anxiety is the subjective state of the individual's becoming aware that his existence can become destroyed, that he can lose himself and his world, that he can become "nothing." . . . Anxiety overwhelms the person's awareness of existence, blots out the sense of time, dulls the memory of the past, and erases the future . . . it attacks the center of one's being. . . . Anxiety is ontological, fear is not. Anxiety always involves inner conflict. . . . Ontological guilt "arises" from forfeiting one's own potentialities.[13]

Miss Rosa, his father, and others fervently tell Quentin stories about people who have lived fervently on a level of action; Quentin, even considering that he is young, has no life of action himself about which anybody could fervently tell a story. Even fervently telling a story is an action, but Quentin himself tells the Rosa-Sutpen story to Shreve in a kind of bewildered, impotent, static voice that Faulkner gives us in a controlled series of fragments. Far from motivating him to live a life of action that might embody the values of the Old South, both the tellers and the tales only make Quentin aware of how empty his own life and consciousness are. Quentin is passionate only in the last line, as Meursault is passionate, yelling at the priest, only at the end of *The Stranger*. When Shreve asks Quentin, "Why do you hate the South?" Quentin's hysterically anguished denial, "I dont hate it!" is true. His existential dilemma is that, having a self so famished, he doesn't even hate himself.

In *Absalom*, his father, Miss Rosa, and others offer family and public history for their own varied reasons, but they provide a way for Quentin to transcend his subjective sexual impotence and his emotional, imaginative, and intellectual paralysis. Given Quentin's inability to respond as an active receiver of the legacy, Faulkner implies that Quentin's dilemma is deeper than incestuous longing, that it is the existential dilemma of being and nothingness. Quentin is now and always has been a shadow verging on nothingness, amazed and anguished at the spectacle of richer lives of action or of active preservers of the lives of more active people of the historical past. Quentin, who ends in suicide, helps us see why Faulkner himself, who in life merely posed as a warrior and man of action, who *may* have considered suicide, turned to creative re-creation, with war and its aftermath as the human action with the greatest range of possibilities in life and in literature. Meditating on Quentin, my student Melissa Wilkinson, in a moment of intellectual ecstasy, exclaimed, "It's wonderful that Faulkner could make so much out of nothing!"

Many critics see Quentin as Faulkner's alter ego, his most autobiographical character.[14] Quentin was one of his favorite characters. He might have said, Quentin c'est moi! If a writer's life is most truly expressed in the subjective act of creation, rather than in a recital of external events, *Absalom, Absalom!* is Faulkner's autobiography as a person via Quentin and as an artist at work creating Quentin. Paradoxically, Quentin's narrow, single-minded consciousness is at the center of Faulkner's myriad-minded consciousness.

Quentin is listening, subconsciously, on the deepest level, deeper than the Henry-Judith incest implication, he is listening to the basic meaning of Sutpen's design, which is a calculated effort by the boy Sutpen to exist by creating a mansion and all that went with a plantation way of life, because turned away from the front door of a mansion, the boy had an intuition of existential anxiety, the fear of nonbeing. Sutpen's design ends in catastrophe, maybe a suicidal overreaching. As both reader and Quentin listen to the Sutpen stories, Faulkner enables us to imagine Quentin's thoughts and emotions.

Faulkner, I imagine, and Sutpen felt the same anxiety, but Sutpen distracted himself by building an empire, which failed him and his community; Faulkner distracted himself from anxiety by creating his Yoknapatawpha saga, as a work of art that triumphs like John Keats's urn, did not fail him and will not fail his readers, if they work with him as his collaborators by responding not only to the surface complications but also to the implications that the shirting contexts generate. Faulkner's ideal reader will then feel unbearable pathos for a character such as Quentin in ways no other novel can stimulate.

Poem X in Faulkner's *A Green Bough* has been referred to as "Twilight," an apt title for Faulkner's meditation on the Quentin beneath the line-by-line surface of the novel: a terrific figure on an urn—

> caught between his two horizons,
> Forgetting that he cant return.

This an allusion to the town emptied of its folk in Keats's "Ode on a Grecian Urn." And Edgar Allan Poe's poem "From Childhood's Hour" evokes a sense of Quentin's life:

> From childhood's hour I have not been
> As others were:
> I have not seen as others saw:
> I could not bring
> My passion from a common spring . . .
> And all I loved, *I* loved alone.
> *Then*—in my childhood . . . was drawn
> The mystery which binds me still . . .
> From the cloud that took the form
> Of a demon in my view.

For Quentin, the demon is not Sutpen, whom others called demon, but the spot of grease on the road where Quentin merely wished he could have more fully existed.

Rediscovering a Major Civil War Novel

Joseph Stanley Pennell's *The History of Rome Hanks and Kindred Matters*

Joseph Stanley Pennell's *The History of Rome Hanks and Kindred Matters* is the most autobiographical of Civil War novels. The protagonist's drama of consciousness occurs around 1940. Consequently, in *Rome Hanks* more than in any other Civil War novel, a clear understanding of the author's life and of his complex use of the point-of-view technique is essential if the reader is to respond most fully. The novel is the "record of the author's search for the answer to the questions: 'What am I? How did I get to be what I am?'" (*Current Biography 1944*, 542).

Asked to comment on his life and work for *Twentieth Century Authors: A Biographical Dictionary* in the early 1950s, Pennell (pronounced as in *kennel*) responded with details that very closely described Lee Harrington, the protagonist of *The History of Rome Hanks and Kindred Matters* (1944) and of *The History of Nora Beckham: A Museum of Home Life* (1948), the second novel in a trilogy, the third volume of which was written but never published:

> I was born in Junction City, Kansas [on the 4th of July, 1903], when it was still a "tough" town. For the place is three miles from Fort Riley; and all famous cavalry regiments—including the Seventh—knew "Junktown" well. The "Wild West," however, had gone. By the time I began to notice things most of the townspeople had forgotten James Butler Hickok. [And Jeb Stuart and Custer and Armistead, and by 1991 most seemed to have forgotten Pennell himself.] And I do not remember the saloons and bawdy houses of my native town. Nevertheless, when I left the town in 1947 there were still respectable women of earlier generations who would not walk down the "saloon side" of Washington Street.
>
> My Grandfather Pennell [Judd Harrington in the novel] served with the North Carolina troops in the War-Between-the-States; and my Grandfather

> Stanley [Tom Beckham] fought in the Ninety-fifth Pennsylvania Volunteers (Goslin's Zouaves) in the Civil War. My great-grandfather (Rome Hanks) on my mother's side, a major in the Fifteenth Iowa Volunteer Infantry, went through the battle of Shiloh and the Atlanta campaign. I am both a Rebel and a Damyankee.

When he was sixteen, Pennell's father, Joseph Judd Pennell, left North Carolina with his father and crossed the plains. He went from making coffins to taking photographs that have earned him a place in the history of American photography. A distant relative was Joseph Pennell, a still famous graphic artist.

Photography played an extremely important role in the Civil War and in Pennell's life. Pennell's father is represented in American Heritage's *American Album* (1976) by a "curious patriotic scene," the unveiling of a monument in Junction City, Kansas (166). In the two novels, Pennell captures facets of the life of the small-town photographer—Robert Harrington is the son of a Southern veteran of the Civil War who moved to the West. Pennell is haunted by his father as photographer and by the photographing process and the photographs themselves. Lee thinks he could have stayed home and become a studio photographer, after his father. He remembers watching his father take photographs. "As Lee lay squinting in the night, this series of pictures of Papa—almost as if he, Lee, were a camera Dry Plate multi-exposed—passed in his mind quickly, not flat as on a screen, but deeper and sharper than life, as are the braces of photographs mounted on a card and looked at parallactically through a stereoscope. . . . The camera of experiences bats its lens a timertwo" (304–5).

The two novels are Proustian researches, recapturings of things past and contemplations of selected images, photographic in nature. Mythic metaphors emerge from those memories, accompanied by many storytelling voices. Photographs of men at Shiloh reunion, 1889, "seem now as mysterious" as stereopticon views of Pompeii (11).

Pennell's mother, Edith Stanley, to whom he dedicated *Rome Hanks* but who died before it was published, was a pioneer woman. She "might be said to be the daughter of pioneers, as she did a lot of traveling in covered wagons and saw a lot of Indians." He had a love-hate relationship with his mother, who was the model for Nora Beckham in the two novels.

"I was educated in St. Francis Xavier's School, the Junction City High School, Kansas University [one year], and Pembroke College, Oxford University [three years]. I chose Pembroke College because it was known (and still is) as one of the most 'literary' of English speaking colleges." He left there with a BA in 1929. In *Rome Hanks*, Lee's numerous direct and indirect allusions to history, religion, literature, and art reflect Pennell's own classical education in England and contribute to a rich external context for the novel's Civil War events.

Pennell started writing for newspapers during summer vacations while in college.

> As a newspaper reporter, I "broke in" on the Denver *Post*, worked for the St. Louis *Post-Dispatch*, the Kansas City *Star*, the Los Angeles *Examiner* and the Los Angeles *Post-Record*. I was, for a couple of years, managing editor of the Huntington Park *Signal* (California). During hard times, I worked on the radio station KMO of St. Louis (as everything from end man in the minstrel show to continuity writer and announcer for the Farm Hour [heard also twice a week as "Professor of Microphone English"], taught in the John Burroughs School and acted in a St. Louis stock company. (Even now I occasionally see a former fellow player on a movie screen.)

In most fiction and nonfiction (see especially Sam Watkins's *"Co. Aytch"*) about the Civil War, writers draw quite frequently upon the theater for key metaphors and similes (influenced in part by their reading of such images in Shakespeare, "all the world's a stage," etc.). As Pennell had been, Lee and Christa, his lost love, are actors in the repertory theater in St. Louis. Pennell adds to his own repertoire of theater metaphors several movie metaphors and devices. He alludes to movie directors (94) and invokes the good name of the great Russian director Sergei Eisenstein (155). As Thomas Wagnal, a major character, tells about Shiloh, Pennell links key, summarizing images, as in a movie montage, with such phrases as "I saw . . . I heard . . . I remembered" (109).

In the mid-1930s, Pennell abruptly returned to Junction City. Supporting himself by renting his father's photography store, he wrote in an apartment above. No one except his mother and Thelma Baker, town librarian, knew that he was writing a long novel, that he was not what he appeared to the townspeople to be, an idler taking a seven-year vacation. Before going into the army, he also wrote a draft of *Nora Beckham* there.

The image of Pennell as a recluse reading and writing is illuminated if we remember Nathaniel Hawthorne's years as a recluse in his dead father's house in Salem, Massachusetts, and recall the several ways he worked his own life into his early tales and novels. But Pennell was more a modern-day writer as man of action—he interrupted his work to go off to war. The jacket photo shows him in his officer's uniform. The fact that the novel appeared in the summer of 1944 and that the author is pictured in uniform would have caused readers of the novel quite naturally to think of World War II, and readers today will see many similarities to various wars since, especially Vietnam. The trilogy Pennell planned was another one of those strange artifices writers have used to write autobiography; he used both the fictional mode, as Thomas Wolfe, James Joyce, and Ernest Hemingway did, and the third-person device as Henry Adams did in his autobiography *The Education of Henry Adams*.

"As far back as I can remember I have always wanted to be a maker of things. I think it was at Kansas University that I began to think of myself as a writer, a maker of books. It was, however, much later, in time and burned manuscripts, when I began to write *Rome Hanks*. That book took more than five years of my time."

He studied Mathew Brady's famous photographs; Brady is depicted at work in several passages (see especially 74, 75). He "read scores of books, looked at many others," about a thousand, including the 128 volumes of the *Official Records*. Lee also names Civil War diaries, histories, songs, novels, and magazines. He

> searched long in diverse obscure corners of obscurity. For my grandfathers had told me little of their part in the Civil War; my grandfather Stanley had recollected a thing or two—but he always exploded into a rage of fine cuss words when he began to tell of how the Rebels let maggots get into his wound when he was a prisoner on Belle Isle. And Grandfather Stanley and Grandfather Pennell called each other "Mr. Stanley" and "Mr. Pennell" whenever they met.
>
> Aside from the newspaper stories I wrote, I published an article on Americans at Oxford in the *North American Review* and some verse in Miss Harriet Monroe's *Poetry, a Magazine of Verse*. These, I believe, were my start.

Poems open both of Pennell's novels and appear in them as the work of Lee Harrington. Poems frame *Rome Hanks*; just as Pennell puts his dedication into a poem, Lee the young poet ends his long meditation with his four sonnets to Christa (novelist-journalist Martha Gellhorn in real life).

Part of *Rome Hanks*, "The Courtship of Tom Beckham," appeared in *Mademoiselle* in September 1943. A short story, "On the Way to Somewhere Else," appeared in *Harper's Bazaar* in 1944 and was reprinted in *Best American Short Stories, 1945*.

"After I finished *The History of Rome Hanks*, I joined the army [1942] and served for two years as a private and subsequently a second lieutenant of antiaircraft artillery." He was public-relations director for the antiaircraft training center at Fort Bliss. "*Rome* was published while I was still in uniform."

After the war, Pennell returned to Junction City but left after a dispute over the city's failure to stop the noise of a merry-go-round that disturbed his writing. He had worked on *Nora Beckham*, titled after the granddaughter of Rome Hanks, who married Robert Harrington, the photographer. This is a much quieter book, which is similar, reviews claimed, to Marcel Proust, Joyce, and Wolfe. As in *Rome Hanks*, there are many side stories, but Lee, again the center of consciousness, becomes clearly the focus of the novel.

In *Rome Hanks*, Lee frequently alludes to famous paintings: "The Night Watch," "The Anatomy Lesson," and "The Age of Innocence " (15, 17, 89). In the last line, "He watched the spider climbing up the wall over his desk toward an engraving of Friar Bacon's study over Folly Bridge." *Nora Beckham*, the second volume in Pennell's projected trilogy, ends with the same image and thus deepens our understanding of what happened to Lee as a result of his meditations and his service in World War II.

> Ah, Lee said, Ah. Nothing's become of me—And my father's dead and Nora's dead and Dee Given's dead and Wagnal's buried in Potter's field. He took another drink and looked at the red and silver artillery shield and the silver bar on his forest green shoulder loop. He buttoned the firegilt buttons and put the cap on his head. The spider—a spider—was again climbing up the wall over the desk toward the engraving of Friar Bacon's study over Folly Bridge. (350)

Some time after 1944, he married Elizabeth Horton, an army nurse, to whom he dedicated *Nora Beckham*, "with all my love." She drew the portrait of him on the cover. Thelma Baker, the librarian who had helped him research *Rome Hanks* and gotten it read at Scribner's while he was in the army, when she was told of Pennell's marriage, exclaimed, "That can't be! He loves *me*!" She lived in Junction City for many years; apparently, she never married.

After Elizabeth committed suicide, Pennell married her sister. "I now live, with my wife, Virginia Horton Pennell," he wrote for *Twentieth Century Authors* around 1955, "on Tillamook Head, a promontory overlooking the Pacific Ocean" near Seaside in northern Oregon. And that was the last the literary world heard from him.

In Junction City, Pennell had worked on the third volume of *An American Chronicle*, entitled "The History of Thomas Wagnal"; Wagnal was a major character in *Rome Hanks* and *Nora Beckham*. About Wagnal, Hemingway remarked to Charles Scribner in 1949 that the old soldiers who write to him praising his own war fiction "are like that wicked old man that boy you have in your stable wrote so magnificently about in The History of Rome Hanks. Parts of that were better than anything ever written in America and parts were worse" (*Selected Letters*, 1917–1961, 1981, 669). But his alcoholism impaired Pennell's creative faculties. Lee is talking to his bottle of ale throughout much of *Nora Beckham*.

Having started a biography of his father, Pennell was working on a straight autobiography when he died of pneumonia in Oregon in 1963 (the year of Evelyn Scott's death and a year after William Faulkner died).

Thelma Baker submitted *Rome Hanks* to three publishers; it was returned unread. *Rome Hanks* arrived at Scribner's late in 1943, when Pennell was thirty-five, just before his induction into the army, says Stephen Berg in *Max Perkins, Editor of Genius* (1978). "Another of those damned works of genius," Max Perkins overheard his associates say (423). Berg claims that Pennell had been inspired by Wolfe and that his book "bore many similarities to Wolfe's work" (424). Many reviewers made the same observation, but all Wolfe's fiction, except for a novella, is cast in the omniscient point of view and Pennell's is third-person central intelligence, to use Henry James's term. The Wolfe parallel derives from a misreading of the point of view; it is Lee Harrington who is Wolfian, not Joseph Pennell. "Perkins spoke of the book to everyone," says Berg, "for none in years had excited him so much" (426).

Perkins wrote to Pennell, "I am having a grand time reading it, and I should like to tell you that a colleague here showed me that Pickett's charge piece, and I really do not believe I ever saw a war piece that excelled it, not forgetting Tolstoi" (424). But the novel had two problems, Perkins said. First, Christa, Lee's beloved, was too much like her real-life model, Martha Gellhorn, who was then married to Hemingway. Second, it was open to the charge of obscenity. Through the mail, they worked on those two problems, and others, over most of the year, until Christa was less based on Martha Gellhorn, and the so-called obscene elements were reduced. Gellhorn refused my request to allow publication of her letters to Pennell. (*Note:* I was in touch with her until her death in 1998; she is a minor character in one of my novels.)

The novel was banned in Boston for "vulgarity," thus increasing sales. On July 26, 1944, Perkins wrote to Pennell to tell him that sales were about one hundred thousand, that the novel had been picked up by a book club and had gone into an armed-services edition (*Editor to Author: The Letters of Maxwell Perkins*, 1997, 263).

Orville Prescott correctly predicted that *Rome Hanks* would cause more debate than any other novel of the year. It was certainly the literary event of 1944, when these other novels also appeared: Lillian Smith's *Strange Fruit*, Ben Ames Williams's *Leave Her to Heaven*, Kathleen Winsor's *Forever Amber*, Niven Busch's *Duel in the Sun*, Charles Jackson's *Lost Weekend*, Somerset Maugham's *Razor's Edge*, Saul Bellow's *Dangling Man*, Harry Brown's *Walk in the Sun*, John Hersey's *Bell for Adano*, Jean Stafford's *Boston Adventure*, and Caroline Gordon's *Women on the Porch*. Since 1938, no major Civil War novels had appeared and only two more would show up in the forties: Clifford Dowdy's *Where My Love Sleeps* (1945) and Ross Lockridge Jr.'s *Raintree County* (1948). Sinclair Lewis called *Rome Hanks* "one of the richest and most pungent novels of the decade."

The novel was praised and damned (and defended by Perkins in a letter, 255) for its gruesome depiction of the killing and maiming of soldiers and its descriptions of bodily functions. "We saw the rebel officer's face splash the water in a puddle" (18). The woods "smelled like piss and powder" (20). "It was almost dusk then—and I kicked something. I picked it up before I saw that it was a young golden-haired head with its blue eyes open" (25). "Once I fell down and put my hand in the mouth of a corpse" (26). "Nights in bivouac sounded like the turn-on of a thousand hoses" (4). There are many instances of sex, including masturbation, buggery, and whores. Wagnal even imagines that Katherine fantasizes General Stuart in bed with them (214).

In chapter 10 (80), Lee dotes on his own body and its infirmities, augmenting the effect of Wagnal's descriptions of the effect of war and disease thus far and anticipating Lee's memory of Pinkney's various descriptions of the body. This is the only chapter that is completely italicized, suggesting that Lee's meditation on his body comes some time after the meditation that ends the novel. This chapter suggests two metaphors for the novel, the body politic and war as an anatomy lesson. Wagnal's early references to the body snatchers (7) and to the resurrectionists (139) of Edinburgh suggest a parallel to the way old men snatch the bodies of the young and hurl them into war. At the end, imagining his birth, Lee returns to the infirmity of his own body since birth, weak lungs (359).

Even before Norman Mailer's *Naked and the Dead* (1948) and James Jones's *From Here to Eternity* (1951), Pennell had gone beyond Hemingway and other war novelists in rendering the speech of soldiers realistically, although all four still used "f——." *Rome Hanks* was banned in Boston and in a few other places at a time when *Strange Fruit* was banned for the single use of the word. Many copies of both novels were sold to readers searching out such words and left unread once the thrill wore off.

The obscenity charge and certain references to explicit language in reviews may have stimulated sales, but the confusion noted in reviews suggests that many who bought it were unable to read it with enough comprehension to get through it. By 1957, when Robert Lively in *Fiction Fights the Civil War* put *Rome Hanks* on his list of the fifteen greatest Civil War novels, very few people remembered it.

Professor of history Paul Rossman of Quinsigamond Community College in Worcester, Massachusetts, impressed most by the description of Pickett's charge that had impressed Max Perkins, wanted to use *Rome Hanks* in his class, but it was out of print. The trouble he had getting *Rome Hanks* reprinted was far greater than Thelma Baker's difficulty in getting it published. Rossman sent it to one hundred publishers for reissue before Second Chance Press took it on in 1981. To the publishers of that small press, it was one of the greatest books ever written. But it sold only six thousand in hardcover and paper. However, it was the first fiction ever offered by the History Book Club, which bought 1,500 copies. Historical Times Book Club also offered it. And David Donald, a major Civil War historian, assigned it in a core curriculum at Harvard. There was some film interest too.

Both *Current Biography 1944* and, ten years later, *Twentieth Century Authors* summarized reviewer response to *Rome Hanks* as being "sharply divided"—from "self-indulgent, confused, torrential style and undisciplined, sprawling construction" to "a permanent acquisition to world literature." However, having taken a close look at the reviews themselves, one must conclude that they were mostly positive, though many critics had serious reservations, generally having to do with structure and style. Even the negative reviewers made some strong positive statements: "obscure" but "powerful and promising"; "not a true historical novel," but "it will appeal to adults who enjoy adventure and spice"; "the method of the book is pretentious and clumsy," but "you can piece together a bottomside view of the Civil War that is worth putting beside Brady's photographs, Grant's 'Memoirs,' 'The Red Badge of Courage,' and J. W. De-Forest's 'Miss Ravenel's Conversion'"; "surface absurdities and wild overwriting," but its "repetitious style . . . develops considerable force"; and "perplexing, irritating . . . masses of formless, purposeless experimental writing," but it is a "brilliant, powerful" novel. The *Newsweek* reviewer called it "haphazardly put together" but had high praise for Pennell's descriptions of Civil War battles as being better than the descriptions that journalists on the scene were offering of World War II battles (Pennell himself was then in the service).

Novelist Hamilton Basso expresses the double attitude generated by the book's effects:

> Mr. Pennell, like Wolfe, commits just about every sin known to literary man, and, again like Wolfe, thinks up a few all his own. His book is chaotic, undisciplined, and formless, it is extravagant and sentimental, its prose is so emotionally supercharged that it often sputters all over the place, and by and large, it will give those who appreciate novels like Mr. Brown's "A Walk in the Sun" [a short World War II novel, written in simple, economical style] a very bad attack of chills and fever indeed. Despite this, however, and I readily admit that it is a lot to despite, Mr. Pennell's book strikes me as being a work of unusual talent, and, among other things, the best novel about the Civil War I have read, with the natural exception of "The Red Badge of Courage." . . . Mr. Pennell, with any luck at all, ought to have a long career as a novelist and, I hope, a happy one. He should be leery, though of anybody who urges him to walk in Thomas Wolfe's shoes. He can get places on his own.

Like all the other reviewers, Basso failed to see that Pennell's command of point of view already placed him less in the company of Thomas Wolfe than in that of Henry James, James Joyce, and William Faulkner.

Neither generally negative nor positive reviewers revealed an understanding of how point of view works in fiction. Diana Trilling rejected the novel, partly because "Mr. Pennell tells us simple and obvious things so elaborately as to make us believe he is being profound." On the contrary, Pennell as author says very little because the novel is set in the emotions, imagination, and intellect of the protagonist, Lee Harrington, on whom the author sustains focus. Ms. Trilling makes the amateurish mistake of attributing to the author the thoughts of his character, a mistake in no way mitigated by the fact that Lee *is* one of the most autobiographical characters in fiction.

The style derives directly from the third-person, central-intelligence point of view. Reviewers noted, often disdainfully, a certain experimentation in style, apparently unaware that it is Lee and/or Wagnal, not Pennell, who indulges in Joycean wordcrafting, such as "wishing for the lip-salved lady with the viciousdashing look on her" (56) and "they were clothed in roughandready plainasanoldshoe garments" (173). Midwesterners Lee and Wagnal share Pinkney's Southern love of the sheer sound of words, such as "plowhannels!" (157). Kansan Pennell is more convincing in his use of Southern dialect than most purebred Southern writers. (See the long paragraph on page 116.) Lee, as young poet, would be quick to use literary and lyrical phrases (see 169–70) and indulge in wordplay as a way of making the past his own through inventive expressions.

The absence of quotation marks in dialogue and the grouping of speeches by several different characters within paragraphs, extremely unusual in 1944, were cited on reviewers' lists of confusing experimental features of Pennell's novel. Given that there is so much storytelling within storytelling, readers should consider how confusing the use of quotation marks would prove to be. Apparently, reviewers and readers blithely ignore the author's own explanation for omitting quotation marks in "Note to the Reader": "to make the narrative flow from one alembic without entailing either too much cloudiness or clarity."

In his intelligent and overwhelmingly positive review on the front page of the *New York Times Book Review*, on July 16, 1944, Nash K. Burger called the novel "a landmark among novels of its type" and claimed that "there is considerable experimentation of style and structure in the work, and it is all very well done indeed," but he too fails to illuminate for his readers the author's point-of-view technique. One may safely assume that the reaction of reviewers is likely to be that of readers as well.

Pro or con, *no* reviewer describes within a context of clear understanding how all the elements and techniques work together to produce a work of art. Many of those techniques Pennell's readers might have encountered in Herman Melville's *Moby-Dick* and in Proust, Joyce, John Dos Passos, Faulkner, and Joseph Conrad. *Rome Hanks* may have seemed (and may seem even today), next to Faulkner's *Absalom, Absalom!* and Evelyn Scott's *Wave*, the Civil War novel most original in conception. In these three, more than in other Civil War novels, point of view is the crucial technique, and Pennell's use of it posed problems of orientation for reviewers and other readers.

Readers may make the mistake of taking Lee as merely a point-of-view device the author is using to present battles and other Civil War experiences.

On the contrary, Lee is a direct result of the author's autobiographical impulse; more importantly, *Rome Hanks* is a work of art, produced in large part by Pennell's use of point of view, not as reviewers suggested in spite of it. Pennell's Lee Harrington is like Faulkner's Quentin Compson, especially in *Absalom, Absalom!* Quentin is Faulkner's most autobiographical character, in spirit more than in fact. Pennell's Lee, on the other hand, is much more literally an autobiographical character than Quentin is. Quentin is an ostensibly marginal character whose marginality in several stories and novels is developed artistically and thematically in such a way that he becomes the major character. A major difference between Lee and Quentin is that Lee, unlike Quentin who tells stories to his Canadian roommate Shreve, has not yet surrendered to a compulsion to tell stories of the war (he has told Christa only what little he knew at the time and only to impress her romantically).

For the reader who keeps Pennell's point-of-view technique clearly in mind, what seems experimental to the untutored reader may follow quite naturally after the first three chapters.

Pennell opens with a device he will use often: italicization to set passages off for various purposes, another feature of experimental writing before 1944. Except for "Note to the Reader" and the dedicatory poem, Pennell uses italics for the same practical reason most people do: to signal that the passage functions in some way different from the main body of the text, and for that reason its importance is stressed. On page 302, near the end of the process, Lee will remember this opening passage verbatim. The reader who grasps the function of this technique at the start may experience the passages more intensely. This first instance provides Lee and the reader with a compressed impression of most of the major narrative elements, character relationships, and themes, while employing one of the major techniques that will create artistic unity—italicized passages that anticipate key moments to come.

Lee remembers three stories simultaneously: his recent relationship with Christa (around 1940) and the Civil War stories Wagnal and Uncle Pinkney told him soon after.

The compulsion to remember makes the more general, distilled images come to Lee out of chronological sequence. Here are the major instances of his recollections, with the chronological event in parentheses: prelude (see 302); 5 (see 111); 55 (see 62); 136 (see 147 and 214); 157 (see 225); 338 (see 352).

In the two italicized paragraphs that open the novel, Pennell suggests how the reader is to read *Rome Hanks*. *"You awake, Lee thought"* indicates that the point of view will be third-person central intelligence; every element of the novel will be filtered through the perceptions, sensations, emotions, and consciousness of a single character, Lee Harrington.

When Lee awakes "*in the vast night of all the years*," he cries out: "*How could I have known?* [about the war]. . . . *All night!* . . . *I go back and look again and heed and look again and heed. . . . forgetting why (Christa's face and hair and bored voice).*" Here, we are told why he went North to seek out Wagnal to implore him to tell him about his Yankee great-grandfather, Rome Hanks, and why he went South to seek out his Uncle Pinkney to implore him to tell him about his Grandfather Judson Wade Harrington—it was because of Christa's disdainful response to his feeble attempt to impress her with his glib recital of only the few facts and notions about his Grandfather Harrington he then possessed.

This passage opens the first chapter: "Yes, Christa said. Yes; I'm sure your Grandfather must have been a fine old Southern gentleman." It is in that chapter that Pennell more securely sets up the third-person, central-intelligence point of view. The first line of the second paragraph, "She is bored, Lee thought," and the opening of the third paragraph, "And now here he was, Lee Harrington, sitting across the table from the most beautiful and proudest girl he had ever seen," paraphrases Lee's conscious thoughts at that time and place. Then Lee repeats in his own thoughts the statement she had made in Pennell's third-person narration.

The space break indicates a leap in time from that scene in the department store lunchroom with Christa to his own room years later, after her statement has stung him into seeking out Wagnal and Uncle Pinkney and after he has read a great many books about the Civil War. "Lee looked at the photograph and the four sonnets he had pulled out from under the desk drawer." The implication is that the photograph is of Christa who has rejected him and that the sonnets are love poems to her. As he launches into the remembering process, he creates a parallel between himself and Christa and Dante and his ideal love Beatrice. Christa is his muse, as Beatrice was Dante's, even though Christa is, ironically, a negative inspiration. Another implication of the parallel is that Lee as Dante has a Virgil (Wagnal and Uncle Pinkney combined) who will guide him through the divine comedy of the American Civil War.

Pennell frames the novel with that scene in Lee's room (4–5). Having referred to them at the start and several times during the course of his meditations, "Lee picked up the four sonnets and began to read them to the photograph" (361). "Thus, Lee said sententiously to the photograph" of Christa, "love ends" (362).

Lee has failed as a lover, as a poet, and as the last line of chapter 1 intimates, as a citizen in his hometown: "I *am* an exile—an exile, Goddamn them all to hell!" Lee's compulsion to recall and, with slow deliberation, to fix in memory the stories he has listened to about his ancestors in the Civil War prompts him again, in the italicized opening of chapter 2, to reach forward to remember Wagnal's distillation of his entire story: "*God help me, boy, I'm old and Katherine is dead and Dick's dead at Savage's Station.*" Then Lee tries to put his memories into some chronological order by recalling his mother and her attitude about himself and about Wagnal. Because his mother used to ask, "Whatever is to become of you, my poor boy?" we may suppose she is among those from whom Lee feels exiled as he remembers his own and his ancestors' pasts.

In the opening of chapter 3, Pennell continues to orient the reader to the pervasive third-person, central-intelligence point-of-view technique with such phrases as "Lee remembered," "Lee thought," and "Lee said." In passages only a few lines longer, now and then, the author's presence is more clearly sensed. "Yes, Lee said aloud, it is strange—damn' strange. He looked at the sonnets with warm, hypnotized eyes. Strange, he said, strangely" (114).

For two hundred pages after that passage, Pennell seldom offers such passages of author narration because he has established the third-person, central-intelligence process—and because Lee begins to imagine the lives and thoughts of others. With so few passages in which the author narrates—always from Lee's point of view, however—the reader, to remain securely oriented throughout the novel, must avoid the misapprehension that Lee is writing, because Lee has never even attempted to write about his own life or his ancestors, nor is he speaking to a person in the room. He is remembering, thinking, or speaking aloud to himself or to some creature (the spider) or object (the photograph) in the room. The reader overhears, so to speak, his memories and meditations. Again, the primary narrator is Pennell, though always through Lee's consciousness.

It is Wagnal and Uncle Pinkney who have a compulsion to tell stories, responding to Lee, the listener. Again, Jane Eyre says, "The eagerness of the listener quickens the tongue of a narrator." As Lee remembers the various stories, Pennell reorients the reader frequently with such phrases as "Wagnal said," "Pinkney said," and "Lee remembered." To keep the focus on the storyteller-listener process, Pennell also has Wagnal and Pinkney address Lee directly. "I saw your grandfather beneath the bluff," Wagnal tells Lee. He calls him "boy" or "sir." Uncle Pinkney calls him Lee—"Now Lee . . . mark what I tell you, boy!" (194)—because Lee's father was named Robert Lee after General Lee and because Lee and Pinkney are bound together in kinship: "You and I can sit here under the honeysuckle vine and talk about war; and I can tell you . . . how we . . . " (182).

With the opening of chapter 4, the alert reader will have become fully oriented to Pennell's complex use of point of view.

As stated earlier, most of the negative comments made about the novel on its appearance derive from the inability of those reviewers to perceive the workings of Pennell's use of the primary technique of point of view, which affects style and every other technique and device and the narrative, character, and thematic elements in any work of fiction. But technique not only enables a fiction writer to organize and control all the elements of a work; technique in itself expresses a major aspect of the work, and that is especially true of Pennell's novel.

For instance, Pennell uses the technique of juxtaposition to create an expressive pattern. Lee is fighting the war, in memory and imagination, simultaneously on both sides, and that process is dramatized several times when Wagnal telling stories is juxtaposed to Pinkney telling stories. Pinkney's world is contrasted, by juxtaposition, to Wagnal's (167) and then Wagnal's is juxtaposed to Pinkney's (177); their personalities and styles of speaking are contrasted. They are juxtaposed again at pages 204 and 236.

And at one point Pennell juxtaposes Lee's imagining his grandmother Myra's frontier experiences to Uncle Pinkney's storytelling (225); next, to Wagnal. Pennell clusters three kinds of narratives, all remembered by Lee. Lee's final memory of Wagnal's storytelling, mostly about Rome Hanks—"That's it, Wagnal said. It was an old song"—is juxtaposed to a contrasting chapter in which Lee imagines his great-grandfather Rome's meditations: "Rome would awaken again. . . . Again and again now he would remember" (297). Pennell's use of the technique of juxtaposition expresses Lee's active desire to connect the voices of both sides of his family in a single flow of memory—a kind of reconciliation.

One effect of juxtaposition is the profound sense of simultaneity for both Lee and the reader. Two things when experienced simultaneously are felt more intensely. For instance, as Wagnal tells about the fall of Vicksburg on July 4 (100), Pinkney will tell about the high tide of the Confederacy on the same day, same year, 1863, at Gettysburg (183); readers who know even a little Civil War history will experience both events simultaneously at both points in the novel.

At Lee's birth on the July 4, 1904, fireworks suggest Vicksburg and Gettysburg. With the firing of a cannon (even though it is one from the Spanish American war), Lee's entire life within the context of the Civil War is dramatized (353). In Lee's omniscience-reaching imagination, all three events occur simultaneously. The effect of simultaneity is one of the major achievements of the process Lee has been going through.

Pennell's controlled repetition of words, phrases, lines, and passages, and his use of the device parallel, help reinforce simultaneity and enable Lee to see and feel a rich and complex historical context for his meditations on the Civil War. For instance, Pinkney invokes the Revolutionary War by declaring that his father fought at King's Mountain.

Another major effect of the process Lee is going through is his sense of parallels between characters: Rome is to Wagnal what Reeve is to Judd Harrington; Doc Gaines, who delivers Lee, is ironically a comic version of Lee as he comes to be obsessed with the war; Clint Belton parallels Bull Pettibone in

Pinkney's story. Wagnal's cabin parallels the room where Lee will remember the stories Wagnal told in the cabin. Above all, the romance of Wagnal and Katherine parallels Lee and Christa.

Listening in memory to Wagnal and Pinkney side by side, Lee discovers that grandparents on both sides were guided by or obsessed by the pursuit of the ideal and of a woman as the embodiment of that ideal. "Maybe if women were not watching," Lee imagines Rome thinking at the end of Rome's meditation, just before he hears Clint's footstep on his porch, come to kill him for being witness to his disgrace—cringing in fear under the bluff (293). Lee, who has held Christa up as the ideal woman for himself, names, in the last chapter, ideal women throughout history (360).

Some reviewers were appalled by what they called Pennell's cynicism. Again, it is characters not Pennell who pose both the concept of the ideal and the attitude of cynicism produced by the corruption of the ideal. Wagnal refers to "the uses of man as a first-rate absurdity" and says of Katherine's sister Una, "And it was Una who was already planning the evolution of an imperial purpose to satisfy the cold perfect pattern of her geometric vanity" (98). In the mansion's garden, he observes that "the little temple was built as a ruin," suggesting the South's "Lost Cause," to which Uncle Pinkney also scornfully refers. In the midst of battle, Pinkney the Southerner asks, "Where am I? And, what, in God's name, am I?" (183). For Wagnal, "The Great West" beckons, but its promises remain unfulfilled.

Before he began to write, Pennell himself experienced the process that his autobiographical protagonist, Lee, experienced. The novel's primary purpose then is to enable the reader, also, to go through that complex process, that experience. It is *not* simply to tell the story, interesting as it is, of Rome Hanks or of Lee's other kin, as the title may lead readers to expect.

Pennell stresses the importance in that process of the oral storytelling tradition. Lee tried to tell stories to Christa, a cynically reluctant listener. Both Wagnal, the Yankee, and Pinkney, the mountain Southerner, tell stories to Lee. "Boy, Wagnal said, everything is strange: You sitting there on that kitchen chair," the eager listener (112).

In serious fiction, first-person narratives are always about the narrator, and it is as much to the narrators, as revealed in storytelling, that Lee responds as to the various stories they tell about his kin and their friends and enemies.

In addition to Wagnal and Pinkney, Lee recalls several other, minor storytellers, making his own consciousness all the more complex. Long ago, Grandpa Tom Beckham told Lee a little about his war experience. Even as Lee remembers Wagnal telling him about Grandpa Beckham, he recalls things his grandpa said: "I can hear my grandfather now, Lee thought" (281). Katherine told Wagnal the bizarre and violent story of Jabez (126–35); Wagnal retells it to Lee; and Lee later remembers the tale.

The author and the reader experience what Christa's attitude denies her: the process of "looking and heeding," a process that transcends storytelling alone. Lee experiences that, too, as he listens to Wagnal. But stories are only the inciting events; they are elements in a process.

Because she clung to stereotypes and clichés, Christa did not even experience the storytelling. Many confused readers of *Rome Hanks* were probably like Christa, reluctant to respond, bored, even hostile, and confused. The ideal reader will *want* to experience the kind of process Lee is experiencing.

Remembering, thinking, and speaking aloud, Lee does not always reveal how he feels about what he has heard and read. It is the reader who may imagine the effect on him, which is profound, considering the fact that he recalls everything in such extraordinary detail, even allowing for the natural enhancement his emotions, imagination, and intellect bring to the details he has heard and read about.

The effect of this complex process on Lee is suggested by the effect on Wagnal of his own storytelling, especially as contrasted with the effect one may imagine Uncle Pinkney's storytelling has on *him*. Wagnal's stories are less *about* Rome Hanks and others than they are expressions of Wagnal's own character. Wagnal is somehow changed, as is his listener, Lee. Pinkney, on the other hand, seems relatively unaffected; primarily, he is a deliberate, self-conscious Southern Appalachian Mountain storyteller in the way he uses words and pours on the Southern accent.

As Lee searches among his kin and kindred matters for his place in the life-death pattern, he traces, like the spider, a web—of blood kin relationships, following Southern kin who fought in the North at Gettysburg, and Northern kin who fought in the southwest at Shiloh. The "kindred matters" referred to in the title includes Wagnal who, as nonkin storyteller, affects Lee as much as the actual kin he tells about—even more than Uncle Pinkney affects him.

Chapter 1 is mirrored and climaxed in the final chapter, lending a certain symmetry to the novel, but some readers may feel that the novel ends most effectively as Wagnal ends his last story on page 296. Near the end, after about page 315, the storytelling style and tone of the novel seem to change. Lee begins to use some of the phrases of the omniscient, sometimes satirical narrator: "On the day when we see the covered wagon of the Beckham family nearing the Town . . . " (328); "It is to be noted that Nora said nothing" (342); and the satirical style of the two chapters describing his own birth (347). The question arises, Were the last fifty pages written first, or is the change to a more prevalent omniscient imagining a natural development in the process Lee is going through?

As part of that process, Lee speaks aloud but not necessarily to himself; rather, he is speaking as a way of remembering the stories more clearly and forcefully. "Wagnal was all at sea now, Lee said aloud" (7). As we experience

Lee's stream of consciousness, it is dramatized when he suddenly speaks aloud, as if the oral tradition has taken hold of him, even though he isn't ready to make another attempt, after the deeply abortive one with Christa, at telling other people.

But like most recluses, Lee does talk to himself. "Now, Lee said, his voice falling to a soft chant, I am afraid of cities when I am walking along alone at night" (52). Sometimes Lee speaks to himself about Uncle Pinkney even as he remembers his uncle remembering (199). Sometimes he speaks to Wagnal, contributing to Wagnal's own memory and meditation (110). Lee talks to the spider, weaving a web as *he* is: "Lee posed the question to the spider" above his desk (36). Talking aloud, he animates the inanimate. "Look, Lee said fiercely to the blank wall. Look!" (50). "He was my grandfather, Lee said tenderly," to the four sonnets he has written for Christa (58).

Reviewers put Pennell's scrambled chronology on their lists of experimental devices. Again, an understanding of point of view would have cleared up any confusion. Events for the storytellers are finally structured not in chronological time but in memory time, and so are Lee's memories of the memories others have told him. Remembering, Wagnal and Pinkney *tell* Lee mostly about *other* people, and then as *Lee* remembers, what they told him becomes part of his own life.

Lee's meditations on his body (chapters 10, 80) suggest that while memory, imagination, and intellect can move at will from past to present, the body is always dying in the immediate present. Phrases such as "Now I know" remind the reader of the present (98). Pennell is delineating a young man's meditations on the past, within a framework of the present, and quite naturally Lee would mesh present and past, returning to his relationship, for instance, with Christa at those points where he remembers Wagnal's stories about himself and Katherine. "Wagnal sobbed a little—like distant thunder, Lee thought. And I sobbed with him. For I loved Katherine too—as I loved Christa and Anne and love——" (135). The past is still alive in Lee's total response to the way it is alive in Wagnal's remembering voice. About a hundred pages later (257), after Wagnal has told of Katherine's death, he (or Lee) recalls an event before her death; and for Wagnal and Lee and the reader, she, one of the most vital characters in the novel, is alive again.

Pennell suggests in his note to the reader that memory is more important than accuracy and facts. "All anachronisms are conscious, as the narrative is filtered through the memories and desires of several narrators who may be either ignorant or untruthful—or both." Wagnal himself tells Lee that his memories of battle (34), and of Katherine (121), may be inaccurate.

Many lines attest to or suggest the importance of memory. For instance, "And each memory is a shock that racks this big, clumsy arthritic frame. . . .

No. . . . I cannot stand the light over these things, for when I see it over them, I know again that I was young and I am old now" (169–70). And Lee remembers his affair with Christa up to the point where she rejected *his* stories about his Civil War great-grandfathers (148–57).

Forgetting is a torment. "Well, I'll be Goddamned! they had forgotten everything" (36), says Wagnal, who about one hundred pages later exclaims, "I forget. . . . I forget how it was then exactly" (146). Uncle Pinkney feels the pathos of being forgotten. "Who remembers gen'l Dick Garnett now?" (198). Lee has set for himself the painful but exhilarating task of *not* forgetting.

Many major American novels from *The Scarlet Letter* to the present are novels of meditation on events that illuminate American history, the American Dream, and the American character. The character relationship that embodies that meditative process is the hero-witness relationship. Rome Hanks and Lee's other kin, and Wagnal as well, are heroes who stimulate the meditations of Lee, the witness.

As the characters remember and meditate, their imaginations come into play—Pinkney's imagination less than Wagnal's, and Lee's is most pervasive. Wagnal imagines General Ulysses S. Grant's thoughts (last paragraph, 254). Wagnal is obviously imagining the event in Clint Belton's life with Katherine's sister, Una, and their thoughts. (See especially chapter 28, at 236.) Later, he imagines Clint seeking out Rome to kill him. Having heard Wagnal tell what he has had to imagine, Lee himself is able to imagine Rome's thoughts up to Clint's arrival; Lee then remembers Wagnal's telling him about the Clint-Rome confrontation as Wagnal had imagined it.

Having heard all the stories, Lee, as early as page 55, feels a compulsion to imagine his grandfather Tom Beckham's life, until he merges his own consciousness with Tom's: Tom "lay there for what seemed a long time, for the flies were not only at his thigh but at his face and hands. Jesus, they bit, Lee thought reverently. And he could hear them droning" (71, 311).

From about page 271 on, through the power of his imagination as it thrives on fragments he has picked up during his life, especially from listening to people talk, Lee becomes, in a sense, his grandmother Myra too and his father Robert—and his mother Nora: Lee goes from "Why, I can see my mother, drying her eyes" to "She saw herself as she leant against the screen door at dusk" (338–39). And then he even imagines his mother giving birth to himself.

Even before the novel begins, Lee has gone through a long awakening process: "*You awake, Lee thought, in the vast night of all the years,*" opens the novel. "*How could I have known? I tell you, I didn't know!*" (2). The process of *waking* to *knowing* becomes part of who he becomes, a creature of his own meditation.

The dynamics of storytelling and listening, remembering and meditating, and imagining, in a sustained process such as Lee undergoes, produces as one achievement of human consciousness a kind of omniscience, the sense of which is profoundly exhilarating. Lee and Wagnal, who are in many ways so much alike, acquire this power most obviously. In all his stories, Wagnal aspires to know and do everything: "Everything was going on in the world; nothing was stopping until I could finish what I was doing and go see it happen, go take part in it, go everywhere and be everything" (137). For him, strangeness and fascination become pervading experiences of consciousness (112–13).

The lives of Wagnal's friends are so important to the formation of Wagnal as a person that he not only tells what they did that he actually witnessed but also imagines and then tells Lee their very thoughts. Lee must have sensed that Wagnal has achieved a kind of omniscience, because one of the effects on Lee of Wagnal's omniscient-like storytelling is that Lee himself begins to imagine the lives of others.

Lee even imagines Rome, also aspiring to a kind of omniscience. Rome once told Wagnal that curiosity "should be directed . . . toward a history of the world in general terms" (54). Lee imagines Rome meditating on this larger view: "Rome saw all the world as lying simultaneously in dark and quiet . . . places which he had never seen except on the lantern slides of his brain" (285). And later Lee imagines, "Now Rome had begun more and more to see the wide continent of North America spread out before his mind's eye in one great nocturnal panorama" (299).

Why does Pinkney seem not to aspire to omniscience? Perhaps because in his Southern culture many people already tended to think of themselves within a larger context as a habit of mind.

When he met Christa, Lee "had not even vicariously lain under the bluff at Shiloh" (48). But he finally achieves a degree of omniscience, as this passage suggests: "I have lain under the banks at Shiloh," Lee thinks, "and talked to the pale major from Springfield, Illinois and heard the boy from Fairfield, Iowa blubber. I worked Webster's guns on the landing and lay wounded all night on the banks of Owl Creek. . . . I am the soldier who never fired a shot. . . . I buried no dead. . . . Yet because of something that happened before my grandfathers came to Kansas, I know these things. I know" (see long passage, 43–44).

The compulsion to remember stimulates Lee's own imagination, and that phase of the process is the most crucial. Point of view generates that process; style and several other techniques and devices control that process to create a work of art. Confusion of style, chronology, and other "problems" are the product of reader inattentiveness, not of a lack of artistic power in the author. In the imagination, humankind transcends captivity in "self," in the limited sense of that word. We do not often reimagine the facts of our own past, as Lee does not *his*, but in making the humanistic leap to imagine the lives of *others*, he most truly creates himself. Lee fails as lover and poet but succeeds as a human being by becoming, at the end of the process, the man who remembered, imagined, and meditated on his and his ancestors' pasts. (Thus, he is brother to Willis Carr, protagonist of my Civil War novel *Sharpshooter*.)

Such a man is capable then of passing that experience, in artistic form, on to others; Lee does not yet do that. That is what Pennell himself does, in a great novel that puts the reader through the stages of the same process. The Civil War and its impact are freed from the inertness of mere facts and stereotypes to become real and vital for each person within his or her imagination. It is first there that it has either emotional impact or meaning; without that process, the Civil War as a public experience that all Americans can share in a wide variety of ways remains inaccessible.

The History of Rome Hanks and Kindred Matters page citations are to the 1944 first edition; the pagination is the same for the 1983 Second Chance Press reprint.

The Innocent Stare at the Civil War

Madison Jones's *Nashville 1864: The Dying of the Light*

The innocent stare, a fixed stare in his first novel *The Innocent* (1957), is reiterated in all Madison Jones's work, especially *The Forest of the Night*, *A Buried Land*, *An Exile*, *A Cry of Absence*, and *Passage through Gehenna*. One has only to compare *Nashville 1864* with Jones's most ambitious, complex, and finest work *A Cry of Absence* to see that the basic Jones art can serve him well. In *An Exile*, for instance, all the elements—character, conflict, theme and techniques, point of view, and style—cohere to create an intimacy with the protagonist that is almost unbearably intense and immediate.

All Jones's fiction is about the Civil War and Reconstruction. That claim derives from my often-stated conviction that in a profound and pervasive sense all fiction written by Southerners is about the Civil War—and thus Reconstruction. One may say of certain novels that do not ostensibly deal with the Civil War, therefore, that they are among the great Civil War novels: *Huckleberry Finn*, *Absalom, Absalom!* and even *All the King's Men*. That Jones turned late in life to the Civil War in *Nashville 1864: The Dying of the Light* (1997) is not an expression of an acquired interest so much as it is a more direct expression of effects of the war and Reconstruction that underlie all his work. I do not mean literal depictions of the war that we may find in isolated passages of Jones's fiction. *An Exile*, for instance, has few direct or implied references or allusions to the war, but the characters, the setting, and the cultural milieu are a creation of the effects of the war and Reconstruction. An even more expressive Civil War novel is *A Cry of Absence* because it deals head-on with complexities of the lingering effect of the war and Reconstruction as it exploded during the decade of the Civil War centennial and the trauma and upheaval of the civil rights movement.

Given my premise about Southern writers in general and Jones in this instance, by devoting an entire, though very short, novel to the war, Jones invites the question, What is the achievement of *Nashville 1864*, winner of the Michael Shaara award (sponsored by the United States Civil War Center) and the T. S. Eliot award, as a late expression of Jones's vision? Also, how does Jones's novel compare with Civil War novels by other Southern contributors to the genre, such as William Faulkner, Allen Tate, Ellen Glasgow, Caroline Gordon, Margaret Mitchell, Evelyn Scott, his friend Robert Perm Warren, and his teacher Andrew Lytle?

The general story is very simple: thirty-six years after the war, in 1900, Steven Moore writes a memoir of the two days when he, as a boy of twelve, searched for his soldier father during the Battle of Nashville. Because many Civil War novels for young adults depict similar searches by children for family members, some readers have assumed that Jones's novel was written for young adults. Because the boy is accompanied by a young slave, one recalls the opening chapters of Faulkner's *The Unvanquished* (1938), which render the adventures of a young man and his young slave and give a similar impression of appealing to young adult readers—the characters and the action are simple, and the style is clear. But *The Unvanquished* continues into adulthood, and Faulkner develops a very complex vision of the war and Reconstruction. Whether Bayard Sartoris is writing or telling his story is left ambiguous. Allen Tate, however, in *The Fathers* (1938), makes the act of writing a memoir of the year before the war, also involving a slave, the primary vehicle for delineating a vision of antebellum life as it prefigures aspects of the Civil War and Reconstruction Southern mentality.

As my own short novel, *Sharpshooter* (1996), evolved over fifteen years of rewriting, I was aware of its moving into and within the tradition of novels about adolescents who fight in or witness the war, searching for family members. The narrator, thirteen when he goes to war, begins to write his story ten years after the surrender. All four novels are short. The crucible in Faulkner's, Tate's, in my own novel, and in Jones's is the relationship between a young white boy and a slave. These similarities attracted me to Jones's novel.

Nashville 1864 falls into another category of Civil War novels, those that re-create but do not reenvision the war. For 136 years, Americans, especially Southerners, have been staring at the Civil War and Reconstruction—an innocent stare, because both Northerners and Southerners have, from the start, missed almost everything that happened back then and ever since. Out of that prolonged innocent stare, all fiction by Southerners, but none by Northerners, has been directly or indirectly, and profoundly and pervasively, about the legacy of the Civil War and—we should stress, as Shelby Foote does—Reconstruction ("There are two sins for which America can never be forgiven—slavery and

Reconstruction.") Unfortunately, that innocent stare has achieved few visionary insights into the Civil War itself. The child's stare serves as an apt metaphor for the innocence that sees too little.

Paradoxically, it may be more difficult for Southern than Northern writers to produce artistically successful Civil War novels. They often strive so hard to re-create faithfully the Southern way of life, before, during, and after the war, and to re-create battles, that they neglect the art of fiction, which enables writers to render complex character relationships through a coherent conception that projects a vision. That is the problem I see in Madison Jones's *Nashville 1864*.

His protagonist, as a boy in 1864 and as an adult memoirist in 1900, seems to be fixated upon faithfully rendering battle details, depicting "benevolent" master-slave relationships, and attacking Northerners for destroying God's creation of a superior civilization in the new Eden of the South. I say "seems" because Jones's previous works (from 1957 on) and their artistry encourage a possible conclusion that unintentional ambiguity may be the source of a likely impression that the novel is neo-Confederate in attitude and performance. The element of the novel that is most promising but neglected is the relationship between the white boy and his young slave, enhanced by the narrating voice of the boy as an adult thirty-five years later. I will examine the elements that dilute the impact of that relationship: the content and tone of the memoirist's and his grandson's commentary on slavery, Northern aggressors, and modern times; the fitful development of the relationship between the white boy and the slave boy; the rather perfunctory preoccupation with the details of battle; and the lapses in the art of fiction, especially in style.

Drawing upon a convention of the earliest novels, Jones presents a fictitious descendent, a grandson of our time, who finds the manuscript, feels a duty to get it published, and writes a foreword. "I had become a rather serious-minded fellow, a good deal less than pleased with what I saw happening in Nashville and elsewhere, and the reading of the memoir went straight to my heart. . . . But it was only recently, here in my old age, that I decided to seek publication for it. My hope is that it may affect others as it surely has affected me" (x). That arrogant assumption produces the obsessions of neo-Confederates—not that one may understandably expect others to be interested in the war, but that others may share the convictions and attitudes that sustained the Southern participants and that haunt their descendants. "We live in a time when it has become routine, at least in the most influential quarters, to view the Old South as a veritable nest of evils. This view was already there in its infancy even at the time when my grandfather wrote, and there is good reason to think that some part of his intention here was to counteract it. For me, at least, he quite successfully did so" (xi).

After the foreword by the present-day grandson, the adult Steven in 1900 declares in the first paragraph of his memoir that his case is special because there was in his character, then and now, "what was already abundant in Southern people generally: an ideality that almost no facts in a case could mitigate" (1). My worry that Jones may share, to some degree, the views of both the grandson and his paternal grandfather was aggravated by the eagerness with which the adult Steven knowingly launches into a digression defending slavery, while decrying its excesses, very early in his memoir. "Here I suddenly find myself digressing into the realm of polemics. . . . Certain things cry out to be said in our defense." While granting that slavery was already dying out and should not be reinstituted, he indulges himself in the tired old arguments we hear to this day, such as this: "The intimacies common among us . . . were, though qualified, indeed family-like. Hence our feeling of betrayal when defections began to occur" (17). The prevalent response today is that maybe the slaves had an *ideality* too—of freedom.

My apprehension derived from my impression that Jones does not seem to be preparing a context in which to accumulate implications that assure the reader that the old man's arguments are not the author's. I began to wonder what inspired him to create once again a character with whom readers are familiar to the point of tedium. The adult Steven's un-nuanced hyperbole that "the institution of slavery was an inherited one, passed down from time immemorial to the first American settlers" is generally regarded these days as a contemptible defense, especially when we recall that millions of Americans said it was contemptible as early as 1820. Steven also trots out the divine sanction argument, blames the African and the New England slave traders, excoriates the abolitionists, quotes Grant's lack of interest in fighting to free the slaves, and concludes that "largely financial reasons and not slavery caused the war" (19).

Steven seems to argue that the Confederacy was justified on all grounds and that the maliciously destructive invasion of Northern armies only reaffirmed the justice of its cause. He tacks on the cynical argument that no field slave would trade places with a wage slave in the sweatshops of the North, as if being free were not a cherished difference. All that is so numbingly perfunctory that readers of all Jones's works will hesitate to conclude that he is offering this American citizen of 1900 as someone to care about. The early pages of the novel fly then like a Confederate battle flag, and the effect is almost as offensive, for African Americans at any rate. While Jones clearly has not created a raving racist, he also is not creating a character whose capacity for rationalization is monstrous; the adult Steven is too one-dimensional to take on that kind of interest for a serious reader.

Jones's subtitle is "The Dying of the Light," a phrase quoted from one of the most famous modern poems, "Do Not Go Gentle into That Good Night," a villanelle by Dylan Thomas. "Old age should burn and rave at close of day, / Rage, rage against the dying of the light" is the other two lines of that first stanza. One is inclined to wonder, in Jones's imagination, who is raging against the dying of the light, and what light is dying? In the absence of any other source of "light," one is inclined to conclude that the adult Steven is raging against the dying of the light shed by the South's heroics in battle and by its glorious civilization, blessed by God.

God gets the boy Steven, his father, and an old lady who befriends them through tribulations, and when Steven kills a Yankee soldier, it is he who trumpets God's "vengeance by my hand" (124). The very last words of the novel are those of the old lady, who cannot "believe God would ever forgive" the Yankees for destroying "civilization"—Southern, she means. "They might have been my father's words," says the modern-day son. "Or my own words, even now, though thirty-five years have passed" (129). Faithful blacks, a cherished image throughout, are waiting at home for their masters to destroy the enemy. On the next to last page, Steven assures his reader that the father of the slave boy, Dink, killed during Steven's search for his own father, never blamed him. It is Steven's perception that the faithful slave, now free, kept his "friendship with me through all the years till his death." Steven presumes even to impute feelings to the ex-slave: "His feelings were real. I feel sure he went down to his grave still yearning for that old vanished world." Unprompted by Steven, readers may pose the question, From where may come forgiveness for the slave owners and the fire-eaters who inflamed them?

Expressed in the first twenty pages and reiterated at the very end, the rhetoric and tone of Steven's and his grandson's convictions pervade all the rest of the memoirist's narrative.

Despite the slavery-justification polemics, the early stages of Jones's delineation of the relationship between the twelve-year-old white boy Steven and the twelve-year-old slave boy Dink led me to look for a possible contradictory line of thought, to be alert for the gradual creation of a context that would ironically reinterpret for readers today those antiquated but still destructive convictions.

The story begins when the Moore family receives a letter that the father is wounded. Sister Lisa, sick, "lay there limp and wasted." Mother is failing, and might die if the father doesn't come home. One may wonder how compelling a reason that is to risk a child's life in the midst of battle to search for him. The first thirty pages are devoted to preparing for the search. The next sixty pages are devoted to the search, ending with the death of Dink, the slave boy, and the finding of the father. In the aftermath of forty pages, the boy takes the father home, with the aid of an old lady, and shoots a Yankee on the way.

I will follow now the relationship, in action, between the two boys, Steven and Dink. Steven, as adult narrator, says, "I, along with Dink, set out on my mission" (31). When they encounter a black Yankee soldier, Dink asks him, "You ain't never been a slave?" Steven tells us, "The word, in Dink's mouth here and now was a kind of shock to me" (38). I hoped this moment might be the beginning of a series of minor but cumulative revelations that would transcend the white boy Steven's immersion as witness in battle as he searched for his father.

When Dink tells the black soldier, whom he calls "a Yankee nigger," that he is himself a Confederate, I thought the image of a black slave child as a self-proclaimed Confederate was another lunge at justification of slavery, but I expected there would be later on some ironic reversal.

Stereotypical descriptions of Dink and his behavior also seemed to be Jones's setup for reversal. Steven the grown man still describes Dink in danger as "standing beside me now, panting and white-eyed" (62). That description recalled the depiction of breathless, wall-eyed, scared "darkies" in B and C movies of the thirties. Dink is reluctant to go further into danger but will follow his master, saying, "I ain't afeared if you ain't." He then says, "I'm a Conf——." The broken word "confederate" is immediately juxtaposed to the boom of a cannon (40). Then the adult Steven offers his readers the stereotypical and sentimental image of white and slave children sleeping together: "We slept on the ground inside" a soldier's tent, "wrapped in one blanket close together against the bitter cold" (49). But I expected that situation might prove to be one of several preparations for a change in their relationship that would undermine the proslavery polemics.

When they wake the next morning, Steven announces that they must keep moving, but Dink, "rolling his eyes," observes that it is too cold. Steven recalls that "over the years I have a thousand times in memory profoundly regretted this, my forcing him to go along. . . . This was what it meant to be a slave. This fact . . . was the source of my discomfort with the word 'slave.' . . . So it was against his will I led him into dangers in no way his to face" (56–57). Surely, this passage would signal the possibility of Jones's intention to develop in some complex way Steven's conduct, emotions, and thoughts about his relationship with Dink.

The passages richest in actual development of the relationship come in chapter 7. The boys see Yankee troops attacking. "Suddenly, 'Them's niggers!' Dink's pitched voice had said it" (74). As Dink watches "nigger Yankees" fighting his master's Confederates and getting slaughtered to free slaves like himself, a change comes over him. "The tone of his voice was strange, new to him. So was his expression, gloomy and sullen as I never had seen it before" (76). "Dink followed, but not up close anymore" (76). Continuing his search for his father, Steven becomes hesitant in his pace because, he says, "From the start it was clear that the grisly event back there by the railroad cut had shocked Dink deeply—as, in a way less acute, it had shocked me. But his lagging, his persistent and sullen silence as we went on, increasingly weighed upon me" (78).

This time, Dink accepts with reluctance Steven's invitation to sleep next to him to keep warm. Sensing what is on Dink's mind, Steven declares, "They were Yankees too, come to take our country away from us. We got to fight back." "The silence again, but this time it was brief. He said, 'They was niggers just like me'" (80).

The most dramatic event in the story is a change in the *secondary* character Dink, not in the protagonist. I expected therefore that Jones would develop in the remaining fifty pages of this novel (or, at 129 pages, is it a novella?) some internal conflict within Steven.

But drifting off to sleep, Steven thinks only of his father, his mother, and his sick sister. Distant firing wakes him, and Dink comes closer. Then Steven regains consciousness after an explosion and sees "from under a slanting beam," Dink's "dim face" appear.

The title of my essay turns upon the passage that comes next: "His eyes were looking at me. 'Dink,' I said. His eyes looked . . . but did not look. It was some long time before I understood that this was a death stare I was facing" (82–83).

That death stare is a charged image that embodies everything most powerful in the novel's potential—in character relationships, plot, style, theme, and conception—but it is here that the book implodes; it is here that Jones misses a great opportunity, because the most expressive metaphor for the war, Reconstruction, and our legacy of the war is the innocent's stare, witnessing the war while alive, in later life remembering the war, and in death still staring at the war, even as we Americans stare at it a hundred years after Steven wrote his memoir. The innocent stare at battle, at death, and at the past not in a positive, workable vision but, for many Southerners, transfixed, is an ideal rotten at the core, transmuted into the Lost Cause. It is such a stare that Faulkner in *The Unvanquished* and Allen Tate in *The Fathers* asserted sixty-three years ago and that I assert in my own novel, the stare of children. In Jones's novel this childhood stare, recalled in late middle age by Steven, is merely a floating metaphor, no more expressive than any other.

Steven's too weak to extract Dink's body from the debris. "I thought of Dink, and stopped. 'I've got to go back,' I said." But a young soldier urges him on, and he complies rather readily (89). Thereafter, Steven the boy merely alludes to Dink, as the adult Steven conscientiously devotes himself to recalling details of battle, bemoaning the defeat of the Confederate army, and ironically, on the same page where one of those allusions to Dink occurs, bemoaning the destruction of Southern civilization, but not at any depth the loss of Dink.

He refers to his "long nightmare" as beginning *after* Dink's death, at the sight of "a gory pile as high as my waist of severed arms and legs," suggesting dead Confederates are more "harrowing" for him than Dink's death (92). The effect on him of Confederate defeat in the battle "were the moments that remain most vivid in my memory" (95). The scene in which General Stephen Lee rallies his men "till this day . . . is alive in my imagination" (102). He comes to a cabin where a black woman and a black man befriend him, reminding him of the blacks at home, especially Dink's father Pompey. He sleeps. "It was long but never much of a sleep. Dink kept coming back, and Pompey behind him, blaming me" (111). His hatred of the Yankee soldier he encounters on the road is more powerful than his brotherly love for Dink. "I was suddenly wrung with a hatred for him" (117). Dink's attitude toward the enemy changed, but Steven's did not, not even with Dink's change as example. Five pages from the end, he finds his father but does not speak to him of Dink.

Jones attributes to Steven the boy only one more serious observation, twenty-four pages before the end: "And suddenly, with a throb of bitter pain, Dink was in my mind. There was a murmur of voices, speaking of Dink, and accusing eyes fixed on me" for deserting him, or his corpse, a mildly ironic reversal of the adult Steven's condemnation of slaves who desert their masters (105). But the force even of that line is diluted by adult Steven's declaration on the next to last page that Dink's father never blamed Steven for the boy's death and that the father, in fact, remained a friend of the family until he "went down to his grave still yearning for that old vanished world" (128). On the final page, Dink is alive in Steven's memory only in reference to "remnants of the house where Dink had met his end." More important for Steven as a final memory is the spot where Steven had "unknowingly witnessed 'the great mistake'" that caused the Confederate defeat in the Battle of Nashville. Thus, Jones creates in Steven a character who recalls Dink and his death only incidentally and with no more emphasis or implication than he thinks of his father and his mother—rather idealized, one-dimensional characters who in no way compete with Dink for the reader's interest.

Having become keenly aware that the relationship that had been developing between young master and young slave in the search for the father had become, over halfway through the novel, far more interesting and meaningful than the search itself, I was forced to conclude that Jones was not developing a dramatic internal conflict that was working its way outward into an external conflict. Steven and Dink stand in an old house "as if expecting some painful issue" (70), but Jones does not, it later turns out, have a major developing issue between the boys themselves in mind.

Narrating his experiences with the young slave, Steven does not convey in the past, or in the present, any feelings about him that would even suggest a change of mind and heart about the slave himself or about slavery in general. Coming so early and expressed so fervently by Steven in later life, the master-slave family-tie ideality (or fantasy) reduces the relationship of Steven and Dink to the status of a mere illustration of that wishful claim, a claim that is presented, examined, but usually deconstructed by hundreds of Southern fiction and nonfiction writers.

Whether the convictions expressed by Steven's descendant in his foreword and Steven in his memoir reflect to some degree the author's own perspective remains for me ambiguous but not, I feel inclined to conclude, in the positive sense of an author's deliberate ambiguity meant to encourage a range of possible insights.

The relationship between the white boy and the slave boy, even though it ends with the slave's death midway in the book, is intrinsically interesting, because while the narratively uninteresting search in battle for the father has a routine beginning, middle, and end, the boy's relationship with his slave playmate has a potential that, though only partially actualized, may haunt the reader more lastingly than it does Steven and his older self. We are left with a rather overwrought re-creation of battle that fails to transcend the vacuous literalism of reenactments and a dogged mimicry of the kind of memoir a witness might write. Madison Jones stares at the war, his boy character stares at it, and the boy thirty-six years later stares at it, but the stare remains a fixed stare, unenlightened. The rage against the dying of the light is hollow, and the light itself dies without illuminating.

As the boy Steven wanders into the battle zone and onto the battleground, I expected the adult Steven to try to recall the past in such as way as to enable the reader to experience the shock of battle *as the boy experiences it*, but although descriptions of stages of the single battle of Nashville that Steven witnesses take up most of the novel, the author and his narrator are so enamored of battle details that they provide a full, knowledgeable re-creation that undercuts our immediate experience of the lost boy's shock and confusion. Steven's depiction of the battles themselves has the air of a Civil War roundtabler's obsession with the facts, as if a full re-creation is as important to him as the recovery and understanding in memory of the major events and issues in his own life. In pursuit of that re-creation of heroic acts and glorious defeat, the narrator mixes indiscriminately specific events he witnessed as a boy with what he has learned over the years about the general setting of the battle.

Jones does not create a tension between the elderly man's command of the facts and his memory of the boy's limited experience; the one seems merely to enhance the other. The effect, however, is that the adult Steven's compulsion to fill in the surrounding facts distracts us from the boy's immediate experience and dilutes its impact. Jones and his narrator, like many Southerners attracted to the war, seem to feel obligated or eager to render the battle fully in an attempt to enhance for his reader Steven's very limited and ignorant exposure to it, with the effect not only that the battle is vague and tedious, as is usually the case when the compulsion to render every detail prevails, but also that the boy's own unique experience is swamped for us by generalizations and facts he could not have known at the time. "The action was in fact a feint on the part of the Yankee army. . . . What Dink and I observed from our position on the hillside was not the main action" (67). Jones also attributes to the boy an unlikely perception of details and to Steven as a man an unlikely memory of such details (112). The boy's experience seems then to have had an effect on the man no deeper or greater than to motivate him to re-create the battle events. Everything is directly stated and, in the mode of nineteenth-century rhetoric that Jones adopts for the narrator, overstated, and so the reader experiences almost no implications.

As an old-fashioned narrative technique, Jones has Steven announce what's to come, mechanically, in general terms: "In April and May of '63 there were two events very damaging, and also disillusioning, to us" (16). "Two times, in '62 and again early in '63, Father came home . . . that first time. . . . His second time . . ." (22). "The worst times, of course, were yet to come. The year of '64 was much harder than '63" (26). "In the midst of this came unexpected news. . . . But this one had already happened" (29). "In April there were two events that I am not likely to forget. . . . But this came later in the day" (77). "We saw down below a sight that abruptly stopped us" (73). "The wonder, however, was something that came to me only in retrospect, from what I was later to learn" (101). The effect is to undercut the illusion readers crave—of events happening *now*.

The action of the search is too simple. Neither Steven nor Dink ever really initiate an action along the way, although Steven, almost as the author's narrative afterthought, in the last six pages, shoots a Yankee to defend his father and the old lady who helps him. Chapter 8 ends thus: "It is ironical that this, the memory of our soldiers constructing those works, should have left me feeling reassured when real sleep finally took me. For in fact, I was to learn in after times, I had been eye-witness to a most crucial error in the making" (88). The use of this device prevents the reader from sharing a major experience with the boy and also from experiencing with Steven as adult a deep insight about that missed experience. It is simply noted and left to dangle.

The most dramatic event of the novel (or novella) remains the death of Dink. Steven does not initiate action of any magnitude, certainly not a line of action that produces external conflict the reader can follow with increasing interest; the action around Steven lacks imagined complications, and the rendering of battle actions is routine. Large episodes are rendered in much the same perfunctory way as such small episodes as this: an officer tells Steven and Dink to go to a house and eat. They go. They eat. They sleep. Up to page 31, Jones doles out routine summaries of routine daily life, with nothing unusual and everything very basic, namely, what we find in numerous other Civil War novels. Halfway through, I wondered, What is being developed? In the absence of protagonist-initiated action producing conflict, the reader expects an internal conflict, which I have argued is ambiguously posed but fitfully and finally inadequately developed.

Except for Dink, the characters are one-dimensional, even though we get the hero both as a boy and as memoirist narrator at age forty-eight. The object of the search, the father, presented early as a heroic image on a horse, is reduced to a stumbling blind man. The mother exists not much more than in this line: "I will never lose the vivid memory of my mother on that wagon seat with the lines in her hands, stiffly erect" (15). The passage goes on with a routine physical description of a woman the reader never really gets to know.

Adult Steven's direct references to the act of remembering and writing also undercut for the reader the immediacy of the boy Steven's experiences. The context in which we respond to every word of Steven's memoir is that of self-conscious recall and writing. That could be a dimension of the experience that enriches our apprehension of it, but nowhere does Jones seem to be developing a pattern of implications, ironic or any other kind. Steven is still doing it eight pages from the end: "I need give no very detailed description of that long ride, continuing into the night, before we met with the brief but harrowing ordeal in store for us" (121). That experience, summarized in that way, cannot then be a "harrowing ordeal" for the reader. The most blatant example comes earlier, when Steven quotes a Yankee officer to make "my account as complete as possible" (98). The battle as a whole upstages the boy's experience of it.

From page 3 onward, the narrator mentions his memory at numerous points, calls attention to its imperfections, and thus undercuts the effect of the experience being rendered. "It is difficult for me to be even sequential, much less complete in my account of events following that shell's explosion" (99). Had the author involved the reader intimately in the boy's perceptions, the question of completeness would have seemed irrelevant, especially in a novel so brief. On a single page, Steven says, "I remember" three times, without significance (100). Time frames such as Jones uses here (looking back from 1900 to 1864) usually serve to illuminate, but this one does not. There is no sense of rediscovery and new discovery, revelation, or insight into self or community. The constant reminder by the adult Steven that he can or cannot remember, or only vaguely remembers this, that, and the other, provides the reader with only superficial insight into the memory process and the frustrations of writing a memoir. Neither the experience itself nor the writing about it seems to have affected the narrator very deeply. In novels of complexly delineated irony, for instance, the facets of a narrator's failure to achieve revelation is a primary experience for the reader. The grandson's foreword too fails to add a perspective or attitude that might render the memoir more meaningful. We are left with a rather overwrought re-creation that almost fails to transcend the vacuous literalism of reenactments.

The memoirist's style also dilutes the effect of the relationship between the white boy and the slave boy. In his foreword, the grandson assures us that Steven's memoir is well written and that factual accuracy, necessarily enhanced by imagination, is one of its virtues. Jones's own stylistic imagination seems quiescent in this re-creation. The style is pretentious, pseudo-literary, full of formal phrases, in imitation of many memoirs, I suppose, but Sam Watkins's and General Ulysses S. Grant's memoirs show how to avoid those stylistic trappings. Style, the life breath of a literary work, here undercuts every element it renders—especially the boy's relationship with the slave boy and battles.

Descriptions of extreme events are stilted. A cannonball takes a man's head off. "They fell silent . . . all, I guessed, with visions in their mind's eyes. . . . I suppose that, given the shock and terror my experience included, this is not surprising" (67). "I said it out of a throat drawn painfully tight" (70). "Then and for an unmeasurable time thereafter, with the cannon blasts above . . ." (71). "These registered only as stock events of the battle," an attitude that produces stock phrases in style (72). "Even when I saw that he was gone, distress remained like an object lodged too close against my heart" (84). "My confusion came back, increasing. In something like panic I strained at the knob, then knocked" (104). This stilted, formal quality infects the dialogue as well, sometimes ringing false to this Tennessean's ear.

When a writer is not in control of point of view and style, even an astute reader and writer can get the style and the time of narration wrong, as does novelist Madison Smart Bell on the cover: "The language of the child-narrator is tone perfect for those times." It is not the child who narrates in 1864 but the man, in 1900. Bell inadvertently touches, however, on the problem: the narrative might have been more effective had the boy at eighteen or nineteen written or orally told his story and dealt fully with Dink, as Bayard Sartoris in *The Unvanquished* dealt with Ringo, only with greater complexity, because Bayard's compulsion to tell a story sprang from several other characters as well.

Paradoxically, it is the innocent stare of the very young that sometimes provides a more meaningful view of the antebellum, war, and Reconstruction eras as compared with adults who seem compelled to heap facts, out of a misdirected sense of obligation to authenticity, upon the heads of readers, diluting the impact of direct experience. The adult Steven brings to that past experience no fresh perspectives and derives from the act of memory and memoir writing no significant insights about either his personal experience or the national tragedy. To the extent that the art of fiction fails, all else in a novel fails.

Less obviously than Jesse Hill Ford, a Southern liberal who fought hard in life and in literature for the civil rights of blacks in Tennessee (but who ironically shot and killed a black soldier who trespassed on his estate), Jones has taken humanistic positions, especially in *A Cry of Absence*, on civil rights, never quite taking a liberal position, because his basic conception is of the limitations of human nature. Because *Nashville 1864* was written late in his life, one might expect to find either a departure from the consistent Aeschylean stance that M. E. Bradford posed for Jones's work to a critique of the South's position on slavery as expressed in the war or to an outright conservative apologia. My reading of the novel is that it lacks the one thing vital for the capstone of a distinguished career: a fresh perspective or vision of the war, whether liberal or conservative, that might enable us to reinterpret the body of Jones's work.

O. Henry's Civil War Surprises

Thomas Wolfe had never been called a Civil War writer until I made that claim in *Thomas Wolfe's Civil War*. Here's another surprise: O. Henry was a Civil War short-story writer. And only here has that label ever been slapped on his work. Nor has he ever been called primarily a Southern writer, although a few thousand of his millions of readers over the past century worldwide know that he was born and raised in the South. Neither has anyone, *Cabbages and Kings* in hand, fudged a little to call him a South American writer. Forty years ago, however, he was called a Western, a Texas writer, based mostly on his collection *Hearts of the West*, and augmented by a new collection of the other Westerns. *The Gentle Grafter* collection makes calling him a prison writer, in the tradition of Miguel de Cervantes, easy. Peeling labels make labeling a risky business, so I wouldn't do it were it not for the lamentable fact that his well-sustained, century-long reputation is founded firmly upon the stories in such volumes as *The Four Million*, *Strictly Business*, and *The Voice of the City*.

It is a distorted tribute to O. Henry that his reputation as one of the international masters of the short story—in the Boccaccio, de Maupassant mode—rests monumentally on the tales set in New York City. Over nearly a century, O. Henry's major achievement has been considered to be his unique way of depicting life among the lowly as in "The City of Dreadful Night" and "The Gift of the Magi," his most often reprinted story. But only about half of his three hundred tales are set in Manhattan. He moved there specifically to be close to editors who provided him with a living, and he sentenced himself to a grueling task of producing a story a week for the rest of his short life. About thirty of the stories are set in the South, thirty-two in Central and South America, and eighty in the West. Even though they are among his first, his last, and his best, his Southern stories are scattered throughout his collected volumes. The South American, the Western, and the "grafter" genres, added to the Southern tales, make up over half of O. Henry's three hundred stories.

"I take my pen in hand to say that I am from the South," wrote O. Henry, "and have been a stranger in New York for four years. But I know a restaurant where you can get real Corn Bread." Alphonso Smith points out that many of his friend's stories "stage a contrast between the North and the South or the North and the West," especially in "The Rose of Dixie," "The Duplicity of Hargraves," and "Hygeia at the Solito." The narrator of O. Henry's "Municipal Report" says, "I desire to interpolate here that I am a Southerner. But I am not one by profession or trade. . . . When the orchestra plays Dixie . . . I slide a little lower on the leather-cornered seat and, well, order another Wurzburger and wish that Longstreet had—but what's the use?"

O. Henry's way of depicting experiences in the South offers a new cast to our picture of Southern fiction. If we recall the O. Henry of the Southern stories, we enable readers today to see vividly an O. Henry who has been too long kept in the dark beyond city lights.

If I were assembling "O. Henry's Civil War Surprises"—and perhaps I will—the contents would include the following: "The Guardian of the Accolade," "Two Renegades," "The Emancipation of Billy," "Thimble, Thimble," "The Rose of Dixie," "A Municipal Report," and "The Duplicity of Hargraves."

"O. Henry's Civil War Surprises" promises not only a different focus but also, for most readers, a distinctly "new" perspective on O. Henry and his tales. Frequent themes in all types of his stories are especially appropriate to fiction about the Civil War: reformation, regeneration, atonement, and rehabilitation. I use the term "Civil War" to include the Reconstruction era, which lasted almost three times as long as the battle era. Most of O. Henry's stories are set in the era he knew first hand, Reconstruction.

I offer here an iconoclastic challenge to the legend according to which O. Henry is the Caliph of Baghdad on the Subway. I argue instead that O. Henry is fundamentally a Southern writer, all of whose fiction, including the New York tales, derive from the style and technique of the Appalachian Mountain oral tall-tale-telling tradition. No matter where his stories are set—and they are set all over the United States and in several foreign countries—at the heart of each is the oral tradition of the South. The surprise ending for which he is famous is a salient feature of that tradition.

Turning to writings about O. Henry, I find that his friends, biographers, and a few critics have pointed out the importance of his North Carolina roots in general and of the influence of Southern humor in particular. But it is my own conviction that O. Henry should be regarded as first and foremost a Southern humorist of the highest caliber.

We see O. Henry most truly when we see him first learning tale-telling techniques in the small, foothills town of Greensboro, North Carolina, where he was born and where he lived and worked until the age of twenty, and then as a young man and a family man who spent most of his adult life in the small, state capitol town of Austin, Texas. William Sydney Porter (O. Henry was his pen name) was born in 1862, on the eve of the battle of Antietam. Three years old when his mother died, he had to move with his father to his grandmother's house in the last year of the Civil War. He grew up during the Reconstruction turmoil. The tales veterans and townspeople told were colored by major differences between North Carolina and other Southern states. There had been few slaves in North Carolina; and the state had reluctantly joined the Confederacy, and few battles were fought there, although it lost 20,600 men, almost a fourth of the total of Confederates killed in battle (disease claimed almost twice as many). At Gettysburg alone, 714 of North Carolina's 900 men were killed; Virginia, where most of the great battles were fought, had the next highest losses at 6,947, only a third as many as North Carolina. It was in Greensboro, where no battles were fought, that President Jefferson Davis prepared his final escape from the Confederacy. O. Henry's father worked in the military hospitals as a doctor; he became an alcoholic recluse, working on such inventions as a perpetual-motion machine.

Judge Albion Tourgee, the town's most famous and suspicious carpetbagger, wrote a celebrated Reconstruction novel, set in Greensboro: *A Fool's Errand: By One of the Fools*, an exposé of the Ku Klux Klan. O. Henry himself became one of the few Southern writers in his time to criticize and satirize professional Southerners who promoted Southern aristocratic manners and pretensions about pride and honor, as we see, for instance, in "Vereton Villa: A Tale of the South" and in "A Blackjack Bargainer."

O. Henry relished listening to people talk and assumed his readers would too. His powerful, authoritative voice as all-knowing narrator—the engagingly self-conscious voice of a creator of settings, characters, and dramatic events, always with humorous overtones—evolved out of his youthful participation as listener and teller in the Southern tale-telling tradition. He opens "The Emancipation of Billy" thus: "In the old, old, square-porticoed mansion, with the wry window-shutters and the paint peeling off in discolored flakes, lived one of the last of the war governors. The South has forgotten the enmity of the great conflict, but it refuses to abandon its old traditions and idols."

My contention, that as we read any of his stories we do well to think of O. Henry as a Southern writer, becomes more trenchant if we can agree that the effects of Reconstruction pervade Southern consciousness up to the present moment and that in a vital sense every work of fiction by a writer raised in the South is about the Civil War.

Although the term "the South" may embrace Texas, the claim is stronger when we note that the features of the mountain tall tale also characterize O. Henry's Western stories. It's often with surprise that one remembers that the Cisco Kid (one of the most famous Western heroes who was the inspiration for two silent and twenty-three sound movies, followed by radio and television series) is O. Henry's creation in "The Caballero's Way"; it is included in his fourth collection, *Heart of the West*, a roundup of his favorite Western stories. Few readers today are aware that he wrote about half as many Westerns as New York stories. The stories in *Heart of the West*, along with his many other Westerns, offer a unique perspective on the West. O. Henry was the Mr. Scheherazade of Austin Nights long before he was called the Yankee de Maupassant.

Accused in Austin of embezzlement, O. Henry became a fugitive. His friendship down in South America with another fugitive, the notorious train robber Al Jennings, increased his stock of Western lore. A good example is "Two Renegades," set in Central America. It is also a Civil War story, involving two veterans, one a Yankee, the other a rebel, who finally regard each other as "part human."

Finally, O. Henry surrendered. In prison, he wrote fourteen other stories, more of which were set in the South than anywhere else. Two were published while he was in prison. Several others written there were published later before he arrived in Manhattan, including some of his best stories set in the South: "Georgia's Ruling," "Whistling Dick's Christmas Stocking," and "A Blackjack Bargainer."

To the end, O. Henry had the South in mind. He had outlined a series of stories about the modern South. Near death, he was planning to write his first novel at long last. "The 'hero' of the story will be a man born and 'raised' in a somnolent little Southern town."

On June 5, 1910, at the young age of forty-eight, O. Henry died in a hospital in New York City deep in debt. At about sunrise that day, he had said, in his pronounced Southern accent, "Raise the shades. I don't want to go home in the dark."

The Last American Epic

The Civil War Novels of Father and Son, Michael and Jeff Shaara

Young Jeff Shaara first saw Gettysburg when his father took the family on a visit to the battlefield in 1964. Six years later, Jeff, then eighteen, helped his somewhat frail father as he walked Gettysburg battlefield in the early 1970s, researching a Civil War novel (*The Killer Angels*). Out of such little moments, a great literary and cinematic epic depiction of the American Civil War began. We may imagine Homer's father taking him over the battlefield at Troy, actually or orally. A major difference is that both father and son are authors of the epic Civil War literary tetralogy: *The Killer Angels* (1974), *Gods and Generals* (1996), *The Last Full Measure* (1998), and within the sesquicentennial years, *A Blaze of Glory* (2012), *A Chain of Thunder* (2013), and *The Smoke at Dawn* (2014).

Michael Shaara is the author of the novel *The Killer Angels*, which won the Pulitzer Prize for 1975. Writer-director Ronald Maxwell's highly successful, now classic movie adaptation *Gettysburg* appeared in 1993, five years after Shaara's death, and stimulated sales of the novel to about three million copies. Maxwell became a kind of father figure for Jeff, encouraging the young rare coin dealer to write a prequel to his father's famous novel. Only three years after the movie *Gettysburg* appeared, Jeff Shaara's *Gods and Generals* was published; he tells the story of the same generals over a five-year period before their separate, parallel paths converged on Gettysburg. Ironically, unlike his father's novel, it was an immediate bestseller, and work on the film began only three years after publication.

Publication of *Gods and Generals* is a unique event in the history of American literature. Never before has the child of a prize-winning writer published a novel on the same subject, featuring the same characters. Furthermore, what we have here is a very interesting reversal: the son does not take up the story where the father left off; he goes back to 1858 to throw the lines of the narrative forward to the point where the father's novel began.

This question arose immediately: do the son's boots fit the father's footprints? If brute curiosity is a crude motive, I am glad to report that it is well satisfied, and on a high plane. In every sense, even when compared with the father's celebrated work, the son's uncommon skill has produced a Civil War novel that stands out among all others. Therefore, to paraphrase Mark Twain, persons attempting to find exploitation in this literary event will be shot.

In *Gods and Generals*, Jeff Shaara does indeed deal with epic mythic figures—Robert E. Lee and Stonewall Jackson—but he also deals with lower-ranking officers, such as Joshua Lawrence Chamberlain, who were led by generals. With the national consciousness of the father, the son presents the war from both sides (the Shaaras are from New Jersey and lived in Florida). As in *The Killer Angels*, the chapters of *Gods and Generals* bear the names of the historical figures, two Southern and two Northern, on whom Jeff Shaara concentrates: Generals Lee, Jackson, and Winfield Scott Hancock and Colonel Chamberlain. Shaara alternates among characters, drawing the reader into the novel's fifty-eight chapters, first through Lee's perspective. The focus falls less frequently on Chamberlain and Hancock than on Lee and Jackson. Now and then, other characters, Northern and Southern, are favored: Jeb Stuart, Oliver Howard, and William Barksdale. Each man marches on parallel lines with the others toward the explosive convergence at the obscure little crossroads town of Gettysburg. Most of the novel is devoted to the major battles in Virginia and Maryland that preceded that march into the North. A narrative this complex would be a risky venture for any first-time novelist.

Because the son's novel stands on its own feet, not on the father's shoulders, comparisons by no means prove odious. The son has a greater conceptual power than his father had. His narrative covers more time and space, with a pace that begins in a meditative mode and gradually achieves a marching cadence. There are more long stretches of sustained narrative and more variety in the dramatic scenes; they are more fully developed, and the dialogue is more natural. Jeff Shaara gives us access, as did his father, to the subjective experiences of his characters, but with greater brevity. And the sequences in which all those elements are represented are more skillfully controlled. And *Gods and Generals* is more truly epic in scope than *The Killer Angels*.

"*The Killer Angels* opened an enormous door for me," the son tells us in his acknowledgments; "[it] allowed my apprehensions to be set aside, and brought forth the first words of this book. [My father's] greatest wish, what drove him through a difficult career all his life, was the desire to leave something behind, a legacy to be remembered. Dad, you succeeded."

Shaara has said that in writing *Gods and Generals*, he discovered his true vocation and that in General Grant (hero of *The Last Full Measure*) he discovered his own special subject, one that put his new vocation as a writer to the test.

> I loved writing about that man. I wanted to shatter the myths about him and tell his story fully and truthfully. I liked being able to bring out the differences between Lee and Grant. People are emotional about Lee, a beloved figure, an inspiring figure. But Grant is cool and aloof, so I wanted to bring him alive for the reader. Writing about him was a little like writing about Stonewall Jackson in *Gods and Generals*—exciting, discovering the man as I tried to recreate him as a real person, not just an awesome legend. Both men were hard to get close to in life.

Readers of *The Last Full Measure* may be struck with certain parallels: just as Grant developed his talent in the Mississippi Campaign, the young novelist developed his talent while writing about Grant after that campaign; and both President Lincoln and Jeff Shaara found their man in Grant.

Of all the heroes in the trilogy, Shaara felt two men were most like his father as a man and as a writer pursuing his vocation. "As a man, my father was most like Joshua Chamberlain. I think my father felt an affinity with him. My father was idealistic (although he became a cynic in his later years), an intellectual, a scholarly kind of man, like Chamberlain." Until Jeff's father wrote about him in *The Killer Angels*, the general public knew little about Chamberlain; he lifted Chamberlain from obscurity into mythic status in the American consciousness; and he continues to play an important role in Jeff Shaara's two novels in the trilogy.

> And then the other side of my father that I was quite aware of as I wrote comes out in General Hancock. Hancock is very good at what he does. After Reynolds died, he was perhaps the greatest Union general in the field. Like Hancock, my father had no patience with incompetence, stupidity, inefficiency. You know that scene in the newspaper office when Hancock reaches across the desk and grabs the newspaperman by the throat? I felt my father guiding me as I wrote that scene.

And he felt that the only way he could "describe that murderous battle of the Wilderness was through someone who was there in the thick of the smoke and the fire. But describing Hancock wounded, suffering, I knew that scene was my farewell to my father."

Like both father and son, Ulysses S. Grant is a great stylist, which is partly why Ernest Hemingway declared Grant's autobiography to be one of the masterpieces of American literature. As Jeff wrote from Grant's point of view in

The Last Full Measure, Grant's style influenced Shaara's own. "I tried to catch the simplicity and the flow of Grant's style when writing inside Grant's mind and I worked to change my style to be more appropriate to Lee when writing from his point of view." Although his style is similar to his father's, Jeff Shaara has forged his own distinctive style. "Lee nodded, wanted to say more, to break away from the thoughts of Jackson, but the image was still there, would not go. Lee turned back toward the march of the men, felt the wetness again."

Jeff Shaara continues to use his father's background and structuring devices. "I wanted all three novels to have the same basic features." But in *The Last Full Measure*, one sees a difference in his handling of the structure. As omniscient author, he goes into fewer minds than he and his father did in the first two novels—mostly from Lee's to Grant's to Chamberlain's. He consciously worked at creating that difference.

> I agonized over that. I worried that there might be an imbalance between Union and Confederate points of view, but I really couldn't think of a Southern general of great enough stature or interest for me or the reader. Longstreet gets wounded and is no longer of use to Lee. Stuart gets killed. I go into their minds once only to show that everybody is fading out, leaving Lee alone. It's subtler in General Gordon's one chapter because he can see, as Lee cannot, the futility of opposing Grant. One by one, all the great generals go—Jackson is already dead—and Lee misses each of them. So of the Confederate generals, I decided to show Lee's mind isolated. Lee who was the symbol of the whole war, of the whole confederacy, is out there by himself, facing Grant.

Jeff Shaara handles that point-of-view structure much more effectively now. Although he devotes a few more chapters to Grant and Chamberlain than to Lee, it's important to stress that he sustains a major achievement that distinguishes this father-son trilogy from most other Civil War novels: he gives the American public a balanced experience of the temperament, sensibility, character, and convictions of generals on both sides of the battle lines. Ideally, the Homeric Civil War epic that Americans have longed for depicts both sides evenhandedly and compassionately, encompasses major battles led by major leaders, and appeals to all readers, North and South, young and old, and men and women. The trilogy begun by the father and finished by the son is that epic.

Shaara intentionally juxtaposes Lee's mind to Grant's most often and most consistently to show contrasts between them and to ignite Chamberlain's contrast with both Grant and Lee. "And Chamberlain is there also because I wanted to continue to tell his story. He's such a wonderful and unique character. And I was continuing my father's original focus on Chamberlain, taking him beyond Gettysburg." Halfway through the novel, I realized that one great effect of giving the reader deeper insights into Grant is that Shaara provides, by the method of contrast, a much clearer sense of who Lee is, and Lee, in turn, illuminates Grant. The juxtaposition of Lee to Grant also enables us to feel the sting of irony, as when Grant at Cold Harbor thinks, "There is no one to blame but me," and the reader recalls Lee thinking at Gettysburg, "It's all my fault."

The scenes between Mark Twain and Grant at the end of the novel are so appealing and moving one can imagine a play dramatizing their relationship. "When I learned that Twain commissioned Grant to write his autobiography I was ecstatic. Twain is such a public icon, he's worked into Westerns, even science fiction movies as a character. The parallel between Twain and Grant talking together with Huck and Jim's conversations on a raft on the Mississippi River rings true to me."

My question earlier was, Can Jeff Shaara's *Gods and Generals* possibly be as good as his father's *The Killer Angels*? My answer was, Better. The haunting question since then has been, Was *Gods and Generals* merely a high level act of filial mimicry? My own answer is a resounding no, and my evidence is *The Last Full Measure*. But some people who admired *Gods and Generals* worried that it might be just a fluke. "So," Shaara has said, "did I." Shaara proves once and for all that, though influenced by his father, he has a voice and talent all his own. The two million readers who revere the father's novel now have to contend with the praise of those who have read the son's first. I recommend turning to the son's depiction of pre-Gettysburg events before reading the father's rendering of the battle itself. Both experiences will prove memorable and perhaps inseparable. Jeff Shaara's *Last Full Measure* brought this unique and monumental father-son trilogy to a triumphant conclusion. On the threshold of the new millennium, the Shaara father-and-son vision of its origins in blood and courage illuminated American's future.

In the three novels, the focus is divided equally between North and South, but because of the nature of movies, Ron Maxwell's plan had to be somewhat different: *Gettysburg* focuses on North and South equally, *Gods and Generals* focuses on Generals Lee and Jackson, and *The Last Full Measure* will focus on General Grant. Because the third movie in the trilogy is still in an uncertain planning stage (as of July 2014) and thus most people are unaware of the overall balanced perspective, a controversy has arisen over the seemingly sympathetic view of the Confederacy in the movie version of *Gods and Generals*. Equal focus on North and South was relatively easy in *Gettysburg* because the battle took place in a single small town in only three days. But because it takes place over several years and several battles, *Gods and Generals* had to focus upon a single hero, General Stonewall Jackson. Even with that focus, shifts to

Chamberlain on the Union side slow the character-based narrative pace. Not even excepting Grant and William Sherman, the two generals in whom there has always been the greatest interest, not only in both the North and the South but also around the world, are Lee and Jackson. Given the danger of shattering the focus, cinematically that is imperative enough for concentrating on them.

The unfortunate result is the unfair accusation that *Gods and Generals* is pro-Southern and, in the minds of quite a fewer number of critics and viewers, therefore neo-Confederate, but not, one hopes, pro-slavery. As scriptwriter and director, Maxwell enables Chamberlain to attack slavery and even has Jackson wish freedom for his black cook. Moviegoers who view the Confederacy as evil might concede that it is in the nature of drama in all genres that the more colorful character steals the show and seems at moments to skew its meaning, the classic instance being John Milton's epic poem *Paradise Lost*, which sets out to "justify the ways of God to man," and in which the risen son of God cannot compete for our interest with the fallen angel, Lucifer.

In Homer's epic poem *The Iliad*, heroes on both sides are flawed. Homer avoided the serious risk of immersing the reader in too many battles and too many characters by compressing the ten-year war of many battles into a single battle and by having one clear-cut hero on each side, as Ron Maxwell was able to do in *Gettysburg*. But the actual nature of the American Civil War—many officers and men in many battles on many different battlefields—and Jeff Shaara's novelistic conception for *Gods and Generals*—gave Maxwell a scriptwriter-director's cinematic nightmare in which his choices were dictated and limited. The battles (minus Antietam on the cutting-room floor) are among the most powerful ever filmed. And the focus on Jackson, enhanced by Lee's hovering presence, gives the viewer one of the most moving death scenes in recent memory. If we do not quite have a blind Homer in the combined novels of father and son, in the films we have a Homeric vision that is uncannily clear. The novel trilogy and the movie trilogy are true examples of epics.

Given that this is the age of interdisciplinary studies, one may wonder why historians are perceived by some to have a lock on the Civil War. In the general public's experience, however, it is not the historian who dominates the subject but the novelist and the moviemaker. Most historians have a limited audience. James McPherson may be an exception, but in the popular imagination, Shelby Foote, novelist-turned-historian in the 1950s, remains our greatest living historian. In the realm of popular culture, of mass communication, the study of the war has always been multidisciplinary if not interdisciplinary. More recently, it has also been multicultural and has thus come under fire as being politically correct. The spectrum of interest now is educationally, politically, and culturally quite wide, varied, and extremely but understandably complicated.

As I have said in other essays, the serious novelist, like the historian, begins with facts. But the historian must cleave to them, while the novelist draws upon the emotion-charged memories of individuals and of a culture at large, transforming private memories into public metaphors. The novelist goes further, into the private imagination, shaping and transmitting truths that transcend facts alone to stimulate public enlightenment. I don't write historical novels; I write novels about the struggle of unique individuals in history with facts, memory, and imagination. I myself am not an academic historian; I am a novelist and a teacher of literature and creative writing in all genres.

What, in fact, caused the Civil War? One answer is that the cause is everything anybody at any time in the past and the present declares to be the cause, whether it be slavery, preservation of the union, economics, states rights, or all those and other causes interacting dynamically. As Ambrose Bierce rendered in his short stories, perception is everything. Our hearts and minds as Americans are affected, influenced, and shaped by perceptions, which may be based less on facts than on a tangled web of illusions, lies, distortions, bad memory, or some oscillating combination of those things. Stress on facts has very seldom changed the popular mind in the past or in the present.

Even though the Civil War was on some levels, but not all, thoroughly documented by its participants, major novelists know—and show—that facts alone are far from enough. They write out of an awareness of the fact that both Northerners and Southerners, civilian and military, entered the war ignorant of each other, that individuals and groups often fought the war in ignorance of vital facts, and that in the national consciousness, the war is what memory and imagination make of the facts we know, facts that are too few and undependable, except as stimulants to the creation of myths and metaphors that light our way through successive epochs of our history.

The events of each decade in American history provide a fresh perspective on the Civil War. Professional historians, amateur historians, and ordinary citizens revisit, rediscover, and redefine this central event of the American experience. Thus, we reflect on the past, experience the present, and enlighten the future by the fitful light of shifting interpretations. The decade of the civil rights movement was a perfect time for a centennial reassessment of the Civil War, which failed to deal with black participation. In the 1980s, several books, the movie *Glory*, and Ken Burns's PBS documentary *The Civil War* gave us a sharp sense of the role of African Americans and of women in the war.

Each epoch in American history through the Civil War, from the voyages to Massachusetts and Jamestown to the revolution, the War of 1812, and the Mexican-American war has transpired on an epic scale. The epoch of the Civil

War, with its antebellum prelude and its Reconstruction postlude, was the last in American history to produce the elements of an epic.

In its simple form, the definition of an epic is that it is a long narrative poem of many related episodes depicted on a grand scale, rendered in an elevated style, and that it is about the adventures and deeds of warrior heroes, relating the history and expressing the aspirations of a nation or a people. A clear example is Homer's *Iliad*, the story of the Trojan War, in which the Trojan Hector and the Greek Achilles are heroes in a conflict that defined the identity of both their countries.

If we are to use the term *epic*—and I am arguing passionately that we should and must—we need to achieve a much-needed fine-tuning of our understanding of the definition. One way to do that is to compare it with other terms. *Epic*, *tragedy*, and *satire* are terms among many that have been so often used and misused they have been robbed of their original aptness and vitality to the point where they now have a keener life as clichés than as truly useful terms. For example, television news often attempts to wring emotion out of the death of a drowned puppy by calling it a "tragedy" for the little boy who lost it, when "pathos" is the appropriate term. When it is also misapplied to the fate of the 2,996 victims of the World Trade Center slaughter, little room is left for Aristotle's definition as illustrated in his prime example, Sophocles's *Oedipus Rex*, which basically is the fall of a great individual because of a fatal flaw, such as pride.

"Satire" is more frequently applied than "sarcasm," when the work being discussed is actually no more than mere sarcasm, which in Greek means "the tearing of flesh." "Tragedy" and "satire" are used far more often than "pathos" and "sarcasm," when the latter terms are far more to the point. The reason is that "satire" and "tragedy" are honorific terms; their use elevates the subject and lends it an aura of high-level importance.

The same is true of "epic," as when a novel or movie is called an epic simply because it is long. "Epic" makes any novel or movie sound more important than it can possibly be. Because the term "epic" has been overused and misused, I notice that critics withhold the term when they praise novels and movies of great value, so that few critics have used it even when praising Civil War novels and the movies.

What the hell difference it makes is this: the use of the term "epic" to characterize the events and the poems, novels, and movies of the Civil War is, for Americans caught up in history, unusually apt. The importance of the accurate use of the term for the historic event and as a genuine honorific for novels and movies that deal with the war on a grand scale is that when we feel we are experiencing the magnificent exploits of heroes on a high level, our response to such works is magnified and elevated, and our sense of the war as being relevant to our lives today is deeper.

By contrast, "tragedy" and "satire" are far less appropriately applied to the Civil War. To call the war a national tragedy, or even to invoke the adjective "tragic," is to abuse the term, as Claude G. Bowers did in the title of his Civil War history, *The Tragic Era*. We want very much to apply the term "tragic" to the assassination of President Lincoln, but the key phrase in Aristotle's definition—"the fall from a great height of a noble person because of a fatal flaw in his character"—does not apply. It is not on record that a "fatal flaw" killed any of the war's heroes. Discussing a Civil War movie he greatly admires, Ron Maxwell rightly declined to indulge in the honorific term: "*Ride With the Devil* examines a tragic subject without being a tragedy." So-called satires were written about Lincoln and other key figures and events in the war, but amid much "tearing of flesh," no true satire has been written about any aspect of the war.

On the other hand, parallels were early and readily drawn between the war and Homer's epic poem *The Iliad*; to this day, many parallels have been noted and they are revealing, but many remain not yet clearly drawn. In 1956, Otto Eisenschiml's *American Iliad* and in 1991 Charles P. Roland's *American Iliad* helped draw limited public attention to the basic parallel.

But who is our Homeric poet of the war? In the very first weeks of the Civil War, poets started firing off poems, and although most misfire, the war has kept marching in millions of metric feet ever since. It is a scandal and a shame that so little great poetry has come out of the Civil War. America deserves an epic poem on the war by a poet of much greater genius than Stephen Vincent Benet, whose 1928 Pulitzer Prize–winning *John Brown's Body* has stood as a modest monolith. Now and then, an unpublished poet asks my advice about submitting an epic poem to a publisher, and I cannot be encouraging. Although we often speak of our Civil War as an American *Iliad*, no major poet has been lured by that phrase into testing his or her talent to the limit. Not even, despite his piecemeal effort, did the author of that maritime allegorical epic novel *Moby-Dick* go that far; about the war, he gives us only a miscellany of poems, *Battle Pieces*. Not even clear-sighted Walt Whitman, who served as a wound dresser during that time when "America was turned into one vast hospital," could give us the Homeric epic for which the war's events clearly provided raw material; instead, he left us the poems in *Drum Taps*—some of the finest of the war—and the notes in *Specimen Days*, in which he stated that "the real war will never get into the books." In 1962, critic Edmund Wilson echoed Whitman in *Patriotic Gore* and in 1973, literary historian Daniel Aaron took up that theme again in *The Unwritten War*.

Well, both were wrong about that, as we know by looking at the greatest achievements in memoirs, journals, histories, stories (Ambrose Bierce's, to be exact), and the truly epic novels: the Shaara tetralogy; Mary Johnston's *Long*

Roll and its sequel *Cease Firing*; and Evelyn Scott's trilogy (*The Wave* is the best known of the three). Both Johnston's and Scott's works include antebellum and Reconstruction eras, thus illustrating the most inclusive definition of the Civil War novel.

To reach further ahead of Whitman's time to film, a medium he might have loved, we see *Birth of a Nation*, *Gone With the Wind*, *Glory*, Ken Burns's documentary, *Gettysburg*, and *Gods and Generals*. Because the epoch of the Civil War is intrinsically epic, the application of that term to almost any novel or movie of the war may come naturally to most Americans. "Facts reveal battle strategies, political maneuvering, and casualty lists," said Leah Wood Jewett, second director the United States Civil War Center, in a headnote to her interview with Ron Maxwell in *Civil War Book Review*. "But it is the fictional accounts produced over the past 130 years that convey the intimate, human moments that pierce our hearts and illuminate our imaginations. The novel—and in modern times, the film—speak to our souls in ways that no other medium can," Ron Maxwell elaborates. "Poetic license is the art of what might have been. It is like a retrieved memory, an illumination." And Jeff Shaara summarizes: "Naturally, the novelist, filmmaker, and historian can each bring a particular contribution to the same account. What works for the audience is, ultimately, all that matters." In Homer's time, the only choice, but a good one, was poetry. For a narrative of some length, prose works better for many people today. And for many more, movies work best.

Jeff Shaara is as aware as the critics who praise his epic impulse and his achievement in the realm of epic prose so that three of his novels deal with the other two major epics in American history: the revolution (*Rise to Rebellion* and *The Glorious Cause*) and the Mexican-American War (*Gone for Soldiers*). Before Maxwell challenged him, he had no thought of becoming a writer, but only a natural-born writer could produce almost three thousand pages of expertly researched historical fiction in less than a decade. His next project was World War I, and there is the logical expectation that he might plunge into 1812 or Korea. But the world wars meet far fewer criteria for the American epic than the nation's earlier wars on native soil.

Application of the classic definition of epic to key players and events in the Civil War may produce several patterns. For example, although the Trojan War was not a Civil War, the American Civil War provides an even deeper, more complex, and relevant portrayal of the national consciousness than would a war with another country; a conflict among brothers produces a deeper, more lasting psychic wound than one against foreigners. If we imagine one possible pattern of parallels—that General Lee is like Priam, King of Troy, and Hector is like General Stonewall Jackson and that Agamemnon is like Lincoln and Achilles is like Grant—we may see that the actions of heroic leaders and their heroic followers are more relevant expressions of the national character when the actors are brothers of the same national family. If emancipation of slaves instead of captive Helen is the prize of the victors, we may again see a greater relevance of the American epic to lasting serious issues in our national story.

The style of the Shaara trilogy is elevated, though it suffers by comparison with Homer's, but Maxwell's use of the poetics of cinema must be allowed to stand without comparison, except with that of other writer-directors of the few American epics we have. When we compare the impact of the epical Trojan War and Homer's epic upon Greece as a nation, and the Greeks as a people with that of the Civil War and Shaara-Maxwell's epic, we may with some justification conclude that the American war had a much deeper, clearer, more lastingly powerful, direct effect. The impact of the Shaara novels and the unfinished Maxwell movie trilogy as expressions of that war and its effects is too recent to inspire much more than a confident prediction—which I will now make. Unless another novel and another movie come along to challenge them, these will stand as our Homeric epics—our finest means of understanding how our national identity has been shaped.

As I have said in earlier essays, by understanding the Civil War as our last American epic, we can understand ourselves in the world today, both our dark problems and our bright prospects. Facts alone fail us. Imagination alone fails us. Emotion alone fails us. But emotion, imagination, and intellect, acting together upon the facts, make the facts stand up and speak.

SOME POPULAR CULTURE FORCES THAT HAVE CREATED OR AROUSED AND SUSTAINED THE GENERAL PUBLIC'S INTEREST IN AND PERCEPTION OF THE CIVIL WAR AND RECONSTRUCTION

A question frequently asked by bewildered Northerners and beguiled Southerners is, What is it that draws people in increasing numbers to reinvestigate the Civil War era? I imagine that profound needs in the public psyche, of which most people are unaware, respond to the newest popular culture force—as to the first great force: Harriet Beecher Stowe's *Uncle Tom's Cabin*. The public mind does not normally take into account the ways it has been prepared for the next force to take effect, but the ground had been plowed, seeds sown.

Release of the film version of *Gods and Generals* raises this question: What is the obvious distinction between the romantic notion of the Civil War era and the more assiduously academic, and "accurate" (problematic word in this context), representation of the war? Over time, there have been changes in how the Civil War has been and is being depicted. These forces are so powerful that they do not just appear and eventually fade; they endure and, as an accumulated group at any point in time, function simultaneously, so that *Gods and Generals*, a force itself, draws added strength from the energy, still vibrant, of earlier popular culture forces.

The following list does not include a single academic historian because I am examining in this particular essay forces that have the greatest impact on the American consciousness, and my contention is that, generally speaking, Americans' interest in the Civil War has been monumentally stimulated by popular culture events and works far more than by academic history books. Each item listed has restimulated interest in the war and in previous events, novels, and movies about the war, as when the movie *Gettysburg* resurrected the novel *The Killer Angels*, reinvigorated the reenactor movement, and inspired Jeff Shaara to write his five Civil War novels. Without Ken Burns's documentary, I doubt that a sufficient audience would have been prepared to respond to and make a great success of *Gettysburg*. Burns, as a force, came on the scene in 1990 when interest was relatively low, although the movie *Glory* (1989) certainly aroused interest; all Civil War works and events thereafter owe a great deal to the success of those two movies.

Uncle Tom's Cabin (1852) was an internationally best-selling novel and very long-running play and silent and sound movie. When he met Harriet Beecher Stowe, Lincoln said, "So this is the little lady who wrote the book that made this great war."

Reconstruction (1865–1876), the great effect of the war, was over twice as long as the war itself and far more powerful in prolonging, especially in the South, its effects: violence, economic depression, racism, and mistrust of government, among many others, a legacy alive today. In 1999 or so, Shelby Foote, on a panel with me in New Orleans, said, "There are two sins for which America can never atone: slavery and reconstruction."

Family Histories (Oral and Written), Monuments, Family Photographs and Portraits (Mostly in the South), and the Ruins of Mansions, and So On

Miss Ravenel's Conversion from Secession to Loyalty (1867), first major Civil War novel, focuses on a Louisiana family, by John William De Forest, a Union officer.

Battles and Leaders, four volumes, Century Company, 1887. Personal recollections and drawings. Here historians and the general public interested in the war meet.

Ulysses S. Grant's Memoirs, published and promoted by Mark Twain, 1885. Hemingway called it a great work of American literature.

Creation of the National Park Service battlefields, especially Gettysburg (1895) and Vicksburg (1899).

The Red Badge of Courage (1895), by Stephen Crane, is a great force, even though it is more about courage and war per se than about the Civil War; the famous battle scenes are lifted almost verbatim from Forest's novel.

Books of Civil War photographs, especially *Miller's Photographic History* (Mathew Brady et al.), 1911.

The Birth of a Nation, 1915 (based on *The Clansman*, 1905, by Thomas Dixon). Sustained Southern resentment over Reconstruction; slavery apologia.

Poet Carl Sandburg's multivolume biography of Lincoln, appearing from 1926 to 1939.

Ordeal by Fire (1935), by Fletcher Pratt (paperback title: *A Short History of the Civil War*); almost everybody's favorite all-time short history. Pratt was not an academic but wrote many military works.

Gone With the Wind, novel (1937) and movie (1939). (The movie had the greatest effect on my own perception of the war. I read no books on the war until I began writing my own Civil War novel, *Sharpshooter*.)

Civil War Centennial, 1961–1965 (mainly controlled by academic historians, but many novels and nonfiction works were produced; reenactors were stimulated; the focus was narrow; and it was less meditative than celebratory, commemorative).

The Civil War: A Narrative (1958, 1963, 1974), by novelist Shelby Foote (see his novel *Shiloh*, 1952).

The Confederate flag controversies, from the civil rights era to the present.

Glory (1989), movie; fresh perspective on the war: paved the way for Ken Burns's documentary.

The Civil War (1990), documentary movie, by Ken Burns (stimulated much greater interest in Foote's history).

The United States Civil War Center (1993). I was founding director; resigned 1999.

Gettysburg (1993), movie, by writer-director Ronald Maxwell. Stimulated resurrection of *The Killer Angels*—published in 1974, not a big seller at that time, even though Pulitzer Prize winner. The movie was a major reinvigorator of the reenactor movement and of Civil War roundtables and, unintentionally, neo-Confederate organizations, as was Burns's movie.

Cold Mountain (1997), Pulitzer Prize–winning novel (and film, 2003).

Gods and Generals (1996). While all his novels prove that he is a worthy successor to his father, Jeff Shaara should be regarded as a fine novelist in his own right. Takes a myriad-minded approach, thus setting a vitally new pattern for others to follow in all genres and venues.

The Last Full Measure (1997), by Jeff Shaara. Sequel to *The Killer Angel*, with a focus on General Grant.

Gods and Generals (2003), movie, by writer-director Ronald Maxwell. Focuses on Generals Jackson and Lee; Joshua Chamberlain provides Northern perspective on slavery.

My Personal Choice of the Twelve Best Civil War Movies

Birth of a Nation
The Civil War
The General
Gettysburg
Glory
Gods and Generals
Gone With the Wind
The Horse Soldiers
Major Dundee
The Raid
Ride with the Devil
Shenandoah

My Choice of the Twelve Best Civil War Fiction Works

By Northern Writers

The History of Rome Hanks and Kindred Matters, Joseph Stanley Pennell
In the Midst of Life, Ambrose Bierce
The Killer Angels, Michael Shaara
Miss Ravenel's Conversion from Secession to Loyalty, John William De Forest
Raintree County, Ross Lockridge Jr.

By Southern Writers

Absalom, Absalom! William Faulkner
All the King's Men, Robert Penn Warren
Gods and Generals, Jeff Shaara
Gone With the Wind, Margaret Mitchell
Huckleberry Finn, Mark Twain
The Long Roll and *Cease Firing*, Mary Johnston
The Wave, Evelyn Scott

(Twain prefigures the war, and Warren shows its legacy.)

The Simultaneous Burning of Nine Bridges in East Tennessee

An episode in the first railroad war in history that has not received the attention it merits is the burning of the bridges on the 270-mile railroad in the Great Valley of East Tennessee. The novelty and the simple dramatic appeal of the "Great Locomotive Chase" through Georgia in the spring of 1862 has overshadowed the uniqueness and daring of the bridge-burning venture in East Tennessee. Five months before a professional Union spy led twenty-two disguised federal soldiers in the capture of the Chattanooga-bound Confederate train at Big Shanty, William Blount Carter, ordained Presbyterian minister and devout Unionist, set into motion the most complex paramilitary sabotage plan of the war: Unionist citizens simultaneously setting fire to nine bridges at the same hour, as preparation for the federal invasion of East Tennessee.

By the mid-nineteenth century, East Tennessee had evolved into a unique Southern region. It had a society and economic system that had less dependence on slavery than most of the South, with political leanings divergent from Middle and West Tennessee. East Tennessee also had a heritage of independent action evident in the State of Franklin movement in the 1780s and the desire for separate statehood in the 1840s. Thus, most East Tennesseans saw little future in joining a rebellion of Southern states in which they had little at stake and much to lose. When Tennessee governor Isham G. Harris, backed by overwhelming popular support in Middle and West Tennessee, led attempts to withdraw the state from the Union to join the Confederate States of America in 1861, Unionist leaders in East Tennessee organized a powerful movement to prevent secession. They demonstrated their disapproval of Tennessee's steps toward disunion by holding well-attended conventions in Knoxville and Greeneville, and at one point asked that the eastern counties be allowed to separate from Tennessee and create a separate state. When Tennessee voted officially on the issue of secession in June 1861, East Tennesseans cast their ballots by over a two-to-one margin against disunion. Even after Tennessee had officially seceded from the Union, most East Tennesseans never accepted the authority of the Southern Confederacy. Beginning in the summer of 1861, thousands of Union sympathizers from East Tennessee began to cross over the Cumberland Mountains; during the next four years, possibly thirty thousand of them joined the Union army to fight against the Confederacy. Unionists who remained in the rural counties surreptitiously organized and trained forces of up to five hundred men and threatened armed resistance to the Confederacy.[1]

Confederate authorities were well aware of the situation. They were especially concerned over the safety of the East Tennessee and Virginia Railroad, a key transportation link for troops and supplies moving to the Virginia front. Having a large number of disaffected citizens within its boundaries keenly embarrassed the infant Confederate nation in its attempt to win foreign recognition and ultimately independence.[2]

Throughout the summer of 1861, Tennessee governor Harris and Confederate authorities dealt cautiously with East Tennessee, hoping that leniency would eventually bring Unionists around to the Southern cause. But continued resistance by armed "tories" and the refusal of many East Tennessee political leaders to embrace the Confederacy convinced Southern authorities to change their policies. Governor Harris informed the Confederate secretary of war, "I fear we will have to adopt a decided and energetic policy with the people of that section." On August 16, the governor announced a new and vigorous policy of repressing "Loyalists" by arresting hundreds of Unionists, and the war department in Richmond soon ordered several regiments of Confederate troops into the region. Before long, the Confederates had over ten thousand soldiers stationed in the eastern counties, guarding key railroad bridges, supply depots, and important defensive positions.[3]

From the beginning of the secession crisis, East Tennessee Unionists barraged the leadership in Washington with frantic appeals for help. As early as May 1861, Senator Andrew Johnson and Congressman Horace Maynard urged President Lincoln to send military aid to the Tennessee loyalists. William "Parson" Brownlow, defiant editor of the Knoxville *Whig*, the last Unionist newspaper to remain in operation in the South, called for vengeance in his fiery editorials for the many Unionists who had been arrested:

> Let the railroad on which Union citizens of East Tennessee are conveyed to Montgomery in irons be eternally and hopelessly destroyed. Let the property of the men concerned be consumed and let their lives pay the forfeit and the names will be given. Let the fires of patriotic vengeance be built upon the Union altars of the whole land and let them go out where these conspirators live like the fires from the Lord.

Brownlow urged Union men to "hold themselves in readiness for action, action, action. . . . A Union man of high character who will disguise himself and travel hundreds of miles at his own expense to serve true men to him personally unknown deserves to be immortalized and to live forever." The identity of the man to whom Brownlow was referring is not known, but Reverend William B. Carter proved to be such a leader.[4]

One of Brownlow's oldest enemies—in politics, religion, and journalism—was Landon Carter Haynes of Carter County. Among the first East Tennessee Confederates to predict a Unionist uprising and the burning of the bridges along the main supply line in the Great Valley, he wrote on July 6 to secretary of war Leroy P. Walker:

> Mr. Brownlow, in his paper, says civil war is inevitable, and that the Union men have 10,000 men under drill and armed with rifles and shot-guns. Mr. Thomas A. R. Nelson made a speech . . . on Monday last . . . in Carter County, in which he incited the crowd to resist the action of the State. . . . The *New York Times*, in a lengthy article, says that East Tennessee is a vital point to the Lincoln Government; urges the Union men to seize Knoxville, and hold it till Lincoln can give aid.[5]

Throughout the summer of 1861, other prominent rebel sympathizers (especially Knoxvillians William Swan, John Crozier Ramsey, and Doctor James Gettys McGready Ramsey) and Confederate military figures described an explosive situation in East Tennessee and urged President Jefferson Davis to take immediate action against the Unionists. General Samuel Cooper reminded General Felix K. Zollicoffer, commander of the East Tennessee District, that "the great importance of the East Tennessee and Western [*sic*] Virginia road require that it should be closely guarded wherever there is reason to apprehend its destruction."[6]

The fears of the Confederate authorities were indeed well founded. In September, William Blount Carter escaped into Kentucky to persuade federal authorities to rescue loyal East Tennesseans. Carter, whose ancestors figured prominently in the early history of the region, was pastor of a Rogersville church, but ill health forced him to retire from the ministry and he took over the management of his family's farms. During the secession crisis, the forty-one-year old minister spoke impressively against the evils of secession and supported the most extreme measures, including separate statehood for East Tennessee and armed resistance to the rebels.[7]

At Camp Dick Robinson, the large federal recruiting center near Lancaster, Kentucky, Reverend Carter conferred in late September with General William T. Sherman, Andrew Johnson, Horace Maynard, and General George H. Thomas, who had recently taken command of forces in Eastern Kentucky.

Carter's older brother, Lieutenant Samuel Perry "Pawhatan" Carter, whom Lincoln had urged to go on special duty from the navy to organize and drill Tennessee volunteers because he was familiar with upper East Tennessee, informed the group of enemy troop distributions. Someone in the group then proposed a bold plan—the simultaneous burning of all the bridges on the railroads passing through East Tennessee. All agreed except Sherman. But Thomas, who had earlier convinced their superior, General Robert Anderson, "the hero of Ft. Sumter," of the efficacy of an expedition into East Tennessee, answered objections so forcefully that Sherman confessed himself "converted" and ordered Thomas "to push on an expedition."[8]

With Sherman's blessings, Carter traveled to Washington to persuade President Lincoln and General George B. McClellan, Union army general-in-chief. Thomas gave Carter a letter of introduction, boldly declaring, "It would be one of the most important services that could be done for the country, and I most earnestly hope you will use your influence with the authorities in furtherance of his plans which he will submit to you together with the reasons for doing the work."[9]

Lincoln was predisposed to listen to a plan for moving into East Tennessee. On July 23, two days after Bull Run, he had issued "Memorandum of Military Policy Suggested by the Bull Run Defeat," projecting simultaneous expeditions into Virginia, down the Mississippi, and into the loyal region of East Tennessee. He ordered arms smuggled through the mountain passes and desperately desired than the liberation of Union-loving people in East Tennessee from rebel oppression. That he felt their suffering deeply was well known. His understanding of the economic, political, and military importance of East Tennessee was also clear.[10]

In Washington, the plan Carter placed before Lincoln, General McClellan, and secretary of state William H. Seward projected the simultaneous burning of nine main bridges on the East Tennessee and Georgia and the East Tennessee and Virginia railroads between Bridgeport, Alabama, and Bristol, Tennessee. Destruction of the long bridge over the Tennessee River at Bridgeport would prevent the Memphis and Charleston railroad from connecting with the Western and Atlantic, the main supply line from Memphis and Nashville to Richmond. The long bridges at Bridgeport and Loudon were the most expensive, the most strategic, but the whole line was vital. Closely coordinated with the bridge burnings was the planned advance of an army toward Knoxville, sixty miles South of Cumberland Gap. General Thomas would seize and control that key rail center while Unionists rose in revolt against their Confederate tormentors. Lincoln, McClellan, and Seward approved the plan. McClellan promised to keep the Confederates in Virginia too busy to send reinforcements. The details of the burning of the bridges were left to Carter's judgment.[11]

Reverend Carter returned to Camp Dick Robinson with $2,500 allocated for expenses as a tangible expression of federal support of his plan. During mid-October, he left camp with two officers recently detailed to this mission, Captain William Cross of Scott County and Captain David Fry of Greene County. In East Tennessee, Carter recruited six leaders, who then selected five or six men to help destroy the bridges.

From Morgan County, near Montgomery, Tennessee, Carter reported to Thomas on October 22:

> I am within 6 miles of a company of rebel cavalry. I find our Union people in this part of the State firm and unwavering in their devotion to our Government and anxious to have an opportunity to assist in saving it. . . . You will please furnish the bearers with as much lead, rifle powder, and as many caps as they can bring for Scott and Morgan counties. You need not fear to trust these people. They will open the war for you by routing these small bodies of marauding cavalry. . . . Tomorrow night I hope to be near our railroad. I have not been able as yet to gain any information as to my prospects of success.[12]

Five days later, Carter was closer to Loudon and one of the main bridges. From near Kingston he wrote to General Thomas:

> I am now within a few miles of our railroad, but I have not yet had time to obtain all the information I must have before I decide on the course best for me to adopt. If I can get half a dozen men to "take the bull by the horns," we can whip them completely and save the railroad. If I cannot get such leaders, we will make a desperate attempt to destroy all the bridges, and I firmly believe we will be successful.[13]

Troop strength, Carter reported, was 160 at the Loudon bridge; 1,400, mostly ineffective, at Knoxville; and 6,000, only about 1,600 of them effective, at Cumberland Gap. He pointed out that Zollicoffer's hold on East Tennessee was tenuous and that Davis was unable to send reinforcements from Virginia. Meanwhile, despotic oppressions had only intensified the loyalty of Unionists and their eagerness to rise up and throw off their "fetters." Having pleaded with Thomas to ask McClellan for more troops, Carter apologized for presuming, as a civilian, to make suggestions to a military man. Willing to risk his own life, he was about to ask his people to do the same. "I can assure you that whoever is the leader of a successful expedition into East Tennessee will receive from these people a crown of glory of which any one might well be proud, and I know of no one on whom I would more cheerfully bestow that crown than on yourself."[14]

Although he knew that October 22 or 23 was set for Thomas's march south, Carter was unaware of the development of the military phase of the plan. On the 21st, for instance, Colonel T. T. Garrard drove back Zollicoffer at Wildcat Mountain, about forty-five miles below Camp Dick Robinson. On the 25th, Sherman warned Thomas, "Don't push too far. Your line is already long and weak." General Albin F. Schoepf went no farther than London, Kentucky, on the 28th, only forty miles North of Cumberland Gap. From Camp Dick Robinson, Thomas continued to keep the advance into East Tennessee before Sherman's attention, and on October 31 he started South for Crab Orchard.[15]

On November 2, acting through Freemorton Young of Roane County and William Stone of Hamilton County, Carter entrusted the simultaneous destruction of four bridges in lower East Tennessee to the leadership of thirty-nine-year-old A. M. Cate, an active and influential opponent of secession and a highly respected citizen of Bradley County.[16]

Four days before the date set for the raids, Carter was still convinced that his mission was, as planned, coordinated with the movement of federal troops under General Thomas. But as late as November 5, Thomas sounded as if he were still trying to "convert" his commanding officer. Enclosing Reverend Carter's October 22 and 27 letters as means of persuasion, General Thomas assured Sherman that "if we could possibly get the arms and the four regiments of disciplined and reliable men, we could seize the railroad yet. Cannot General McClellan be induced to send me the regiments?" Had not McClellan already committed himself to the combined operation? Was Sherman pretending or insinuating an actual obstruction of the plan by McClellan?[17]

In another letter to Sherman, also dated November 5, Thomas noted that "with my headquarters at Somerset I can easily seize the most favorable time for invading East Tennessee." But the day before Carter's raiders struck, Thomas disclosed to Andrew Johnson that Sherman had quite nearly decided not to execute the Carter plan: "I have done all in my power to get troops and transportation and means to advance into Tennessee. I believe General Sherman has done the same. Up to this time we have been unsuccessful. If the Tennesseans are not content and must go, then the risk of disaster will remain with them." On the same day Thomas wrote to General Schoepf at London: "I sympathize most deeply with the Tennesseans on account of their natural anxiety to relieve their friends and families from the terrible oppression they are now suffering; but to make the attempt to rescue them when we are not half prepared is culpable."[18]

Also on the day before the raids, Sherman wrote to Thomas from Louisville: "Mr. Maynard still presses the East Tennessee expedition. I do not doubt its importance, but I know we have not force enough and transportation to undertake it. Instead of dispersing our efforts we should concentrate; and as soon as possible our forces must be brought nearer together. In the meantime do the best you can." Discouraged by Sherman from moving south, Thomas stayed at Crab Orchard, Kentucky. He had been out of communication since late October with Carter, and even if he had had a way to contact the reverend, it was too late to reach the six leaders to postpone the raids.[19]

Given the initial support of Lincoln, Seward, McClellan, Sherman, Thomas, and his own brother, Lieutenant Samuel Carter, the architect of the plan had, on the evening of November 8, 1861, little reason to be uneasy over his inability for the past two weeks to communicate with the federal army. At his command post near Kingston, midpoint on the railroad and about twenty-five miles from the strategic Loudon bridge, Carter was certain that the bands of Union raiders were poised to put the torch to nine wooden bridges and that General Thomas was poised to invade.[20]

After an eighty-mile ride to Bridgeport, Alabama, Robert W. Ragan and James D. Keener found the river lined with rebel troops at the longest and most powerfully built of the nine bridges. Discouraged by this show of force, the two would-be raiders returned to their homes, having failed to destroy the most important bridge.[21]

Thirty miles northeast of Bridgeport, in Marion County, Tennessee, W. T. Cate, A. M. Cate's brother, and W. H. Crowder rode twenty-five miles and burned two bridges, one belonging to the Western and Atlantic Railroad at Chickamauga Creek east of Chattanooga and another on the East Tennessee and Georgia Railroad leading to Knoxville.[22]

The closeness of the village of Charleston on the Bradley County bank and the hamlet of Calhoun on the McMinn County side lent special hazards to the task of burning the bridge over the Hiwassee River. A. M. Cate led the expedition against the bridge when William Stone, overwhelmed with a sense of his fearful responsibility, returned to Cate's house and laid the task at his feet. Jesse Cleveland, Adam Thomas, and the third Cate brother, Thomas L., had already agreed to take part in the raid.[23]

While waiting for Thomas on a public highway, bathed in brilliant moonlight, the Cate brothers saw a rebel officer leading two squads of troops along the road from the bridge. Seeing no way to escape except to run like a coward, A.M. told his brother W.T. to pretend childlike innocence. They rode past the rebel soldiers without being questioned. When they returned to the meeting place, Thomas joined them. Down the road, Cleveland and his son were waiting for them with pine torches. At about eleven o'clock, the men stopped in a pine thicket almost half a mile from the bridge. Sounds of revelry came from the town, full of rebel troops and citizens. The presence of so many soldiers made Cate suspect that an attack on the bridge had been anticipated. Even so, he decided that if the watchman was alone, he would bribe him with a hundred dollars or kill him and throw him into the river.[24]

At about one o'clock the town was dark and all seemed still. Having determined that the safest approach to the bridge was by the railroad, they gathered up their matches, turpentine, and fuel and set off. Some members of the raiding party tried to persuade Cate to turn back. But for Cate, the time for talk had passed. "Protect me with secrecy," he told them. "Go back if you wish. I have come to burn the bridge, and I will do it or die." The others continued with Cate, passing to the left of the depot. In faint light shining from the guardhouse, Thomas Cate crept up to the window where he observed the watchman fast asleep. Moving silently, Thomas Cate, young Cleveland, and Thomas rushed to set fire to the bridge while A. M. Cate and Jesse Cleveland stood guard. One of the saboteurs cut the telegraph wire. Armed with a holster pistol, a sixshooter, and a three-pound knife, A.M. went to the window where he could see inside and easily reach the door. Cleveland stood nearby, his musket charged, ready to kill the watchman if necessary:[25]

> To Cate, the bridge—several hundred feet long, boarded up the sides, covered and pitched on the top—was a splendid piece of architecture. It was so dry that when the flame set off the turpentine, it flashed to the pitch and seemed to dart all over the roof like electric arcs. Having applied the torch, the saboteurs dashed away. Looking back when the bridge was almost out of sight, Cate saw a blaze that glowed from bank to bank; it seemed that not all the water in the Hiwassee River could extinguish it. Cate divided the money, separated the men, and, after a seventy-one mile ride, was resting at home.[26]

As Cate and his accomplices attacked the four bridges at the Southern end of the Great Valley, raiders who remain unknown found the long bridge at Loudon so well guarded that the attack was called off. There is no evidence that Reverend Carter led any of the raiding parties.[27]

Fifteen miles east of Knoxville, where the line's name changed to the East Tennessee and Virginia, the railroad crossed the Holston River and entered Jefferson County at Strawberry Plains. Riding from the mountains of Sevier County, William C. Pickens led twelve men in the attack on that strategically important bridge. On the Strawberry Plains side, the raiders made an opening in a rail fence and crossed a field to the Holston River. Clouds obscured the moon; the air was frosty. Having made no examination of the site in advance, they left their horses with two men and groped along the bank to the abutment.[28]

Pickens, later described as a "bold, dashing, reckless, good-natured fellow, who delighted in just such adventures as this," and another man climbed up onto the trestlework. Pickens lit his torch and was just about to place it between the scantling and the weatherboarding when a bullet struck his thigh, knocking him to the ground. The fall snuffed out the torch. A small but powerfully built guard, James Keelan, grabbed Pickens. As they struggled, one of the raiders rushed to Pickens's aid, but in the darkness he mistook his colleague for the guard and hacked at him viciously with a long homemade knife. Another raider got up on the platform, sank his knife into flesh, felt himself grabbed by the hair, and felt a dirk thrust into his own body. Other raiders on the ground reached up, hitting the guard box with their knives. More men got up on the platform, sinking their knives into posts and wooden sills on two platform levels of the trestle and firing twenty rounds into the dark. Hearing Keelan fall down the embankment, the raiders assumed they had killed him. But the men still below the trestle heard the guard get up and run, and into the confusion of the darkness they fired at him.[29]

Having captured the bridge from its lone guard, the men searched for their matches, but only Pickens had brought some. In the struggle with the guard, he lost his grip on the box, and it fell into the river. One raider suggested that they secure fire from a nearby house, but the idea was rejected by the others for fear of being recognized. With their leader Pickens suffering a bullet wound from the guard's pistol and a severe knife wound inflicted by one of his own men, the raiders reluctantly turned their backs on the long bridge.[30]

Fifty-six miles further northeast, Captain David Fry, a Greene County native, detailed for "special service" from Company F, Second Regiment, East Tennessee Volunteers, led Jacob Harmon and his sons, Henry and Thomas, Jacob M. Hensie, Henry Fry (no relation to David), A. C. Haun, Harrison Self and son Hugh S., and about fifty other men in an attack on the long bridge over Lick Creek in Greene County, fifteen miles west of Greeneville.[31]

Quickly capturing the guard on the bridge, the raiders surrounded a tent at the west end and took five more prisoners. A few minutes later, the bridge was engulfed in flames. Returning to the tent with a large number of men, Captain Fry cursed the six guards for persecuting Unionists in Greene County. He forced the rebels to swear not to take up arms against the U.S. government.

A raider, sheathing his knife, entered the tent, declaring, "That damned wire's done telling on us now."[32]

Thirty-five miles northeast, in the county named after Reverend Carter's historic family, Daniel Stover, Andrew Johnson's son-in-law, led an attack on the Watauga River bridge at Carter's Depot (Piney Flats). The bristling presence of Captain David McClellan's company of Confederate infantry, however, discouraged that attempt.[33]

Stover then led his men to a second target, the bridge over the Holston River at Union Depot (Bluff City), Sullivan County, within ten miles of the Virginia line. They easily captured the two soldiers guarding the bridge and forced them to swear not to reveal the raiders' names. After torching the bridge, Stover released his prisoners.[34]

In all, seven bridges had been destroyed, and now the raiders anxiously awaited Thomas's army of liberation. Meanwhile, four hundred Sevier County loyalists, certain that the bridge burnings were a signal for the invasion of the federal army, marched toward Strawberry Plains to make a second assault on the bridge. At Underdown's Ferry on the French Broad, a Confederate force, composed in part of Knoxville and Strawberry Plains citizens, fired at them from the north bank. After thirty-four hours of skirmishing, the Sevier countians retreated, losing some of their men as prisoners.[35]

Loyalist activity continued also at Union and Carter's Depot. The Confederate guards released by Stover reneged on their oaths of silence, and under an oath to the Confederacy they identified the saboteurs. When news circulated among the mountain men of Carter and Johnson counties that the bridge burners were to be arrested and hanged, one thousand of them assembled at Sycamore Shoals to resist.[36]

Near Carter's Depot, Unionist pickets fired upon advancing Confederate troops under Captain David McClellan, who was forced to retreat. But at night he launched a counterattack and was repulsed again. Fully expecting Confederate reinforcements to overwhelm them, the Unionists retreated through Big Springs to Elizabethton, then to Doe River Cove six miles beyond, staying there until Colonel Danville Leadbetter broke up their camp two weeks later. As they fled into the mountains, some were captured and imprisoned in Knoxville and Tuscaloosa, but many escaped into Kentucky, where they joined the Union army, fully expecting it to invade East Tennessee within days. Others sought refuge in the mountains until September 1863, when the federal army finally fulfilled Lincoln's promise to invade East Tennessee.[37]

The mass attacks by Unionists in Johnson and Carter counties had very little military consequence, but an element of victory flared in their successful demonstration to Confederate authorities that Unionists would never submit to a revolutionary government. Coming quickly after the burning of the bridges, the "rush to arms" and the acts of aggression by large bodies of men in Johnson, Carter, Jefferson, and Sevier counties alarmed Confederate authorities as no previous acts of resistance had done. These demonstrations "startled the whole Confederacy." For East Tennesseans, however, the bridge burnings brought persecution and strife rather than deliverance. An intense reign of terror raged, as large numbers of suspects were sent without trial to prison, where some died of illnesses.[38]

What happened to the bridge burners? After his triumphant destruction of the Hiwassee bridge, A. M. Cate wandered three hundred miles over the mountains until he reached Somerset, Kentucky, in January 1862. He joined the Union army, rising to the rank of captain. After the war, he was elected twice to the state legislature. In 1871, he petitioned the U.S. Senate and House of Representatives, "praying compensation for himself and others, for services rendered in burning certain important railroad bridges in East Tennessee the night of the eighth of November and for loss of property resulting from said act and their devotion to the United States Government." At one point, he casts a shadow of doubt over Reverend Carter's reputation as the heroic architect of the plan. At Flat Lick, Kentucky, before the raids, Carter paid him $500,

> but to me seemed to be exceedingly careful not to acknowledge himself the supervising agent. . . . I have several times requested of the Secretary of War a copy of Mr. Carter's report, or to be allowed to examine it, for the benefit of the committee, and he positively refused both. We have not only been unfairly dealt with, but I have reason to believe, a large amount of the money appropriated for that purpose went into the pockets of gentlemen behind the curtain, who, outside of their knowledge of the matter, gave it no assistance, except, perhaps, to defraud the real actors and sufferers.

Cate pointed out that because Carter refused to recognize him, "the Secretary of War says he has no power to pay." Cate died the year he made the petition.[39]

Cate's brother Thomas was captured, imprisoned in Knoxville, escaped, recaptured, and imprisoned in Alabama for nearly three months. Near death from disease, he was released. After the war, he became a banker in Chattanooga.[40]

W. H. Crowder, partner of W. T. Cate in the burning of the two Chickamauga Creek bridges, fled to Kentucky, where he joined the army and served two years.[41]

The identities of many of the bridge burners were kept secret for as long as thirty-five years. Captain William Cross, of Scott County, told his family that he had been connected with bridge burning, but he did not take responsibility for the intention of burning the Tennessee River bridge at Loudon.[42]

David Fry managed to slip into Georgia where he stole locomotives, destroyed tracks, and cut telegraph lines on the railroad between Marietta and Chattanooga. Arrested while trying to enter Kentucky with forty others, he was jailed in Knoxville as a spy and a traitor. After being transferred to Atlanta, Fry and some of the Union soldiers, who were convicted of participating in the famous theft of the locomotive at Big Shanty, overpowered their guards the night before their scheduled execution and escaped into North Carolina.[43]

Pickens, leader of the attack on the Holston River bridge at Strawberry Plains, doubled up with one of his men on horseback and led his band to Dan Kenner's house, several miles away, where Dr. James H. Ellis, of Trundle's Cross Roads, dressed his wound. Placed on a sled and concealed with fodder, he was hauled back into the Smoky Mountains through Tuckaleechee Cove, on up into Wear's Cove, one of the most inaccessible parts of the mountains.[44]

In that mountain retreat, where loyal men supplied their every need, including fresh bear meat, they met Parson Brownlow and quite a number of other prominent Unionists. Brownlow's employee, William Rule, had ridden secretly to Sevierville the day after the burnings to warn Brownlow that Confederate soldiers were looking for him as a conspirator in the burning of the bridges.[45]

In January, a pilot led Pickens and his men through the Cumberland Mountain passes into Kentucky, where Pickens became the first colonel of the Third Tennessee Cavalry. Six of his fellow raiders became officers in the cavalry and other branches of the federal army. Pickens died a few years after the war.[46]

Confederate secretary of war Judah P. Benjamin issued orders that the bridge burners were to "be tried summarily by drum-head court-martial, and if found guilty, executed on the spot by *hanging*," their bodies to be left "*hanging* in the vicinity of the burned bridges."

From Greeneville, Colonel Leadbetter informed Benjamin on November 30 that "two insurgents have today been tried for bridge-burning, found guilty and hanged." A third was spared because he was too young. People on passing trains reportedly leaned out to strike the corpses of Hensie and Fry with canes and sticks.[47]

Parson Brownlow, assured that he would suffer no physical harm, left his refuge in the Great Smoky Mountains and surrendered to Confederate authorities in Knoxville on December 6. Imprisoned with some of the bridge burners and many other loyalists, he saw A. C. Haun taken from that jail to be hanged. Jacob Harmon was forced to watch the execution of his son and was himself hanged immediately afterward. Harrison Self, accused like Haun and the Harmons of burning the Lick Creek bridge, was sentenced to hang on December 27, but his daughter Elizabeth, with Brownlow's help, sent an appeal to President Davis, who, along with Benjamin, was already moved by earlier appeals to suspend the execution. Benjamin finally authorized Brownlow's exile to the North in March 1862. "I would greatly prefer seeing him on the other side of our lines as an avowed enemy, than as a secret enemy within."[48]

The architect of the plan, Reverend William Blount Carter, shocked by the federal army's failure to execute the most decisive part of the plan, for which the burning of the bridges was intended only as a fiery prelude to invasion, was isolated in enemy territory, where he quickly became known as the leader of the incendiaries. On November 16, he reported the success of his own part of the plan to his brother, Lieutenant Samuel Carter, and readily expressed his impatience with the glacial pace at which the federal army was keeping its promise to Loyalists in East Tennessee. Eventually the minister escaped his native region, but unlike his brother he did not serve in the army, possibly because of illness. When General Ambrose Burnside entered Knoxville in September 1863, Reverend Carter finally returned to Carter County, where he became the leader of conservative opposition to Lincoln's emancipation policies.[49]

Long after many of them were already known, Carter kept the names of his men secret for thirty-five years, going to his grave in 1901 without revealing any of them. But Oliver P. Temple, in his chronicle of the Civil War in East Tennessee, succeeded in tracking down most of the names and, "with permission from those still living," published them in 1899.[50]

Knoxville historian William Rule's conclusion that the history of the events directly related to the bridge burnings is "imperfectly understood" and can never be "fully written" is still true. Except for Temple's *East Tennessee and the Civil War* and the *Official Records*, little more primary information is available now than then. While the raids were clearly acts of war perpetrated by a paramilitary force, even some Unionists, wrote Thomas Humes, another Knoxville historian, "thought them inexpedient, hurtful to public convenience." Lacking a full knowledge of promised federal military action, for which the burning of the bridges was intended only as support, some Unionist sympathizers criticized the operation for its failure to produce practical results. "The attempt to burn these bridges at this time," wrote Temple, "was, in my opinion, from every point of view . . . most unwise and unfortunate. It did little injury to the enemy, while it brought untold calamities and sufferings on the Union people."[51]

Several features of the burning of the bridges call to mind the "Great Locomotive Chase," which occurred five months later. The two exploits had in common the specific mission of burning railroad bridges to cut Southern supply lines for the general goal of liberating East Tennessee from Confederate rule. Both ventures had military backing, but evaluations of the kind and extent of that backing conflicted then and remain unclear even today. Always in dispute has been the strategic value of the two actions even in conception.

But while the execution of Andrews's raid was indisputably a failure (as had been an earlier raid led by him), Reverend Carter's venture at least produced five burned bridges, with fewer losses. Andrews and seven of his raiders were executed, and fourteen went to prison. None of Carter's raiders was killed in action, and only a few were wounded; five were hanged for burning one bridge, and only four other men went to prison. As a thrilling exploit that captured and has continued to hold the public imagination, the "Great Locomotive Chase" deserves its reputation, but for their own unique venture, Reverend Carter and his raiders deserve more recognition than they have received thus far.

The Sinking of the *Sultana*

A Meditation on Loss and Forgetfulness

The story is deceptively simple: the worst maritime disaster in the history of this nation occurred on the Mississippi River about seven miles above Memphis at 2:00 a.m. on April 27, 1865, when the steamboat *Sultana*, carrying 2,222 known passengers and crew, exploded and sank.

Over 1,500 recently paroled Union prisoners of war were killed by the explosion or drowning; many of the one hundred civilian men, women, and children perished. About 200 of the 586 who were saved died later of exposure or injuries in hospitals. The combined death toll was over 1,700.

They had boarded at Vicksburg, where the longest seize of the war had finally ended in Confederate surrender, ending the Vicksburg campaign, more important, in my opinion, than any battle in the East, because control of the Mississippi River was crucial to the success of the Anaconda strategy that was to have ended the war. The boat exploded, and over 1,500 Union soldiers, homeward bound from Andersonville and Cahaba Confederate prisons, perished. All had suffered the terrors of battle, the loss of close comrades, physical and psychological wounds, the risky confinement of hospital, the humiliation of capture and surrender, escape and recapture, homesickness, boredom, the daily threat of death by starvation, disease, suicide, robbery, injury, or death by raiding bands of fellow prisoners. Unlike their comrades in Ohio and the other Northern states, East Tennessee Union soldiers had first suffered hostilities and atrocities from rebel neighbors and Confederate troops before enlisting. Converging lines of force had brought them all to that safe harbor, to that boat, that haven, with its defective boilers, its greedy or negligent officials, civilian and military, to that explosion eighteen days after the Confederacy had lost the war, twelve days after the Union had lost its president, whose funeral train was even then crossing the country, bound for Springfield, Illinois.

Even after six books, four in the last decade, and many newspaper and magazine articles, this unique disaster has failed to seize the imagination of American readers, even those whose fascination with the Civil War seems endless. The first book was a compilation of the testimonies of 135 of the 500 military survivors, *Loss of the Sultana and Reminiscences of Survivors*. In 1890, when the survivors were old men, one lone individual survivor, Private Chester Berry, later Reverend Berry, as a humanistic venture, out of a compulsion to remind his countrymen, and to fix the disaster in their consciousnesses, set about exhorting survivors like himself to send him their personal testimonials, to help raise the dead up into the great river of our national memory. He published them about two years later in Lansing, Michigan.

Personally, Chester Berry, like the Ancient Mariner, wanted others to hear what he would hear over and over again for the rest of his life: the screams of one victim whom he watched step off toward what he trusted to be safety from the burning, the steeply slanting hurricane deck to the burning wheelhouse, just as the wheelhouse broke up and smashed him, as in an iron vice, against the deck, where he flailed about and burned alive. That dreadful night, Berry, like many others, had abandoned pleading nonswimmers and kicked loose drowning men whose clutch would have pulled him down. Survivor's guilt and what we understand today as posttraumatic stress syndrome may have compelled him to do the hard work of finding survivors almost three decades later, through research in military records and newspapers, but mostly by word of mouth at annual reunions, some responding when asked to tell the tale, others as silent as the dead. Some refused or neglected to respond, and some answered very briefly, even laconically. "About all I can say is that I got very wet and quite cold." A few, like E. J. Squire and C. C. Seabury, gave only basic military and civilian information, with no mention of the disaster. Brevity itself suggests posttraumatic stress syndrome. "I do not think it worth while," wrote A. Shoemaker, somewhat enigmatically, "to give my 'Sultana' experience." We might like to imagine that those who didn't respond wrote something but didn't send it, wrote memoirs later, or wrote letters about it—that will be found someday. Hosea C. Aldrich announced he had published a book of his own privately, but mostly about Cahaba Prison life.

As far as I know, more voices spoke at Berry's urging of this major but astonishingly obscure episode than spoke of any other event of the war on any other occasion or prompting. Among other witness books of the war, compilations or single memoirs, this one is at least relatively unique. The 134 survivors who wrote responses had first spoken aloud, on the deck, in the water, later to friends and family, although some were silent, their voices internal, mingled with remembered voices. We read in Berry's book the words they wrote over a hundred years ago, but between the lines, the voices of nearly

1,500 other soldiers and civilian men, women, and children who died in fire and in water speak to us. Imagine Berry as having called forth those voices. Think of his having quickened the tongues of all those survivor voices as a memorial to the 1,500 whose mouths were stopped with mud. The voices of survivors activate the voices of the dead.

Because he wanted Americans to look upon a face as they read each testimony, Berry provided drawings of faces of some of them, from photographs; too few actual photos are in his book. (More photographs appear in later books, as many as thirty-five in Jerry Potter's *Sultana Tragedy*.) *Let the names be given*, we may imagine Berry charging himself, *of all the victims and the survivors*. Painfully aware of his inability to make his list fully accurate and complete, he wanted the world to know the names of all those who died and those who survived.

Berry wanted, and still wants, the world to know the cause of the explosion, so he reprints the military court of inquiry proceedings that had been available in the early volumes of the *War of the Rebellion: Official Records of the Union and Confederate Armies*, the first of which appeared in 1880.

But first Berry wants the world to see the photograph taken from the bank at Helena, Arkansas, in the afternoon of the previous day. As one gazes upon it, one notices that almost to a man the freed prisoners wanted to be in the picture. They who were about to die almost sank the boat themselves. Thousands of men rushing toward the rail, toward photographer T. W. Bankes, must have stirred a sinking feeling in the pit of his stomach.

We have no photograph of the wreckage, despite the fact that for four months it was visible, as men salvaged machinery and divers went down searching for bodies. Let's be thankful for the passion in the drawing that emerged in *Harper's Weekly* over three weeks after the catastrophe.

What will it take for this event, which caused such vexation on the Father of Waters for a few hours, to earn its rightful place as a symbolic expression, embodying every adjective for sad loss, of the tragedy of the Civil War for all Americans?

Snatched from behind plows in West Virginia, Illinois, Michigan, Indiana, Ohio, Alabama, Iowa, Nebraska, Pennsylvania, Kentucky, Missouri, Virginia, and out of the hills and mountains of Kentucky and Eastern Tennessee, thrown into the boredom of camps, the fatigue of marching, and the fire of battle, captured starved, teeth missing or loosened, deprived of good water, weak, sick, in Belle Island, Castle Thunder, Danville, Libby, Castle Morgan in Cahaba, Alabama, recently standing waist deep in water for five days from the rising of the Alabama River in March, in Andersonville prison pen, hell on earth, "den of death," digging tunnels out from abandoned wells, wounded or killed stepping over the dead line, mourning Lincoln, assassinated, swearing vengeance, and then forced to march. George A. Clarkson wrote, "A killing march on the frozen ground, barefooted and nearly naked," many died on the rough roads, conveyed partway by river and railroad, to parole at Big Black River, a thousand miles from home for some.

Isaac Van Nuys related, "The cruel war was over and their cause triumphant." Elated, they turned their faces homeward. A "jolly crowd" looked upon this boat, the *Sultana*, and trusted it and its captain, J. Cass Mason, to take them home at last. Dreamers, they were driven on board like sheep, packed in like pigs. Absalom N. Hatch: "I was . . . too weak to care what became of me." Several complained the boat was overloaded, one of whom was Major William Fidler, 6th Kentucky Cavalry, commander of the paroled prisoners, whose death was only one of the hundreds of confirmations of the fear of catastrophe. Several noticed repair of boilers going on, one of whom inspected the four boilers himself and moved away from them to lie down apprehensively to sleep.

General Ulysses S. Grant—who had refused to exchange prisoners, condemning, as some saw it then and others see it still, thousands of Union soldiers to die of disease, starvation, suicide, and general ill treatment in Andersonville and other prisons—was asleep in Raleigh, North Carolina, triumphantly befumed of cigar and whiskey.

Several families were asleep in staterooms, going North from Louisiana. One soldier kept a photo of his wife and boy in his pants to identify him, if he were lost.

The boat unloaded three hundred hogsheads (barrels) of sugar in Memphis, left at eleven at night, then took on coal "to last as far as Cairo, Illinois." In St. Louis, the owners slept, profit satisfied.

Isaac Van Nuys: From bow to stern, "we were huddled together like sheep for the slaughter," crammed in next to the paddlewheel housing on the upper deck; on the cabin deck; on the hurricane deck next to the wheelhouse and the bell frame; in the alleyway on the second deck; on the promenade deck between the smokestacks; on the main deck, huddled together along with forty or so mules and horses and other freight, as the *Sultana* "steamed up the great Father of Waters" (Samuel J. Thrasher).

Folks back home lay abed, dreaming of sons, husbands, brothers, lovers, imagining them safe on the boat now, warm, fed, in cabins, as it would be for normal loads; envisaged them lulled to sleep by the swaying movement of the boat, the flow of the river, the steady sound of the side-wheeler churning; pictured them appearing at last at the front door, the sun over their shoulders.

Truman Smith: "Every foot of her deck was covered with men who had fought starvation, vermin and filth."

A light rain was falling—the ex-prisoners were used to much worse in exposed places—but the river was already at flood, over its banks.

General William Tecumseh Sherman, having secured the signature of General Joseph E. Johnston at Durham Station, North Carolina, to a document of capitulation, slept better, one may imagine, than his former enemy. Some lay awake imagining the faces of blood kindred at their homecoming. Michael Brunner is one of many who may have been thinking of the foreign town where they were born, in Ireland, England, Germany, or France.

On the shore, recently emancipated slaves watched the mammoth steamboat chug by. Above Memphis, Confederate guerillas waited, just as many passengers feared. Sleeping on deck—"more like a lot of hogs than men"—some were having nightmares of battle, of prison.

Captain Henry Wirz, commander of Andersonville prison, facing execution, perhaps did not sleep as well indoors as did many of his ex-prisoners in the rain.

Paroled prisoners lay by the side of the icebox, by the rear hatchway to the hold, on the roof right in front and the rear of the pilot house, on the texas roof near the steps, in front of two smokestacks, by the boilers and furnace, by the bell; several slept on the boiler deck in a coal bin, in the forecastle, near the jack staff, on the cabin deck in the curve of the stair banister by the stateroom door, on the main stairway, in life boats. "All the decks were completely covered when all of the boys laid down," almost like the old slave ships, "upon which the eye of an evil planet was resting. I tried to get close to the boiler, but it was full there" (Murry S. Baker)

Epenetus W. Mcintosh, left by one steamer, had gotten on the *Sultana*: "I was sent whirling into the water." The explosion threw one boiler out of its bed. Ben G. Davis was "about to take a drink when the boiler exploded and the canteen flew out of my hand." P. L. Horn: "I was lost in the air . . . whirled in the air." Smokestacks crashed down, one forward on top of the bell, the other twisted backward onto the hole in the decks.

In the projectile breaking up of wood and metal, bones broke, noses were torn off. William Lugenbeal: a spear of timber ran through his comrade's body, "killing him almost instantly." George A. King: "I thought the boat was being fired upon by the enemy." In the explosion, some died in the air, before they hit the water. The deck kitchen was blown off into the river. The night was full of praying, laughing, lamenting, swearing, crying, and "some did not seem to know anything" (W. C. Porter). William Madden and others heard the shrieks of women and children, praying, singing "The Star Spangled Banner," pleading, groaning, screaming, "some uttering the most profane language and others commending their spirits to the Great Ruler of the Universe," and animals, the awful brays of distressed mules, horses, in the "mad waters of the Mississippi." The cries of women, children, the roar of water, comrades calling to comrades, strangers to rank strangers, pleading for help, shouting instructions for survival. Fire, the size of the crown of a man's hat, started up in the coal near the furnace. Madden saw a burning hole open up, like Dante's Inferno.

Back in Memphis, thousands slept in ignorance of the fact that they would jump up as rescuers.

A smokestack fell—broke the upper deck—and Joseph H. Mayes fell through to the lower deck. Scores followed, falling from the upper to the lower deck, into fire, burning under fallen pieces, suffocated from the pressure and the smoke. The son of a steamboat captain—sound asleep on the larboard wheelhouse water-box on the hurricane deck—thought that "if she did not catch on fire we were all right . . . fire burst out where the chimneys had stood. Swim or burn." Albert Varnell: "My face was scalded so as to put out my eye."

A sound like "a hundred earthquakes" woke a man warm in bed on land. From his porch, the fire made such a light "I could have picked up a pin." "Thinking that the boys were throwing water, I jumped up to see who it was, when I heard the cry of fire."

In John Litherbury's boatyard in Cincinnati on the Ohio River, where the *Sultana* was built two years before for Captain Preston Lodwick, tools used the day before in building another boat lay still. The captain named the side-wheel steamer—one of the largest on the Mississippi, a model steamboat with a new but malfunctioning type of boilers—as sultans named their concubines, although other steamers before had been named *Sultana*.

Nathan S. Williams: "Men were scalded and burned, some with legs and arms blown off, and it seemed as if some were coming out of the fire and from under the boiler, and many of them jumping into the river and drowning by squads." A. C. Brown: "The chandelier in the ladies' room was burning brightly." The crippled or maimed were trampled on. Jesse Martin: "When I came to I was down on my knees by a cow, as though I had got there to milk her. If the cow had not stopped me I guess I would have gone on into the wheel house, and then I would not have survived to write this." J. P. Zaizer was lying asleep close to the bell. "The smoke-stack fell across it and split and one-half of it fell over, thereby killing Sergeant Smith, who laid by me." "We went to work to put out the fire to keep the rest of the vessel from burning, sinking, until the fire burned me off." Many got scalded all over, flesh coming off in the hands of men reaching, grasping to help. "So badly scalded that his skin slipped off from the shoulders to the hands."

Hours ahead of the *Sultana*, the steamboat *Henry Ames* was carrying 1,300 fellow paroled prisoners safely from Vicksburg to Saint Louis.

"The steam and ashes smothered us so we could scarcely breathe." James K. Brady: burning coals from the furnaces fell "all over me and my friend was trying to brush it off."

Hundreds were driven off by fire into the river. A great many cried out in despair that they could not swim. Daniel Allen: "Wounded sufferers who piteously begged to be thrown overboard" were thrown into the turbid waters. At one moment near the bow, too many clustered together. Some turned and went aft, hoping to jump clear of masses of heads and flailing arms. "A large white horse fastened to the railing on the stern deck, blocked jumpers." Dead bodies clogged the *Sultana*'s broken side wheel. The surging of the crowd was like a "ram of men."

Living bodies appeared crazy, dashing here and there and stopping in consternation. George F. Robinson: "The deck I had laid on was on top of me." Men were held fast under wreckage. "I had to let him burn to death."

William Lugenbeal thought of the pet alligator, chained in the wheelhouse, and wanting its box, got it out of the closet and "ran the bayonet through him three times. . . . I was about as large as the alligator, seven and a half feet long."

Ben C. Davis: "While the boat was burning, the alligator troubled me almost as much as the fire."

The captain whose greed lost many lives lost his own trying to save others.

The flagstaff burned down.

The paroled prisoners' comrades elsewhere were traveling homeward by land, water, and rail.

Dreaming of home, awakened each day to the horrors of prison, they were dreaming of home, sweet home that night, exploded into fiery nightmare, the pitchy dark river. This river was like the turnpikes they had traveled four hundred miles from Andersonville and Cahaba, three hundred miles to their rendezvous with death, but wider, faster, safer.

In New Orleans, the *Sultana*'s cargo waited for the boat's return.

Joshua S. Patterson: "Two elements of nature ready to devour us: fire and water, with tiger-like fury the fire rushed at us." Men above at the rails fell on men in the water. In the brilliant light of the fire, Ira B. Horner was "struggling and strangling." "I was not very well versed in the art of swimming." Naked except for a diary and pictures of wife and children, Simeon D. Chelf "could not kick another lick." The flames drove the passengers off the boat, away from fallen smokestacks, the stench of burning flesh. One man, his arm fractured, three ribs broken, face scalded, body scarred, and bruised all over, was frozen in the cold water to unconsciousness.

Simultaneously, the body of President Lincoln was crossing country by railroad. Imagine the sadness these men felt, knowing about Lincoln, the pistol fire, explosion, lingering smoke in the theater. Simeon D. Chelf was walking on the road toward the boat at Vicksburg when Lincoln was assassinated: "One of the best men that ever sat in the presidential chair, and if he was alive today we, the rank and file, would be better treated by the law-making powers of the land." Survivors fought long, bitter battles for just pensions.

One man held to a chain at the bow of the boat. Another used hog chains to let himself down into the water; another slid down the stay rod and swam against icy racing water at flood in the dark.

"With his child in his arms, Harvey Annis jumped overboard. Anna Annis followed."

Robert A. Trent: "I was knocked down on some mules that were under me."

Firelight made the screams in fire and water more ghoulish. By the glaring light of the burning wreck, the paroled prisoners used anything and everything and nothing to hold themselves up—bed slats, a plank that had been used in loading and unloading barrels, boxes, a coal box, empty candle box, beer kegs. A dead mule blown off the boat saved George F. Robinson's life.

Peter Roselot: "I got hold of some pieces of plank tied together with a pair of suspenders (doubtless the work of some poor fellow who had perished)."

N. Sheaffer: "I floated down the river on a door to Memphis and was picked up by negro troops."

Clinging to a trap door, empty barrels, cracker, sugar, pork barrels, a horse trough, a jackstaff, a spar, flagstaff, parts of stairs, the alligator box, fighting over debris of the wreck, men struggled in the water. Some men threw window shutters into the river for the men to latch onto. Some made rafts, others held on to bunk board, a bundle of clothes, a steerage pole, a trunk that contained ladies' dresses.

James K. Brady pried loose with his left foot a man's grip on his right foot: "He was taking my sock along with him, but he is welcome to the sock; he sank out of sight and I saw him no more." The foot that almost stepped over the dead line at Andersonville, that marched to the boat, sank in the river, kicking.

Men tackled up to the gin pole, the gangway plank, the stage plank, the wheel and the steering wheel, the rudder, the decking, used coils of rope to tie stuff together. One man used a tent rope to tie slats, to create "my frail bark," "my little craft." Logs drifting on the flood, floodwood, flotsam, roots of a big tree, a sycamore log saved lives, but some for only a little while longer.

A woman pointed C. J. Lahue out to the rescuing captain, saying there was "a little boy on a log, in the brush, out on the river."

Some went down in whirlpools. They were prisoners again, under fallen wreckage on the boat, in freezing river water.

City guards, not knowing, fired upon men who aspired to become survivors.

Now, more were dead than alive.

As passengers drowned, somewhere in Mathew Brady's dark Washington Studio reposed six plates bearing the negative images he had captured in Richmond in front of the door to the basement under the back porch of General Robert E. Lee the day after John Wilkes Booth shot President Lincoln, sold with all his negatives by impoverished Brady, may have ended up as panes in greenhouses or eyeglasses in gas masks in World War I.

Unable to see the stars for the rain, Private Wesley Lee, clutching two boards in the river, saw the lights of Memphis, like stars.

Carried by the flood past Memphis, some men were exposed to riflemen guarding Fort Pickering.

Did the drowning victims see their whole lives, or just the prison ordeal, flash before their eyes? A drowning man gripped A. C. Brown around the neck, but A. C. shook loose: "My whole life, from my childhood down to that terrible moment, passed before me like a panorama with perfect distinctness." And did the survivors then drown all the rest of their lives in the memory? James A. Brady: "That sight I shall never forget. I often see it in my sleep, and wake with a start. . . . I can see it now as I pen these lines."

These paroled prisoners were in another battle, a battle against the hands that reached, grasped, pulled them down by the ankles, among horses and mules screaming, the sounds of fire. East Tennessee Unionist bridge burners who escaped prison to serve, and were then captured again, fought off others to hang on to burning planks. A. C. Brown: "The water seemed to be one solid mass of human beings struggling with the waves." Ben C. Davis: "You could almost walk over their heads." Alonzo A. Van Vlack: "I could place my hand upon their heads as they were going down." "While those in the water would catch hold of one another and go down in squads."

The steamboat *Bostona II* was coming from Cincinnati downriver on her maiden voyage.

Perry S. Summerville: "Three of us from Brazil, Indiana, two were lost." Christian Ray: "They clustered together and went down." George F. Robinson: "There were three or four hundred, all in a solid mass, in the water and all trying to get on top." Commodore Smith saw them "sink to rise no more until the morning when all shall come forth." "It seemed as though we all wanted to get hold of each other." M. H. Sprinkle: "The last I can recollect was they were trying to pry the dead man's grip loose from my leg." Water strangling, bodies falling on bodies, drowning men pulling down strong men, within minutes, "hundreds of souls were ushered into eternity" (P. S. Atchley). Two hundred sank at once: "They went down in squads to rise no more," clenching each other, going down together. Some drowned with arms around a tree.

Near Memphis—where lived the greatest cavalryman of the Confederacy, Nathan Bedford Forrest, the Wizard of the Saddle from hell, who himself had dismounted to a life of peace, although he helped set in motion the night riders, the Klan—these Union cavalrymen from East Tennessee fought their last battle, against fire.

"A sea of heads." "I saw him no more," survivors often testified. Clusters of dead bodies floated. Albert Norris: "My feet became entangled in my under-clothing." Wet socks dangled, got tangled, and caught by drowning hands; some let go of their shirts, some were rescued without a stitch on their backs.

The Arkansas names along the shore are mockingly ironic, from Dismal Point to President's Island, Hopefield, Mound City, and Eldorado up ahead.

"Some to awake in the cold water and some in eternity" (Samuel H. Raudebaugh). "Chilled to death," some suffered leg and stomach cramps, some spiraled down in whirlpool. Mistaking the swimmers for Confederate guerillas raiding by water, trying to capture Fort Pickering, Negro guards fired upon them.

Booth, perhaps shot by his own gun, in the dark, had died at dawn the day before, April 26, on a farm such as many survivors had worked all their lives.

"Many were peppered by buffalo gnats and mosquitoes that ate them alive." Comrades kept buffalo gnats off a man whose skin had burned off.

The *Bostona II* was about to achieve the distinction of being the first rescue vessel to arrive.

P. L. Horn watched as a mule, "another floating waif of this disaster—swam along." Horses struggled in the water, wailing.

The *Lady Gay* and the *Pauline Carroll*, which had docked at Vicksburg nearby the *Sultana*, available for the transport of paroled prisoners, steamed upriver now without a single passenger.

M. C. White: "A good many chilled to death" in the ice cold water, in the water four hours, some eight. Joseph Bringman: "I feel the effects of that exposure and shaking up to this day."

Survivors experienced such moments all the remaining days and nights of their lives.

President Davis was on an escape road, imagining a new life in a new nation trans-Mississippi.

Around the coasts of America over five hundred lighthouses and lightships were alight, but other ships were sinking from neglect, old age, accidents, foul weather, fire all over the globe, their crews and passengers drowning or surviving.

Men watched the hull go by, the boat sink, leaving the survivors in "utter darkness." Hugh Kinser remembered that the "hull of the boat went down, its hot irons sending the hissing water and steam to an immense heights." "That crackling sound" of the flames, wrote Wesley Lee, "you all remember so well."

Chester Berry heard his mother's voice: "God save my boy's life."

George W. Stewart: the *Sultana* was to "carry us homeward, but alas, hundreds passed on to the City of Death, to await their loved ones."

"Horner is that you?"

"Yes, what there is left of me."

"More dead than alive," many said.

The ironclad USS *Essex* and the gunboat USS *Tyler*, explosives in their chambers, pulled victims of explosion into their ready longboats and onto their clean decks.

Native Americans in the West were soon to be set upon by Sherman, Sheridan, and other Civil War generals.

Freed slaves reached out, pulled survivors out of the dark flood.

Some made it to Cheek's Island, and to Hen and Chickens Island above Memphis.

"Then there was a nice large mule swam out to us just after daylight." A snag in the river, a willow, a sycamore, a cottonwood tree saved many, and several spent the night in the fork of a tree nearly submerged by the flood.

At first, not a boat in sight, but then boats, yawls, skiffs, a picket boat, *Jenny Lind*, some men of the fire department, the steamer *Silver Spray*, and a gun boat, the *Pocahontas*, among others, appeared.

Blacks, Confederate soldiers, and civilians worked hard to save lives. William Bracken, colored infantry officer of the picket guard on Wolfe River, wanted to help in the rescue but could not find any boats. Some men were picked off the tops of trees. "I floated into a tree top," Ogilvie E. Hamblin said, "at peep of day." Thomas C. Love, a rescuer: "Our six messenger boys took [a dinghy] and saved the only woman that was saved."

The traveling minstrel band, the Chicago Opera Troupe—the number of its members not known—that had gotten off the *Sultana* at Memphis would remember their good luck for the rest of their lives.

Five Memphis hospitals were taking in 521 survivors, more than two hundred of whom would never leave alive. The surviving paroled prisoners were taken by cabs and ambulances to Gayoso, Overton, and Washington Hospitals. W. M. Carver survived, "but my father was among the missing ones." One of the twelve Sisters of Charity, volunteer laywomen, may have survived.

Walt Whitman was writing *Drum Taps*, his poems about the war he had witnessed as a wound dresser.

On the home front, Eli Finley Provines is unaware that his son would return only in the form of a message of his death and that Eli would rise from the table, walk to his daybed, and die of a heart attack.

Several of those responsible for overloading the boat, despite its faulty boilers, perished too: Captain Mason and some of his officers. His body was never found.

Not so Hatch, who selected the men, not so Williams, who put them on board; they were safe in warm beds in Vicksburg, dreaming of a promotion for ingenuity in transporting so many prisoners in a single boat. Nor did others involved perish but were bedded down miles away and thus deaf to the explosion and the screams and blind to the light of fires in the boat and on the freed prisoners, three men who might have prevented it all, Major General Napoleon Jackson Tecumseh Dana, commander of the Department of Mississippi; General Morgan L. Smith, commander of the post and the District of Vicksburg; and Captain George A. Williams, the commissary of musters at Vicksburg.

Horner was "marching along in the city with only one sock." The Soldier's Home (the name remembered variously as Soldier's Lodge or Rest or Retreat) took many in; many were attended to by the Christian Association, the Sanitary Commission, and the Sisters of Charity, who gave them whiskey, red woolen shirts, and drawers.

They moved on to parole headquarters at Camp Chase, Ohio, and then they diverged, returning to New Sharon, Iowa; Mansfield, Ohio, a prison town; Rockford, Tennessee; Armourdale, Kansas; Medina, Michigan; Albion, Nebraska; Tulare, California; Bolivar, Missouri; La Fayette, Indiana; Buffalo, New York; Brown's Cross Road, Kentucky; and over a hundred other small towns, not only in the North, the Midwest, and the West, the South and jobs, far more to farming than to the many other occupations: miner, carpenter, carriage trimmer, minister ("I am not doing much of anything"), whip-stock maker, shoemaker, railway mail business, brick mason, undertaker, furniture dealer, merchant, engineer, mail carrier ("I am not able to work"), stockbroker, plasterer, wood finisher, traveling salesman, medical practitioner, tile manufacturer, stock raiser, banker, telegraph operator, pattern maker, buggy dealer, blacksmith, shoe clerk, tailor, hardware merchant, fireman, real estate agent ("I am completely broken down"). One survivor became a sheriff in Iowa: "Many men are now languishing within the walls of the penitentiary that surrendered only after a desperate struggle and, overpowered by me, were compelled to give in."

Boarding the boat and as it moved up the Mississippi, many feared sabotage and many of the survivors suspected it was the cause ("some raiding rebel battery had thrown a shell into the boat"). P. L. Horn believed that somebody placed a torpedo in the coal bin; some blamed the carelessness of the captain or the chief engineer; and one man suggested that unloading three hundred hogsheads of sugar tilted the boat and that somehow caused one of the four boilers to explode.

And oh, yes, the rest of the world added events that forgotten night worth recording in chronologies.

Prisoners of war on both sides, spending from one to twenty months in captivity, fought some of the most courageous battles—battles for sheer survival on the personal level, victory on the public level, as one of those who were exchanged. Having survived prison, most of the men on the *Sultana* perished, but almost six hundred others who boarded the boat, many in poor health or wounded, battled the dark waters of the Mississippi above Memphis and survived. To survive war and prison and the marching to the boat and then to die pales the phrase "cruel irony." But seeing the irony may make us feel absolved of experiencing other, more complex thoughts and emotions. Irony is neat, transitory. Some died of irony. A long list of ironies and paradoxes killed them, that they perished in one of the most violent events of the war in an area where there had been relatively less war, Arkansas and Memphis. Our parallels, metaphors, and similes fail them.

Let an account be given: 30,218 Union and 25,976 Confederate soldiers had died in prisons before the end-of-war paroles had begun. The number of passengers known to be on board the *Sultana* was 2,222. The three states with the highest toll were Ohio, 652; Tennessee (mostly East Tennessee mountains), 463; and Indiana, 407, followed by Michigan, 274; Virginia, 18; Illinois, 2; and Missouri, 1. One thousand seven hundred thirty-three freed prisoners perished in the explosion, in the river, in hospitals. Among the civilians, in the Spikes family of nine, only two sons survived. Seven hundred eighty-three were saved, but two hundred of them died after rescue, so that 75 percent of the passengers died, much higher than the *Titanic*, that very much not forgotten, often-celebrated disaster. One thousand seven hundred dead is more than twice those killed at First Bull Run, in the Eastern Theater, and Wilson's Creek, in the Western Theater combined. Compare the loss with 1,733 combat deaths in the Mexican-American War, 385 in the Spanish-American, 148 in the Gulf War. The loss of life was over half that of our most recent war-related disaster—the World Trade Center explosions, about 2,862, in one official count. The toll in the Civil War is 618,000, including 30,000 civilians. Twice as many in that count died from disease as from combat; in the Mexican-American War, disease killed ten times as many as combat.

Newspaper coverage of the disaster throughout the nation has been considered very slim. Why did it dwindle and vanish so soon? And why did not the rest of the world take note of the kind of event that usually seizes their interest, curiosity, shocks, and arouses compassion? Why was simple, brute curiosity not aroused? Why were the basic who, what, where, when, how, why questions not begging for answers, nationwide, worldwide then and ever since?

The river, flooded over its banks that night, was already shifting northeast. Until the Mighty Mississippi shrugged its shoulders, turned its course away from the site where the *Sultana* sank, American history washed over it, already forgetting, the American people forgetting.

The flood receded, leaving bodies far down stream, on eastern and western banks, for rats; war-wracked levees let water fifty miles deep into woods, where corpses came to rest for wild boar and high in trees, like Indian burials, for birds. About one thousand victims were never found or accounted for. Bodies were found as far downriver as Helena, where the rare photograph of the *Sultana* had been taken, others even farther down, among the many never recovered and buried. Many were buried hurriedly on Hen Island, others in Memphis ground. Unnumbered bodies remain in the boat, buried now under mud. For a while, when it was still visible as late as June, two months later, people saw bodies on the boat. So now the boat is thirty to thirty-five feet underground, in eighteen feet of water—a watery grave, covered with black dirt, good for growing soybeans. Our memory of nonfamous people on the nonfamous *Sultana* is sunken.

As they who had slept in rain and mud and in the last days of their lives marched in mud and rain to reach a rescuing vessel remained forgotten prisoners of mud, monuments rose on ground all over the South and a lesser multitude throughout the North. The first meeting of Northern survivors was 1885, and the Southern survivors first met in 1889, in Knoxville, where they erected an impressive monument on July 4, 1916, in Mount Olive Cemetery. Mr. Pleasant Keeble, one of the last survivors, who oddly had not responded to Berry's plea for testimony, helped start that cemetery.

In 1912, a monument was conceived, to be carved out of four-hundred-feet-high Stone Mountain, finally started in 1923, rose slowly, not finished until 1970, rising ninety feet, forty-five feet out of the stone—forty-five years, a visible remembrance, by contrast to the sunken *Sultana*, but the statue is only of general heroes, Robert E. Lee, Stonewall Jackson, and the Confederate president Jefferson Davis. Americans and foreigners can't miss seeing it below as our flights land at Atlanta, congested hub of the universe. As that monument rose ninety feet slowly, the recovered bodies of victims and the bodies of survivors dying one by one filled graves in Mansfield, Ohio; Hillsdale, Michigan; and Memphis, among others, as over the years, some of the survivors were buried all over the country.

Over the years, survivors reading about the sinking of the *Maine*, the sinking of the *Titanic*, the sinking of the *Lusitania* must have remembered the *Sultana*, their own struggle, with greater intensity. At their meeting in 1912, in Toledo, the survivors must have spoken of the April 14 sinking of the *Titanic*, in which 1,523 perished. Both vessels carried about the same total number of passengers. They must have compared the huge, luxury *Titanic* with the *Sultana*, big for a steam-wheeler but small and crammed to hellish overcrowding compared with the *Titanic*, less crowded even than the below-decks compartments, full of trapped Scotch-Irish, as were many *Sultana* victims. Only four *Sultana* survivors remained in 1928; two in 1929. The last reunion was in 1930. The last survivor from East Tennessee died March 4, 1931, in the month before the sixty-sixth anniversary of the horror.

One would expect this disaster to appeal not only to people who have an ongoing interest in the Civil War but also to those who have none but harbor an ongoing interest in disasters. Berry's first sentence refers to the national character trait that responds only to major events. "The average American is astonished at nothing he sees or hears. . . . The idea that the most appalling marine disaster that ever occurred in the history of the world should pass by unnoticed is strange . . . and the majority of the American people today do not know that there ever was such a vessel as the *Sultana*." What event could be more major than this one?

The usual explanation for public apathy then and now is that Lincoln's assassination happened only a week before and his train was crossing the country toward Illinois when the *Sultana* went down, General Lee had surrendered, Booth had been shot. President Davis was on the run, and people wanted now to forget violence, destruction, and death. Even so, distraction and a desire to forget is too easy, too shallow, an explanation.

Today we are sated on movies depicting disasters of every type, disasters on television news, two twenty-first-century shocks being the World Trade Center massacre and the Katrina-Rita disaster. But the Trade Center explosions and the hurricanes sparked international shock, in contrast to the lack of national shock when the *Sultana* exploded. We saw them happen as they happened, each stage, and we watched stages of response and reports on stages of response, and actual heroes emerged—firemen, policemen, citizens—and stories and pictures of the dead, testimonials on TV of the survivors. Only survivors saw the *Sultana* disaster unfold, and Berry's book sold mostly to survivors.

The limits of human nature are well known; people can't imagine the loss of that many lives, as with the six million Jews, fifty years later. Our humanity needs to develop that ability—myriad-mindedness, which enables our minds to apprehend several aspects of an event simultaneously, and a compassionate imagination, a sort of towerlike omniscience by which we may comprehend this and other aspects of history. Myriad-mindedness is a goal for future generations to cultivate—inner space travel, as we have cultivated outer space travel.

Through movie camera lens, we have often visited the still-sunken luxury liner *Titanic*, and we have seen the risen Confederate submarine *Hunley* and recovered the remains of eight men. The *Monitor* became famous not because eighteen men perished but because it was a new type of warship causing a new type of naval warfare. It has been raised. But we have not even seriously contemplated raising the *Sultana* and its passengers in the worst maritime disaster in American history.

Recognition will demand something that transcends the three excellent factual accounts about this preventable accident that appeared in the final decade of the last century: William O. Bryant's *Cahaba Prison and the Sultana Disaster* (1990), Jerry O. Potter's *Sultana Tragedy: America's Greatest Maritime Disaster* (1992), and Gene Eric Salecker's *Disaster on the Mississippi* (1996).

Loading on unwelcome irony, Andersonville prison, in novels, plays, movies, and historical works, including eyewitness diaries and memoirs, has consistently commanded and held the public's interest, although Cahaba is relatively obscure. And yet not even that irony serves to take us by the arm and hold us still long enough for us to grasp the impact of the *Sultana* catastrophe and to open ourselves up to one of the most bitter in the flood of ironies: that the Union survivors of Andersonville perished after all, or survived yet another descent into hell that spring night, as the assassinated president's funeral train was crossing the blood-weary land and Davis's defeated Confederates straggled home on muddy roads.

Missing so far is a conceptual imagination that places the *Sultana* disaster in a "tragic" light. Only the light of an extraordinary imagination can unvex and raise this unique and complexly meaningful event from the ever-shifting muddy bottom of the Father of Waters.

If one ascribes public indifference and forgetfulness to the fickleness of the "vulgar herd" mentality, how does one explain, even perhaps excuse, the failure of most Civil War historians to turn away from their fixation upon "battles and leaders" to explore the lesser-known but important events, such as the *Sultana*.

The toll of the forgotten overwhelms the most compassionate imagination. The pathos is magnified when we realize that even when a vessel is remembered or rediscovered, even resurrected from the bottom of the sea or a river, as was the *Cairo* battleship from the Mississippi, it is not the passengers but some unique aspect or salient historical significance that captures imagination and interest.

In the spring of the new millennium, I was invited by the Association of *Sultana* Descendants and Friends to give a dramatic reading of the chapter in my Civil War novel *Sharpshooter* devoted to the sinking of the *Sultana* at their thirteenth annual reunion at the Mount Olive Baptist Church just outside my hometown, Knoxville, Tennessee. That gathering of about one hundred will forever remember what most Americans a few days after the end of the Civil War forgot as quickly as they could: the sinking of the *Sultana*, a disaster about which most

Americans ever since have known nothing. Growing up in the partly Unionist East Tennessee mountains, I heard many stories but never that one.

Even though I devoted a chapter of my Civil War novel *Sharpshooter* to the *Sultana* disaster, I have struggled in vain for over thirty years to comprehend this brief event, emotionally, imaginatively, and intellectually, at a depth and with a complexity commensurate with its importance. As a rebel soldier, my sharpshooter was on the boat in disguise. A few years out West after the war, he sets out for home. "Crossing the Mississippi River on the ferry, I had to hold myself in to keep from falling into a panic, feeling it all keenly again, that night when we all exploded off the *Sultana*, maybe my kin, too, that night in the river when most of us drowned" (59).

Over the decades following, the explosion, sinking, and losses of the *Sultana* becomes for the sharpshooter the most painfully apt symbolic expression of the pathos of war, which all Americans missed in various ways then and have missed ever since.

> I am always in the guard tower [at Andersonville prison]. East Tennessee, South [all federals] and Ohio, North: union in death. I see all of them clearly and, suddenly, my father in a Yankee prison, Cahaba probably, even Andersonville possibly, who survived and was going home with four hundred other East Tennesseans on the *Sultana*, and I see him, and his countrymen, and all those at Andersonville, together, drown now below me. And Grandfather Mississippi Death has claimed most *Sultana* survivors. (139)

But I want the reader to realize at last that in obsessed attempts to remember (imaginatively, emotionally, and intellectually), the aged sharpshooter (no older, however, than I am at eighty-one) is to some degree not missing and that because of personal, prolonged struggle to remember, all the other soldiers and civilians of that era are, in some sense, no longer missing. But in real life, I feel that all *Sultana* victims, survivors, and descendants (now they too are digging out), and even friends, alike are still missing.

I fervently recommended reprinting *Loss of the Sultana and Reminiscences of Survivors* because of a deep and abiding faith that readers will absorb into their consciousnesses the facts of the catastrophe meshed with the testimony of the survivors. Oh, we all may admit the obligation. But that is as abstract as the death and survival count. As with the incomprehensible six million exterminated Jews of our own era, we must count the dead one at a time, if we are to retrieve and remember. We must have faith that readers of the recent reprint of Chester Berry's battle against forgetfulness will, in empathy and sorrow, feel the sting of irony but go on to accept the need, the actual desire, to imagine that night in all its strangling humanity and will then exert the will to retrieve and remember.

Meanwhile, the darkness of that night still hangs, almost 150 years deepening, over the smoke, the screams, and the prayers of the victims and the compassionate cries of the rescuers, some of them Confederate soldiers along the bank who were also returning home. Readers may strive to imagine the vast, complicated canvas of folly and agony, and then perhaps to ponder the web of implications, absorb into their own consciousnesses the testimony of the survivors. Hopes for a national day of mourning being delusional, even during April, which is Civil War History Month, perhaps national recognition may at least come sometime during the final year of the Civil War sesquicentennial meditation, 2015.

Open Berry's book anywhere, gaze into the eyes of the survivor you happen upon. Read aloud, perhaps with someone who will take turns with you, listening. The repetitions from one voice to another effectively impress the facets of the event upon our minds, making a demand upon us to imagine similar torments and thoughts happening simultaneously.

Now that Berry's book is within reach, Americans may begin to respond emotionally to the horrific sights, the screams, the smell of burning wood and flesh, the bitter taste of the flooded Mississippi, and the touch of the flailing arms of the perishing soldiers—and the civilian men, women, and children whom even Berry neglected to remember in *Loss*. The reissue of *Loss of the Sultana and Reminiscences of Survivors* becomes then our memorial to both the dead of that night and the survivors, who are themselves now seven decades dead. Listening to their voices, we may raise all the dead of our Civil War from the bottom of the Father of Waters up into our streams of consciousness, tributaries to the national sea of memory.

The voices are still speaking.

They won't shut up.

We need to know that they will never stop.

Few people listened and remembered then. *We* might listen now.

Most of them are still down there.

Let us raise them up.

All 1,700—*all* 618,000 soldiers, all forgotten 30,000 civilians.

II

MEDITATIONS ON THE CIVIL WAR AND RECONSTRUCTION BY WILLIS CARR, SHARPSHOOTER

Why, if I am the sharpshooter who shot General William Price Sanders (and I am now almost certain that I am), did I feel then, as *I* do still, that I missed the War?

Willis Carr, Sharpshooter, at Bleak House, Knoxville

The minutes of the October 21, 1927, semi-annual, Special Meeting, of the Knoxville Chapter of the Daughters of the Confederacy were read and approved. On March 21, 1925, the Chapter met at Bleak House in the Music Room. There being no new business, Professor Jeffrey Arnow of the University of Tennessee History Department introduced his friend Willis Carr of Carter County, who shared his reminiscences of his role in the War Between the States as follows:

Lota people wanted me to talk about it, but I haven't talked about it all these years. I *heard* a lot of people talk about it, I listened to people talk, but this is the first time that I've opened *my* trap.

And Professor Arnow doesn't even know *why* that I *finally* said I *would* and that's because—right upstairs—I mean we're sitting in the music room and you all know about that ball that the Yankees fired into the wall. General Longstreet's walking up and down in them big boots down here, I could hear him, and they was a man in the back, painting a fresco while that whole thing was going on between General Longstreet and General Sanders, and reason I came is because I was up there in the tower.

And I wanted to come *back*, and just sorta be where General Longstreet was, where ol' Pete was. I'm not even sure I'll be able to go *up* in that tower.

I tell you, I had a fever from we had marched through the mud and the rain and November cold. And I had a fever, and I didn't quite know what was going on, I was barefoot, most of us barefoot. And sharpshooter, see, he can go wherever he wants to, he's a free agent, that's part of it. So you just naturally gravitate to high places. We saw a house on a hill, highest hill, the highest house, I saw the tower up there, I didn't even *think* about it, I just went on through, past that man that was painting that fresco on the wall, smelled the paint, and I climbed that stair-case, and bunch of 'em came behind me, four, five, or six of 'em, we went up there—windows faced East, West—no, East—North, South, but blind toward the West.

From up there, we could look all around, down on the Tennessee River, down there on what I later learned was Kingston Pike, but I didn't know it was called Kingston Pike, I didn't know nothing. I was thirteen, I was fourteen, I was thirteen when I went in, but I was fourteen time we got here. Looked old for my age. And so we got up there, and I had a fever, and this old boy from Virginia, he was—during a skirmish, wasn't a battle, was a skirmish—he was sighting through the window, and he said, he didn't turn around to me, but he said, "I *got* him!"

And so then he aimed again. I was in a fever, leaning up against the West wall, you know, and I was thinking, I was watching him real tight, like *I* was sighting through that telescope lens, and I was waiting for him to say, "I *got* him!" because he's focusing like he really had this fellow, whoever might be out there. But he didn't. And I noticed between his legs where he was kneeling down, I noticed a little trickle of blood. It come down the wainscoting—kinda fancy up there—flowing out on the floor between his legs. So I thought, well, I'll see what's going on out there, and I got up there in the other window—two of 'em's already wounded, laying over there to the side—and I got up there, and I sighted through the sights of my telescopic lens. And I saw a man, an officer, riding a white horse, *charging* back and forth in front of the Yankees that was firing at us. He's going back and forth like he's daring 'em to kill him. Shoot! Shoot! I'm here! Shoot! See if you can *do* it! Yeah. Riding back and forth. And I thought, Nobody, on their side or our side, is crazy enough to be doing what I'm watching, it's fever, it's fever got me, you know. Why, hell—pardon my talk here—I can just shoot at that feller and it won't even hurt him. That's kinda nice, shoot somebody that you can see plain as day, know it's a fever, you shoot at him, won't even hurt him, I just shoot 'im, won't bother 'im, you know. I pulled the trigger, and I just turned away, I didn't even see if I *got* 'im.

But two years after the War was over, I was coming back from out West, where I'd been out there on a two-year drunk, just drunk—bar, barroom *brawls*, you say that word *brawls*, you almost got the whole thing right there in your mouth, need to spit it out. And I made my living by drawing people. I had the knack for drawing, people say, "Draw my picture," I draw their picture in the barroom, I get a drink, made it to my eighteenth birthday that way, just drawing 'n drinking 'n brawling, and I got enough of it, said, "Hell—'scuse me—I'm going back to Carter County." So coming back through, I stopped in this little ol' town, Pulaski, think it was, and these ol' boys were telling about the War, sitting around telling stories. One ol' boy said—well, I was drawing, that's what it was, I was drawing a man, and this other says, "There's the one's picture you *ort* to draw."

And I said, "Why?"

He said, "Well, he's the one——"

"Don't you start that! That's *private*."

The one man said, "Private, hell, you told everybody that comes through this town, you told *us* thirty times, can't you tell him onc't?"

And he's sitting there mumbling.

So I started to draw his picture, he said, "I ain't gonna pay for it."

I said, "You don't *have* to pay for it, 'less you like it."

I kept drawing his picture, he got to talking, said, "Well, what these boys talking about, what made *me* famous in the War was that I'm the one that shot General Sanders."

I didn't know who General Sanders *was*. I didn't know what he's talking about. Said, "Where?"

He said, "At Knoxvul."

So, I says, "I think I was *in* Knoxvul." You know, my brain rotted from drinking, I was too young to remember everything anyway, so I said, "I think I was *in* Knoxvul."

He said, "Big ol' house that they got down there called Bleak House, I got up in the tower, I shot down, and I killed him, I'm the one, very one that you're drawing a picture of."

I believed him, cause I didn't remember a dern thing, who'd remember a fe-ver dream, so . . .

I just went on, I met a lot of other people, I heard a lot of other people, talking about this and that, the Civil War, and I was wondering, "Well, you know, I was there, but I don't remember all *this*, and why are these people so . . . Why they talk about this all the time, why they want to sit around talk about this, what is it *about* it? That was just something I did, then I went out West."

And so I went back up on Holston Mountain to the cabin where we always lived. I was born up there in 1846, the year that the Mexican war ended. I learned that about twenty years later, I didn't know that then. And my great-grandfather, he *stayed* up there when all the rest of 'em went down to fight. He's old, you know, fact he'd been sitting there beside the fire the whole time since before I was born. One day he came in, said, "I'm a-cold," went over there and stirred up the fire, sat down by the fire, and they say he never got up, just stayed there. "Why don't you go sit in the doorway where you can get some sun Gran'paw? You worrying us to death sitting over there, staring at the fire all the time."

He said, "I got my own sun right here, it goes down at night, and I poke it up in the morning, s'all I need."

So my grandfather and my daddy and my big brothers and me went off to war, and time I come back, my great-gran'paw was the only one left. When I come in the door two years after the War was over, he was of course dead, sitting there by the fire, dead. And I said, "Well, that's the way he'd want to go." I went over and I—I'd been civilized, you know, and I was going to bury him, so I pick him up like he's gonna be heavy, like I was still that little kid, you know, still big man in my memory, you know, I picked him up and jerked up on that chair too quick and he spilled out all over the floor. And somehow that aggravated the fool out of me, and I got the broom and I swept him right in the fireplace. His bones been there, ever since, burned down now, of course.

Anyway, I come back home and I went back to hunting—hunting skins and hunting my meat and everything, and I wished I had my old sharpshooter sights to get bear with. And one time I got a bear in my sights and I—he was coming toward me like—I was looking for my dinner—and he was coming towards me like he was looking at *his* dinner, and I sighted on him and I was about to pull the trigger—and I remembered sighting on that man, that officer on the white horse, and I said, "My God, that was General Sanders," that they all a-talking about, 'cause I'd heard a lot of talk about him. General Sanders. I *think*. I'm not sure.

So that has bothered me, what I been thinking about, studying about for years is—sitting up there on Holston Mountain—trying to understand, you know. Why is it, if, if I was the man that shot General Sanders, and I'm *reasonably* certain that I was, I'm not sure, why is it that I feel that I missed the War? That I missed the War?

So one thing that drew me back *here*—I *walked* all the way here from Carter County, Holston Mountain. Cause I wanted to think more about why did I want to go back there, *why* do I want to come back to that place? I *been* in Knoxvul a number of times over the years, and I never had the desire to go up in the tower before, and I wonder *why*.

So I came back, trying to see if I can find a way, over here, in this house, that I could get some kind of answer I hadn't got——

So maybe I need to go back and just kind of go *over* what I *did* in the War. The events. Lota people writing their memoirs and—you know, people publishing them, and after I learned how to read, I read a lot of it.

Well, we were up on the Mountain, and I was thirteen years old. We were all Union, you see, 'cept my mother, she was from 'lizabethton, she was from a family of Rebel sympathizers. And one day Colonel Stover, Andrew Johnson's son-in-law, came up South Holston Mountain and said to my daddy, my gran'paw, he said, "I want you to go *with* us . . . tonight, because we're gonna burn the railroad bridge over Watauga River. Want you all to come and go *with* us."

And they got ready, they got ready to go, you know, I did everything they did, I hunted with 'em, you know, I did everything that they did, even though I was thirteen years old, and so they got ready to go, and they got on their horses, and started down the mountain, and I went right on with 'em, you know, we gonna go burn the bridge, whatever that is, we gonna do something for the Civil War, whatever that is, we gonna do something for the Union, whatever that is, I didn't know, but I thought it'd be a good idea, it'd be something *different.* "What you doing coming with us!" they said, turn around look at me, "What you think you're doing, you get on back up with the women, your great-gran'paw, and take care of 'em till we get back!"

And *me* the best shot in the family. Not supposed to say that, see, because—My gran'paw once said, "Don't brag on what you can do, Davy Crockett done took care all *that. You* don't have to brag nothing, you just *do* it, and go 'bout your business." So nobody ever said, "You the best," and I never said I was the best either, but I knew it. What the hell—'scuse me—they gonna do without me? So, I—they forgot that I was the best runner, too, 'cause when they took off on their horses, I kept right up with 'em round those mountain paths, I kept right up, running. And my brothers pulled up and they reached down in the path and picked up rocks and started throwing rocks at me like I's a mad dog.

Well, I *was* a mad dog by the time they got out of sight. I was so mad, I said, "Hell, I'm gonna go look"—'scuse me—"look for the War by myself, on my lonesome." So I took out and I—Knoxvul, let's see, that's probably where they got that War. How'd I know? Because my great-gran'paw used to sit by the fire, as I say, and when my granddaddy and my daddy would come back from down in 'Lizabethton or someplace, they'd bring the Knoxvul *Whig*. You all read the *Journal* now, but it was the Knoxvul *Whig* then. Edited by Parson Brownlow. "The meanest man to walk the streets of Knoxville," some of 'em said. "That vile serpent Brownlow," Doctor Ramsey said. "The ugliest man to come out of East Tennessee," Brownlow himself said. And he couldn't wait to get that paper, and when he'd get the paper, I'd be up there asleep in the sleeping loft, you know, and when the rafters went to shaking, I knew he'd got his paper, because he'd read that thing aloud. Only books we had up there was Milton's *Paradise Lost*, the works of Shakespeare, John Bunyan's *Pilgrim's Progress*, and the *Whig*. He's the only one could read. He was too mean to teach *me*. I just didn't know *how* to read. Didn't teach anybody else. And he'd yell out, and they'd say, "Can't you read that paper without all that screaming and bellerin'?" He didn't want words on the paper when it come to Parson Brownlow, he wanted fire, he wanted explosion, he wanted *force*! When he'd get done with the *Whig*, he'd take a hammer and he'd nail it to the wall, just to say, "Look yander. That's it. Right there! What the man said." And one time, he read it out of the paper, "They're taking the Union men down to Montgomery on the railroad and they're putting 'em in prison, and we ought to let the railroad, from Alabama to Bristol, be burned and every bridge on that railroad be burned—cut off the supplies to General Lee." And they listened to him, and that's why they were burning. That night, I learned later on, years later, that when they were burning that one bridge, Reverend William Blount Carter was co-ordinating the burning of nine strategic bridges—Strawberry Plains, up here at Bull's Gap—burning all those bridges at the same moment. 1862.

So . . . I went down there to Knoxvul, I thought, Well, I'd find the War. Walked up to this feller on Gay Street, and I said, "Which way is the army?"

And he said—kidding like, I guess, I wasn't paying any attention—"Which one you talking about?"

I said, "Why, the *Union* army."

Said, "Young'un, come with *me*. I'll show you where we got some Union boys."

Took me down on Gay Street, back towards the river, took me in some old place they called Castle Fox, and some of 'em call Castle Thunder after the one they got in Richmond, and took me down in the basement of this place, they's hundred men laying around, all over, talking to each other, and getting sick, and dying, and scared to death.

Put me in there with them, said, "Get in there with *them* people. S'where *you* belong."

And everybody's so sad, didn't have any, you know, they didn't have any vim and vigor, you know, they just all loping around, moping around, you know, and suddenly the doors open, and these Negro soldiers that was guarding us stood aside, in walked this old man. He walked in with his head up and he had fire in his eyes, and they greeted him like he was a prince. I thought, Who in the world is *that* man? He's gonna turn us all loose or something. Somebody look like that. Turned out it was Parson Brownlow. They arrested him for inciting those men to burn bridges—in that newspaper.

He said, "This is the proudest day of my life. And none a you people should be sad here tonight, you die in a great cause." And he'd raise his arms, and he'd raise his voice, and he'd lower his voice—because he used to be a Methodist circuit rider, you know—and he would dip up and down, and he would go among 'em and touch 'em, and he had 'em all pacified, and then he had 'em all fired up, and then he had 'em all proud, and when he had 'em all the way he wanted 'em, he laid down and went to sleep.

And they come in and they says, "All right, you and you and you."

And I said, "What's that for?"

And they said, "They taking them out and gonna hang them, too, for burning them bridges."

And I heard one telling that they had already hung three of 'em by the railroad track, where people passing in the train could reach out with a stick and beat on 'em, hanging from the trees. Colonel Leadbetter did it. And so, they said, "Well, young'un, you want to go with these people we putting on the train?"

I said, "Hell, no."

And he said, "Well, then, you got your choice. You want to fight in the Rebel army with *us*, or do you want to go with *these* people?"

And I thought, "These people are dummer'n hell"—can't get over saying that—"These people are dumb. They are too dumb to know that as soon as I get out of here in their army, I'm gonna light out for the Union side, because my daddy said that's where I ought to be. And I'll probably find some of *them* over there, too," you know, "I'll just get out of here."

So I said, "Yeah, I'll be a Rebel soldier."

They put a uniform on me, they put me on a train, they put me under General Longstreet, they put me in a camp, and that was nice, because it was like camping up on Holston with my gran'daddy and my daddy and my brothers, and I enjoyed that, just sitting around, those fellers nice fellers, you know, and they was some of 'em our people, and I got to liking *that*. They had tin cans there, you know, lying around, and I'd take some feller's rifle and I'd do a little target practice, and a officer come up to me one day and said, "Son, you got the *eye* for it."

And I said, "For what?"

And he said, "To be a sharpshooter."

That sounded good to me. A *sharpshooter*. Yeah, that's me. A *Sharpshooter*. All right, I'll desert tomorrow or the next day. I'll see what this sharpshooter stuff's like. And what I saw it was like, it was good, it made me feel good, and everybody was proud of me, everybody looked up to me, and I's only thirteen years old. And so I went with *them*. And I *stayed* with them. Stayed with General Longstreet. I was at Gettysburg with him. I was in the Wilderness with him.

Bragg was facing Grant down there in Chattanooga, and he said, "Bring up Longstreet." Lee detached him, and they put us on a train, and we went over there, and we *arrived* just in time at Chickamauga to make a difference. We felt pretty good about that.

Then Bragg didn't much like having a man like General Longstreet around him, so he says, "Why don't you go up to Knoxvul and run Burnside out of Knoxvul? 'Cause he's taken over up there." So they put us on the trains, we got on the train, and we got up to Sweetwater, and the railroad was all *knocked out*, and so we started marching—in the rain and sleet, November, cold, no shoes. Came to Bleak House, went up in the tower.

And Burnside, who thought a awful lot of General Sanders, said—you know, as I figure it out—he said, "You go out there and you hold 'em off till we get the fortifications up here on this big hill that over-looks Kingston Pike. We gonna get that all fortified. The Rebels started it and we haven't quite finished it. You give us time to finish the fortification and hold 'em off, just long enough. You think you can do that?"

And General Sanders says, "I can do it."

So we went up against him.

And one of us—or somebody—shot him. Way that I've heard it, they took him to the Lamar House Hotel over there on Gay Street, up in the bridal suite, and he laid there for a long time, and finally died, and they didn't want the soldiers that loved him to know that he died, so they buried him at night. They didn't give him any music or anything like that, because they didn't want to let us know that some officer had died.

But this good friend from West Point, Captain Orlando Poe, who was the engineer fixing the fortifications, he couldn't stand it, so when they let General Sanders down into the grave at Second Presbyterian churchyard, Captain Poe fired a pistol off as a salute. Some others started singing hymns.

I was still up in the tower, afire with fever.

Seems like I remember drawing the faces of the wounded and the dead Virginia boy on the wall of the tower, but if I wanted to make certain, I'd have to climb up there and look.

Then they called us to go down and take up sharpshooter positions around Fort Sanders. Sleeting and raining, and the next morning, we were to rest up, and attack that fort, which they had renamed Fort Sanders.

And what they did, in the night, they went out and strung telegraph wires among the stobs in the ground, so that we'd trip on 'em in the early morning hours when they expected the attack. They took boiling water and poured it over the parapet so that it would freeze fast and create ice on the slopes. And General Longstreet said, "The ditch——" We would come up to a ditch and "It's very shallow. You can get right across it very easily and you can just climb on up that bank. You won't need the pioneers to go in and cut a place in the bank because that normally has something to grab holt of. You can just stand up in that shallow ditch," because he'd observed a man walk across that ditch through field glasses.

So the men rushed past us—sharpshooter's positions—the men rushed past us and they were ready to take Fort Sanders, they rushed through, they fell in the telegraph wires, got entangled, they fell on each other, they fell on the sharp stobs that were sticking up out of the ground, they all just piled up, and I had to stay where I was and *watch* all that, and there was some officer up there throwing hand grenades—what you call hand grenades now—that he had made, that he had created, fashioned, and he was throwing 'em down at the men. And what happened was that not only was the ditch not shallow, it was *deep*, and what General Longstreet had seen was a man walking across a plank to get across that deep ditch.

And not only was the ditch deep, but Orlando Poe was a very smart man, he said, "It's the tendency of men"—I heard this later—"the tendency of men charging a place to follow the line of least resistance. So we will plow the field in front of it and they will follow between the furrows." And what he did was to lead them into a position where the cross-fire could get them.

And we were just slaughtered. All there was to it. Only one man got in there. And I was a sharpshooter just watching all that, wishing I was back up in that tower.

So then we got the word to go on, march away, and we went on up the Valley of Virginia, and we rejoined General Lee, and we were there in the battle of the Wilderness.

And I was up in a tree, as a sharpshooter, good position. The woods were on fire and wounded men were screaming, on fire. Burning limbs falling down on 'em. The woods were burning, and I was up above it, getting the smoke, able to see everything, but not able to see well enough to shoot anybody, and afraid I might shoot one of our own men, and somebody yelled up the tree and said, "We have *shot* General Longstreet! Old Pete!"

I said, "We have shot Old Pete, what you mean we have shot him?"

He said, "One of our own men mistook and shot 'im in the throat."

And I looked out over—looked out over—looked out over all that, you know. Smoke. Listening to all that screaming. And I said, "Willis Carr, it's time you went home."

I was pretty sure that I could go back the way that we had marched into the Wilderness and find my way to Holston Mountain in Carter County.

But I got lost somehow. It looked like I was pretty deep into Yankee held territory, so I figured I'd better become a Yankee. I shot a stray Yankee soldier and took his uniform. Then I got captured by the Rebels, and they took me to some town called Anderson and took me before a captain who talked with some kind of accent.

Said, "What do you have to say for yourself?"

Said, "Well, I'm just a poor little boy, only fifteen, looking for my daddy and my brothers, trying to find 'em, and so that's why I put on this Yankee uniform so that I could get through Yankee territory, and look for 'em, sir."

He looked in my eyes and I reckon he knew they had seen the War. I didn't look fifteen at all to him. He said. "I believe you that you're not a

Yankee, but I'm convinced you're a Rebel deserter in a Yankee uniform, take him out and shoot him."

So they marched me to this outdoor prison with walls made of logs, great big open area on a hillside covered with ragged, starved men and a creek running athrawt it that I could see from a distance, and they took me over to what they called the dead house, and they stood me up against a wall, but before they could get lined up to shoot me, there was a work detail coming in of Yankee prisoners, and one of 'em yelled, "Hello, Sharpshooter, what they about to do to you?"

And I said, "Well, where did I know *you*?"

And he said, "Don't you remember that time we met in the middle of the Tennessee River, swimming, and exchanged coffee and tobacco and stuff out there?" And said, "We knew you for one of the best sharpshooters in Longstreet's whole army."

And so they marched the prisoners on inside the prison there, and the Rebel captain who was getting the men lined up straight to shoot me, turned to me, says, "Is he telling the truth, are you a sharpshooter?"

And I said, "Well, I can prove it."

And so he took a rifle off the firing squad and handed it to me, and I shot down everything he threw in the air. And he said, "We need guards here that shoot that way, we got just little kids and old men that want to shoot everybody that even sneezes. So we need you up in one of them towers."

So he took me back to the captain and praised me to him, and Captain Wirtz said in that accent, "The first one you let escape, it's right back in front of that firing squad."

So I went up into a guard tower and one day I looked down and this Negro was leaning up against the dead line post, playing, looked to me, like he was reading a newspaper! A newspaper! Brazen as hell, 'scuse me. Well, now that made me mad. Teasing a poor ol' ignorant mountain boy, by pretending to read that newspaper in front of me, knowing I couldn't read myself. I yelled down, "You asking for it."

Said, "What?"

I says, "Acting like you reading that thing."

Said, "Well, I *can* read it, and I'll teach *you* how, if you want me to."

And so he did, taught me how to read, but what he was reading was Cherokee writing that he told me was made up out of nothing by an Indian of the Cherokee nation. Named Sequoyah. Only man in recorded history ever made up a whole new set of letters, and he did it to free his people from the power of the white man's language. This Negro Yankee soldier had been a slave to a Cherokee Indian plantation owner, and his master taught him how to read and used him as a translator between his family and the white man. And when the War started, his master went into the Rebel army and took him with him to translate, and they got captured, and this Negro was forced into the Yankee army, and that's how he ended up in Andersonville prison, with me guarding over him.

He told me that story about Sequoyah making up that new set of letters, and I loved to hear it more than once. Got so it made me want to read and write Cherokee, and so that's how I learned to read and write. After a few months though, he stepped over that dead line and I shot him, without thinking. I wondered, Why did he do that? knowing I'd have to shoot him, and I guessed he thought I wouldn't shoot the man who taught me to read and write. Sure as the world, even though he was a Negro and I was a white boy, I wouldn't shoot him. I've had sixty-five years to wonder about that, and maybe fifteen more to go.

When it looked like we was going to lose the War, we broke up that prison, and most went to surrender, but I sort of drifted West with some that wanted to start a new nation out there in the West. Ended up on the border of Mexico in what was the last battle of the War—well, after the surrender was already over—in Palmetto, Texas.

And I just stayed out in the West, wandering, scratching a living and the price of a drink in saloons by drawing folks' faces to send back East, as I was saying when I first walked in here.

And then after about two years of all that drinking and drawing and brawling and living like a desert rat, I decided, again, "Willis Carr, it's time you went home," to Carter County, up Holston Mountain. So I struck out, and that's where I've been for the last fifty-five years, some odd. And in all that time, what's preyed on my mind is why I shot that Cherokee Negro, and whether I did shoot General Sanders or I didn't.

Nobody can really tell me who shot General Sanders. Folks tell it that General Sanders was riding a white horse down Kingston Pike, scouting out front of his men, when a sharpshooter shot him. But facts have come out that there was this young captain, Winthrop, come over from England to fight for the Confederacy who, when Colonel Nance's charge up the hill went wrong, leapt on his white horse and went charging on his lonesome up that hill, and back and forth in front of these fence rails where the Yankees had taken up position. The Yankees was shooting at him as he rode back and forth, and they wounded him and he rode back down to Bleak House—but he lived. And all this while, General Sanders stood on the brow of the hill, watching Captain Winthrop dash back and forth, and he turned to his aide—who told about it the Knoxvul Journal twenty-five years later—and said, "What a gallant fellow he was!" And as they started down the far side of the hill, to get out of the firing, somebody shot General Sanders. "I'm hit!" They say his last words were, "I am glad I was not shot in the back." I cannot figure out why he said that.

And I always had this feeling all my life since, that I missed the War. So my mouth is down here in the music room telling you my experiences in the

War, but seems like my mind is always in that tower above our heads, me fifteen, watching the blood of that Virginia sharpshooter drip down the wall under the window and between his legs, smelling the paint from the fresco that man kept painting at the foot of the steps all during the skirmish, and I'm drawing the faces of the wounded sharpshooters on the wall and looking out that window through my sniper's sights at that General on a white horse that I was certain come out of fever. I've drug my body one hundred miles a-walking it, to try to match up my body and my mind, and tell the first and last time about it, but I don't reckon I can climb those steps.

Respectfully submitted, with thanks to Matilda Merrit, stenographer for this occasion, by Musetta McArthy, secretary.

Willis Carr Meditates on the Act of Sketching

Hair Trigger Pencil Lines

Having told his story to a live audience of strangers, Willis Carr, in his mountain solitude, felt compelled about a year later to tell his story again, in very different words, words that do not vanish in the very telling, in more detail, to himself, on paper, a kind of detailed meditation.

When I went to the War in 1862, I was only 14 years old, living with my folks, who was mostly hunters, high up on Holston Mountain, which is above Elizabethton in East Tennessee. Like most folks around *there*, we was Unionists, but my mother was from a Rebel family.

Well, way it was, one day Andrew Johnson's son-in-law come up on South Mountain and persuaded my daddy, my granddaddy, and my brothers to help him and Reverend William Blount Carter burn some railroad bridges. Reverend Carter had planned for nine bands of Unionists to burn nine bridges at the same time from Stevenson, Alabama, to Abingdon, Virginia. My family said, We'll do it, but they told me to stay home with the women. I disobeyed and followed them, and that landed me in a Rebel prison in Knoxville, and the Rebels said, "Do you want to hang with your kin folk or do you want to join the Rebel army?" I said I'd rather not hang, and I only went with them because I planned to run off first chance I got, but they made me a sharpshooter and I just never did.

I am back in Knoxville after many battles in many places under General Longstreet and I am up in the tower of a house called Bleak House and I feel like I am about to die of a fever. In the tower now, in addition to the two who had come up with me, were seven more sharpshooters, but when a ball hit just below, the seven new sharpshooters got out of there and on out of the house and scattered.

The sharpshooter from Virginia, who was only two years older than I was, fired from the tower's East window. "I got him," he said, the way you do when your target is somebody special. Too feverish to focus, I had stopped firing, clenching my eyes, breathing deeply of the raw November air that whistled through bullet holes in the thick beveled window panes to clear my head, spent minie balls all around, my feet sticking straight out in front of me like a doll's propped in a corner. The two previously wounded men were half asleep, moaning. I was idly watching the Virginian when I began intentionally watching him, the look of his shoulders declaring that he was taking very, very careful aim—an even more exceptional target. As if to help him see through the telescopic lens more keenly, I held my own breath, and waited for him to say, "I got him." As I stared at him, a suffocating feeling beginning to rise from my chest to swell my head and blur my vision, I saw a narrow stream of blood appear between his knees where he knelt and move toward where I sat against the blind West wall.

So I thought, well, I'll see what's going on out there, and I got up in the other window—two men were already wounded, lying over there to the side—and I crawled across the tower floor to the narrow window beside the Virginian and looked out at the bare hillside that rose across the pike, eastward.

An officer on a white horse rode back and forth in front of the fence rails, *charging* back and forth in front of the Yankees that was firing at us. He was going back and forth like he was daring us to kill him. Shoot! Shoot! I'm here! See if you can do it! Riding back and forth. And when he passed the lone cedar tree, my feverish heart leapt at the magnificence of what I took to be an image of my fever, for he had no business in the real War, being where he was, doing what he was doing. He was too foolhardy to be one of *our* officers riding ahead of the infantry toward the rails, exhorting his men. Nobody, on their side or our side, is crazy enough to be doing what I'm watching, it's fever, just the fever. He had to be my own contribution, an optical illusion my own feelings conjured to fit this occasion. Not to determine whether he was a romantic vision instead of an actual heroic figure but to hold onto the sight that so lifted my spirits, I reached for my own rifle. I was so wobbly, it took me a while to get him in my telescopic sights, but I got him, and I followed him as he rode toward the lone cedar tree again. Exhausted, confused, feverish, knowing it wouldn't kill, I impulsively pulled the trigger, and I just turned away, I didn't even see if I *got* him. I lowered the rifle, thinking, well, my stray bullet may accidentally hit one of the Yankees behind the fence rails. I crawled back to the West wall and leaned against the cold brick, and looked into the wide open eyes of one of the two wounded men who seemed to have been watching my odd behavior.

"Did you *get* him?"

I smiled, closing my eyes, thinking, he is in so much pain, he doesn't even know the Virginian is dead.

I was staring at the North wall where the sun struck, and something about the look of the light on the plaster made me want to stop everything in the tower at this moment, before anybody came up to disturb what I saw. The wounded men were dozing in agony, their heads still.

On the wall, I began to draw, with a pencil I had taken off a dead Yankee and that I rented out to soldiers who could write, the face of one of the wounded men, his mouth open in agony, a very small profile, and as I drew from memory the face of the dead man, who still knelt with his back to me, a feeling of power surged through me, and then I drew the other wounded man, and drew the first wounded man again, the largest of the three heads—they seemed to get bigger as I felt my strength and the act of drawing grow.

Then I noticed that in drawing the first man again, I had enclosed upon his forehead my first tiny sketch of his profile. The first man had a mustache and goatee, the second wounded man had a beard. I noticed later that all their eyes looked exactly the same in my drawings.

And after soldiers had come up and taken the two wounded men down, screaming because the awkward descent hurt, and lifted the Virginia sharpshooter off his knees and laid him out on his back, I saw that the face I had drawn was even younger than his and did not resemble his but that of someone more familiar, one of my brothers maybe, or myself.

I wanted to write "Men who were shot up here" under my drawings of the men, but nobody had yet taught me how to write.

I crawled over there and drew arrows from the words pointing up at each head.

Then I sat back in the middle of the floor, the stairwell at my back, and stared at the faces until the light got too bad.

After Knoxville, I was in the battle of the Wilderness, up a burning tree, trying to kill some more folks—but General Longstreet was accidentally shot by one of our own men, and I said to myself, "Willis Carr, it's time you went home."

But as I passed near Andersonville prison, I got arrested wearing a Yankee uniform I had stolen, and they said, "Do we shoot you or do you help us guard these prisoners?"

So from a guard tower, I had to shoot some poor fellows.

When the War was over, I drifted West and I was on the *Sultana* when it sank in the Mississippi, drowning 1,500 Yankees who had just been freed from Andersonville and other prisons, and I kept moving West and I drew folks pictures in barrooms to stay drunk for two years, and finally, I said to myself, "Willis Carr, it's time you went home."

So here I am on my way home, stopping off in Vicksburg, and wandering the battlefield.

Mud on the narrow, twisting roads and paths pulls at my high Western boots, wears me down, giving me a terrifying sense of walking, a ghost, on the bottom of the Mississippi River.

When I approach an enormous crater, overgrown with briars, vines, and saplings, I rush away from it, wanting distance and height on it.

I fight dense undergrowth, eating a few blackberries and wild grapes as I struggle to get up out of a ravine that I suspect is full of rattlesnakes.

I climb a treeless slope that will give me a higher vantage point on the crater, discover that the depth of the crater is now lost to my field of vision. I am a survivor again.

But the afterimage of it is still so clear, I open my sketchpad and, as if I am a hovering raven, look down on the crater, and begin to draw, feeling that I am the only soul within miles.

But I was not alone. A man's head showed just above the farther rim of the crater, as if he were—just now surfacing—another survivor of the *Sultana*. I felt an impulse to reach for my rifle, get him in my telescopic sights, and blow his brains out. It came to me that I had seldom been any angrier at all the other targets than I was at this man, and that I still, despite two years of drunkenness, could plug a third eye beneath his brows.

He climbed on up and stood there on the rim, on one leg, on crutches. Then he started down, coming *toward* but not *to* me. He was wandering, gazing around, stopping to stare at the ground. Then I lost him. He is not going to make it, one-legged, through that ravine, that morass of vigorous vegetation, if that's what he has set out to do.

But by the time I had completed the sketch, he was shifting to get a look over my shoulder.

"You got the gift." I didn't know enough then about the skill of sketching to contradict him.

I told him I thought the terrain here looked strange, and he said in a Yankee accent, that the siege had torn it all up, and when I asked, "What siege?" he stepped back so abruptly he almost lost his prop and fell back down the slope.

"Why, the siege of Vicksburg in '63."

And I said, "Oh, yes, I remember hearing about it."

And he said, "Where was *you*?"

And I said, "Oh, out West. I look old for my age." I was only 19 that July.

He wasn't interested in me after that, but just like a Yankee, he came right out and said it: "Draw my picture." Usually, it took me two hours to work a man into position to make me an offer, but this one was vain from the start. "If I was to get over there on the rim of the crater, would you draw me into your picture and sell it to me?"

They would say, "Draw my portrait. Or draw my wife from this photograph." But never, "Draw me into a landscape"—especially one I had already rendered. But the word "sell" triggered "sure."

I told him he didn't have to climb back down into that ravine. "I can look at you standing here, sir, and just stick you in it."

"No, it must be authentic," he said, a little offended. Making a snug fit for his crutches in his armpits, he shoved off. "Just give me a little time."

Having plenty of time, I gave him some of it.

Just as I lost him again, his voice rose to me on heat waves. "Can you put a uniform on me if I describe it to you?"

And I said, "No need to describe it, I've seen one a time or two."

I knew that this moment meant more to him than such moments had meant to any of the men whose faces I had drawn from Georgia to Mexico and back.

In an hour, he was back up on the rim, but only a one-legged silhouette against the sun. When he yelled to me, it made me remember the way we answered the Yankee voices at night, or during a truce for burial details.

"I would sure appreciate it, if you would add a leg."

I started to ask, "Whose leg?" but he was in a mood that his eyes had sort of cast over me. And I needed the money.

So I draw him in, so that he's wearing the uniform and standing on *two* legs, and without trying, I magnify his face in my imagination until I see his eyes again, giving *me* that look from deep inside himself, and I keep seeing the cross-hairs of the telescopic sight, and then, maybe it is the sun beating down on me, but I am inside his eyes, looking back out over the ravine into my own eyes.

I waved the drawing above my head. From the moment *he* started back down into the ravine, I knew he already had it clearly in his head, that he had imagined it as I sketched him in, and saw himself now in a special way that would *be* important until the day he died.

That was when I asked myself, "Why doesn't it mean that much to me? The War. Or any particular moment of it?" I started to yell across the ravine to him that I really had been in it. For four years. Starting when I was 14. But I kept mum.

The one-legged Yankee haunted me the whole time, and I began to feel as if I was missing some part of myself.

Drifting East up the Great Valley of Tennessee, I began to seek out men who wanted to talk about the War, at first only as customers to get enough food in my belly to keep going, but after a while, I was drawn to them out of bewilderment. They remembered everything. All I could remember was camp, though in no particular place. The thousand places seemed to be the same place, always in the woods, and by the time I had pulled back and followed them, the fire starter, the water-finder, and the cook, who always seemed to rise up out of the ranks when and where they were needed, had already done their work, and the storyteller was at it, or maybe the song-singer had already begun, and as one of the sharpshooters who helped make it possible for them to camp with some hope of peace, I was welcome to share the fire, the water, maybe even some of the scarce coffee to wash down my hardtack. And I remembered the times I saw General Longstreet.

But most men drawled out the names of places and battles and the dates with no effort at recollection, and I didn't have them to tell. Most of them were gray-bearded men who made me feel they had fought in a different war from the one I had forgotten, because although I was among the very youngest, and certainly the youngest sharpshooter I knew about, they had *all* been young two years before. Like Rip Van Winkle, I thought these veterans were playing tricks on me.

In Pulaski (birthplace, I learned later, of the Ku Kluxers), I was drawing a man, putting a uniform on him, an idea I offered that struck him as real bright and that upped the charge to a silver dollar, when a bystander piped in with, "The feller's picture you *ought* to draw is this one here."

"Why?"

"Well, he's the man who shot——"

"Don't you start that! That's *private*."

"Private, hell, you told everybody that comes through this town, you told us thirty times, can't you tell him onc't?"

I looked at the gray-bearded man who sat in a rocker, back against the hotel wall. He leaned over, spit slowly, just missing the toe of his own shoe, and looked off down the street as if his friend hadn't pointed him out to me.

"I wonder if I could draw him to where you could tell just by looking at it, he's the man who shot—whoever it was?"

"Hear that, Tom? Give him a dollar to see if he can."

"I told you fellers, it's a secret just amongst ourselves."

"Secret, hell, I never heard such braggin' from a human."

"Well, wouldn't *you*, if it'd been you? Instead of one long furlough in Elmira Prison?"

I started sketching him.

"I ain't gonna pay for it."

"You don't *have* to pay for it," I said, working his eyes, "'less you like it."

As I sketched him, he talked and ended up telling it.

"Well, what these boys talking about, what made me famous in the War was that I'm the one that shot General Sanders."

I didn't know who General Sanders was. I didn't know what he was talking about. I asked, "Where?"

He said, "At Knoxville."

So I says, "I think I was in Knoxville." My brain was so scattered from drinking, and I was too young to remember everything anyway. "I think I was in Knoxville."

"Big old house they got down there called Bleak House, I got up in the tower," Tom said, holding still without me telling him. "He rode a white horse, coming down the Kingston Pike west of Knoxville, and I was up in the tower of Bleak House with four other sharpshooters, but they was all dead around me—when I saw General Sanders riding toward the house on the road below, out in front of his men, like he was scouting on his own. I got him in my sights and he was a dead man. Only general of Southern birth killed while serving in the damned Union army. They named the fort after him, and I was in the attack on it. Sunday, November 29, 1864, by god. I killed him, I'm the one, very one you're drawing a picture of."

I believed him, because I didn't remember a damned thing. Who would remember a fever dream?

I began then to become more conscious of what happens to a man when you sketch him. By the time you finish, he's a different person. I reckon that's why nobody ever looks like the drawing of him. Tom told it again, filling in more detail, sheets of ice on the berme, telegraph wire stretched along the ground, blood ankle-deep in the ditch, getting younger under his gray hairs, and told it a third time with even more facts and embellishments, like most men do, answering questions, until I passed my drawing over to him.

"What you want to make a thirty-year-old man look like Methuselah for?"

"You don't have to pay."

But he wasn't reluctant to pay because, he said, he ought to pass something down to his grandchildren, and I wanted to tell him that I, too, was in that tower and in the attack on Fort Sanders, but his story had only just now reminded me, I had not clearly remembered it for a long time, and his telling it had made it come back in vivid images like a blast from a shotgun. So I wasn't ready to tell much of anything, and I knew if they asked questions, I'd feel foolish not knowing what to say, so I kept mum.

When I finally got home to South Mountain in East Tennessee, my home cabin was deserted and my mother was living in Elizabethton and she'd remarried because my daddy, my granddaddy, and my brothers had hanged for burning those bridges, or perished in prison, or killed in battle, or gone down in the sinking of the *Sultana*. I stayed in the cabin and made my living hunting.

One sleety March day on South Holston, I was hunting, that day not for skins but for food. I was feeling faint from hunger and chill, when I saw my supper walking toward me like he was looking at *his* supper. When the bear saw me, it recognized me for a human and turned and dropped to all fours to get away from me, and I propped my rifle on a branch and got it in my sights just as it got too far for good aim and wished I had my Sharpe's rifle with the telescopic lens, and that's when I got a general in my cross-hairs, riding a white horse up the pike toward the house where I knelt at one of the tower windows aiming down at him.

Something, the light, the way the bear had ambled toward me, the way I felt, a little feverish from exposure to rain and sleet, and fatigued from rambling up and down the mountainside, hungry, had brought it back. I was in a tower and two men were shot and one was dead and seven others had run out, but none of them was that one-legged yankee in the Vicksburg crater, nor that old-looking man who had held still for me to draw his face in Pulaski as he told me about shooting General Sanders. He had proved out to be one of that tribe of liars the War had spewed up.

I had shot a General. But was it a *fact* that I had shot General *Sanders*, the man they named the fort after, the fort we attacked in Knoxville?

After I talked to a few people down in Elizabethton, I was pretty sure it was Sanders because only one general was killed in that battle.

The voices, and daily walking, tracking game on the mountain threw up repeatedly the question, Why, if I am the sharpshooter who shot General William Price Sanders (and I am now almost certain that I am), did I feel then, as I do still, that I missed the War?

Out hunting after that day I found only General Sanders in my sights and I broke out in a feverish sweat every time. The sense of having missed everything else kept me in night sweats.

So I ventured off Holston Mountain to find the War again.

I spent two years wandering back and forth over those places where I was a sharpshooter for General Longstreet. I drew pictures of the battlefields, and it got to where what I craved was to listen to men tell all about how they fought in the War, and to search out drawings and photographs. Here are some of my fragmented meditations that I wrote down in the margins of my sketchbook:

We are so seldom told *when* the photograph we are gazing at was taken, *when* this illustration was drawn. And sometimes not even *where.* A photograph is always taken *there* at the place we see *in it.* But *when*? Before, during, or after the battle? A drawing *may* have been made on the scene, or in a studio in New York City, from a photograph, or from a press dispatch—from a word picture—or from imagination, or all three combined. Some sketches I have seen are offered in various books as being of two, three, four different, widely scattered localities—reused, reprinted, redrawn, in crying need of resurrection.

I do not draw as well as those professional artists whose work has appeared after the War. What I am is a born natural, like the common soldier artist I only sometimes see. Were there many portrait sketchers of my sort in the camps and prisons? I vaguely remember some Yankee prisoners engaged in that at Andersonville, but I wasn't doing much of it myself until after I impulsively drew the heads of the dead Virginian and the wounded on the wall in Bleak House Tower.

I did not open *Frank Leslie's Illustrated History of the Civil War* until almost a decade after it was first published in 1866. I saw it again today and noticed some things about it. The anonymous writer of the preface tells me that these pictures were "drawn in the very midst of the strife," "drawn and engraved directly from sketches made on the scene of battle." Frank Leslie had 12 artists at the front (but only one engraver at the factory, I deduce, from the sameness of the woodcut renderings of the 300 drawings—he made them all look stiff). He refers to them as a "corps" of "War artists." General Carr's introduction includes the observation that "nothing recalls the past so forcibly as scenes *taken* at the time and on the very spot" ("taken," as if he were referring to photographs).

Most of the sketchers and photographers of the War were as anonymous as myself. I look in vain in the illustrated histories from 1866 on up to 1883 for the names of the artists—no mention, no list, no tribute. But after the War, some of them became better known. Edwin Forbes' *Life Studies of the Great Army: A Historical Art Work* was published in 1876. I have copied many of the pictures from these books into my own sketchbook, along with the ones I have dreamed up my own self.

Artists drew themselves into their own pictures (as photographers could not—somebody else had to *shoot* them). In the Frank Leslie book, I see an action scene on the steamer *Mississippi*, showing the artist himself, sketching the scene—William Waud, brother of Alfred, the better artist. I've seen a lithograph from a photograph that shows Edwin Forbes on his horse in the field, sketching for *Leslie's Weekly*. Winslow Homer drew a caricature of himself, looking like D'artanian, as a *Harper's* staff artist. His horse Billy behind him, James Edward Taylor sketched himself sketching for *Leslie's*.

Mostly Yankees saw the weekly magazines. Very few Confederate artists were working because very few Southern illustrated weeklies could get paper. Most of the Confederate scenes were drawn by Frank Vizetelly (killed accidentally in Egypt) and published in a London paper. I see some of the Southern artists now in issues of *Century Magazine*, commissioned to reconstruct events and draw them from the South's point of view: William L. Sheppard,

Allen C. Redwood, John Adams Elder, Adelvert John Volck. As my grandfather used to say, "Let the names be given."

But Conrad Wise Chapman, whose father was a distinguished painter, is the best of the Confederate artists. I hear that he was the only special artist at Shiloh. Wounded there, he was sent to Charleston where General Beauregard commissioned him to paint many views of Fort Sumter. By December 1864, though, he was in Rome missing the end of the War.

The history of the War has a history, and part of that history is a history of seeing. North and South, all questions of seeing should be divided: "during the War" or "soon after the War."

I remember seeing a man over on the Union side of the Rappahanock sketching the burned bridge. Later, I saw the sketch itself—the man was Alfred Waud—showing men on both sides yelling back and forth, taunts and propositions for bartering coffee, tea, whiskey, tobacco. One man waves a copy of Waud's *Harper's Weekly*. Some of our boys wanted to trade a Richmond paper for a New York paper, because neither seemed to report the same war they were in.

Did one of them use me as a model for a sketch of a sharpshooter, without my knowing it? I look for myself. Winslow Homer is a famous painter now, of course, but his first adult oil painting, his famous sharpshooter up in a tree, was first a sketch that appeared—and I have found and saved a copy—in *Frank Leslie's* of April 1862. Somebody did a similar drawing, just another angle and a different hat, of a Confederate sharp-shooter that I saw in *Century*. In *Harper's*, I think I saw it, is California Joe, of the Berdan Sharpshooters, lying behind a little rock with a mountain range behind him. He was famous. But I don't see me in any of them. And in a later issue, they showed Barksdale's Mississippi sharpshooters opposing the laying of the pontoon bridges over the Rappahanock. I'm out of the picture, up in that church steeple, looking for a heart to shatter.

A language of the hand precedes facility with a language of the mind, from drawing to listening and writing. But as I listen more, the more facile becomes my pencil, too. (I hear a grind-stone whirring, my intellect the blade, circumstance the wheel, my will turning the handle.)

I know that I experience the War most sharply when I see it through the emotions, the imaginations, the intellect of others—not just veteran soldiers, but veteran civilians, like good Reverend Carter. I'm not sure what I feel and think about that.

I redraw the drawings I see that were made from photographs and published in *Harper's Weekly* and in books. Visiting Gettysburg today, I met a man who once saw a photograph of a dead sharpshooter in Devil's Den on the battlefield. He described the mood of the photograph so sharply, I saw it myself and I carried it around in my head as I wandered the battlefield. Standing at Devil's Den today, drawing the scene from the photograph as I imagined it, I became aware that there was something not right in that scene. I wish I could put my finger on what's wrong.

Things—people and animals and vehicles—must temporarily stop so Mathew Brady's or Alexander Gardner's camera can permanently stop them. Photographers could not photograph action. Sketch artists slowly stop everything so you can look at everything, but they can show you motion.

As a sharpshooter, I was not too far this side of an artist, for the same terms do apply: field of vision, depth of field, perspective, foreshortening, and so forth. And as a sketcher, I remain, of course, a sharpshooter. Artists "sketch" you (quick as a skirmish), but photographers "shoot" you very slowly. A likeness as opposed to an exactness. Both of which lie.

I struggle now to get everything in my sights: images, insights, conceptions. With a hair-trigger pencil line, I am sometimes on target, bull's-eye.

Strange that General Lew Wallace didn't do like John Esten Cooke and write fiction about the War. He wrote *Ben Hur* instead. But he was also an artist. Well, all officers had to learn drawing at West Point, and General Grant was good at it, too; they say he liked to draw Indians before the War. Listening to testimony at the Wirz trial, such a vivid image took shape in General Wallace's mind's eye, he drew a dead man on the deadline, naked, looking, from low on the narrow stream, up at his crown and shoulder, one arm flung back, the cup handle dangling from one finger, the deadline wood rail above his head, his privates a casualty not of our cruelty but of Victorian prudery. Did he imagine the man I actually shot from the guard tower?

Just as some men's impressions became memoirs that somehow got to be matters of record, some sketches made during the War became paintings after. I am thinking of Homer, who left his studio in a tower at New York University when the War started, and who was a freelance sketcher in the Wilderness at the time I decided to freelance home and ended up in Andersonville as a guard, plucked from before the firing squad in that captured Yankee uniform. He later painted "A Skirmish in the Wilderness." I am thinking especially of Confederate artist Conrad Wise Chapman, who made a sketch of a picket sitting on a tree stump near the Diascund Bridge on the Chickahominy Road and who later elaborated his drawing into a painted self-portrait, replacing the picket's face with his own.

Some other artists I admire and so, look for, are Edwin J. Meeker, Walton Taber, and especially Admiral Henry Walke. Walke's are among those I contemplate but do not redraw, and not because of the fact that I never saw the Federal navy, or the Confederate, for that matter, in action, nor even at rest in harbor. Walke, who was known earlier for his sketches of the Mexican war, commanded the action, then drew it—vivid, powerful, convincingly lifelike. In memory I see "Carondelet Gun Explodes" as clearly as the callous on my third finger as I draw or make these notes.

Sketches are imitations, copies, transpositions, metamorphoses. What was seen in the newspapers during the War was second hand, third hand, fourth hand. Alfred Waud, Edwin Forbes, Walton Taber, and others often drew from Brady, Barnard, Gardner, O'Sullivan photographs or drew on-the-spot eyewitness sketches, or came along soon before or soon after a battle, or sketched from someone else's sketches. Waud's "Lee at Appomattox," nameless's "Harper's Ferry" and "Colonel James Brownlow Wading a River to Kill Sleeping Rebels," Homer's "Our Army before Yorktown," an eight-panel wood engraving in collaboration with Waud. Then the engraver got into the act, copying (in reverse image). Many of those sketches were lyrical domestications of violence, agony, and death. The image floats, a life of its own, from, first, the fingers, wrist, through the engraving process to the eyes of the beholder. I recall now Homer's "Trooper Meditating Beside a Grave," as I meditate beside the grave of the War that settles and sinks more each year out in America's back yard.

Not until Eadweard Muybridge's photographic studies came out a few years ago did Waud and Forbes and other artists learn that all of the galloping horses—observed and remembered—in those thousands of sketches were falsely depicted: never do both feet of a horse leave the ground at once. Look again especially at Forbes' "The Newspaper Correspondent."

Albert Bierstadt is famous as the painter of the Great American West. In his painting "The Bombardment of Fort Sumter" and in his "Picket Duty in Virginia," I see more than a record. In his eagle-eye vision, light from the sky conspires with water to make a mere flash of the historic moment at the fort, and the landscape overwhelms the five Rebel soldiers attacking the picket post, as if Nature were already taking over, as when I found what work she had done when I stumbled into the Vicksburg thickets around the crater in 1867.

The photograph of the Rebel Sharpshooter in Devil's Den that I have never seen is more vivid as I write than the photographs and drawings I *have* seen, and I see it even more lucidly when I remember it at *will* or involuntarily. Why then this compulsion to draw it, too, again and again, looking, in memory, at the photograph as my Gettysburg host described it to me from *his* memory of it in 1876?

(End of notes in margin of my sketchbook.)

By the time I had returned to Elizabethton, I had relived the War in many places, in many ways, many times over, and so now I was eager to visit with Reverend Carter, the man who planned the burning of the nine bridges, and who, after I come back from the War and the West, had finally taught me how to read and write.

As I got closer to my cabin on the Mountain, I knew that everything would become clearer.

In January 1877, I was home again.

I went down to visit Reverend Carter and told him everything about my wanderlust.

He showed me "my recent acquisition": Alexander Gardner's *Photographic Sketch Book of the Civil War*. "It cost me a pretty penny. I've been eager for your return so I could show you this one photograph in particular. See here, 'The Home of a Rebel Sharpshooter,' in Devil's Den at Gettysburg?"

"I've seen several different drawings from this photograph."

"Do you see anything wrong with this photograph?" Before I could answer, Reverend Carter plunged ahead. "First, let me tell you that I have seen a photograph of Alfred Waud, the battlefield artist. As Waud sat on one of the boulders in Gettysburg, sketching for *Harper's Weekly*, Alexander Gardner's assistant, Timothy O'Sullivan photographed him. Waud looked as dashing as any cavalry hero.

"Now, look here at this view of rocks," Reverend Carter said. "Notice the white pad lying on the rock on the right. I imagine it belonged to Waud

who left it there. Now here is the question: Did O'Sullivan and Gardner, looking for corpses to shoot, find Waud sketching at Devil's Den?"

"Or did Waud," I asked, my eagerness startling Reverend Carter, "looking for a vantage point from which to sketch from memory, but now from the Confederate sharpshooter's point of view, find O'Sullivan and Gardner there?"

"Or did they meet elsewhere, and did Waud, who had witnessed the battle, lead the two photographers to Devil's Den?"

"And what is it Waud is sketching in O'Sullivan's photograph?" I wondered, aloud.

"Perhaps it is the place where General Reynolds fell, the sketch of his I have seen most often."

"I have put it together this way, sir."

"Let me see," said Reverend Carter, "if I can *imagine* how you have figured this out. O'Sullivan turns from taking a picture of Waud to help Gardner choose and find a scene to capture. They find the sharpshooter's nook—empty. But they imagine a sharpshooter lying dead there."

"They *see* a photograph of him."

"O'Sullivan and Gardner carry a body forty feet—probably a young infantryman—in a blanket—" Reverend Carter persisted, "—because where he had actually fallen, he did not look interesting."

"Up between two boulders," I put in, "high as a tall man, was a stone wall, built in the heat of battle, but nobody lay dead there. So they stretched the corpse out there, turned him into a sharpshooter, into a photograph, there where I had made a wall the night before." I had let it slip out, my identity as a Rebel soldier was there in the room for Reverend Carter to look at, but he seemed not to have caught my blunder.

"It is O'Sullivan who actually exposes the plate." Reverend Carter, flushed, combative, plunged on. "Light becomes an accomplice to their fakery, their fiction, this icon now of the War. Gardner gave him credit in a catalog, but took credit himself when he sold portfolios of his prints in 1866."

"Then *Harper's*, under the woodcuts based on the photograph, gave credit to Mathew Brady."

"Excellent, Willis," said Reverend Carter, his voice weak with some new attitude that his loud applause made me suspect as envy and resentment. "You know, O'Sullivan was among the many War photographers who followed the transcontinental railroad and army survey parties. The indians called him shadow-catcher."

"I imagine him after the War, wandering the West, just after I left there. While I wandered aimlessly, he wandered to satisfy intentions."

"I see," said Reverend Carter, not seeming to see. "I see."

"At Devil's Den, where many sight-lines had criss-crossed three days before," I persisted, "the sight-lines of artists and photographers converged." I saw in Reverend Carter's eyes the recognition that his sight-lines and mine were among them. But now I was on my own, seeing, learning, teaching. "I missed my own death in Devil's Den, I missed 'The Harvest of Death,' but Timothy O'Sullivan and Alexander Gardner faked my death in one of the most famous photographs of the War, famous up to that year mostly in the drawing rendition, however. THE HOME OF A REBEL SHARPSHOOTER, GETTYSBURG. Then the wrong photographers took or got credit for it. I realize that what you and I see is after all a product of Gardner's and O'Sullivan's combined—"

The expression in Reverend Carter's eyes, of one bereft of an insight he had felt unique to himself and had waited eagerly for my return to teach me, abruptly made me stop. And then the startled look of recognition came to his eyes—the knowledge that I had confessed who I was. I was a veteran of the Confederate army whose bridges he and his men, in league with my kin, had burned.

I backed away from him, turned and departed his parlor, knowing I would never be welcome again.

Climbing the mountain paths, I finished my thought, with the intention of fixing it in writing. I realized that what we see in that photograph is after all a product of Gardner's and O'Sullivan's combined imagination, with Waud as possible encouraging witness or even third participant.

Many sight-lines converged in Devil's Den, as mine do now.

I missed my own death in Devil's Den, but O'Sullivan and Gardner missed what those who saw the famous photograph, and the drawings various artists made from it, saw: a young Rebel sharpshooter dead in Devil's Den at Gettysburg. O'Sullivan, who took the photograph, and Gardner, who took the credit, could never, can never see what I saw, imagined.

Willis Carr, Sharpshooter, Meditates on Photographs

I wrote this June 3, 1926
Still up on Holston Mountain
Elizabethton, East Tennessee

I always intended to hand these fragments I have been writing since 1875 down to my descendants, but I have never had a wife and children. Except for the varmints—the ones I hunt and the ones I don't—I am by my lonesome up here. I am 79, but not yet ready for the Messenger.

In 1893, I declared that I was finally ready to write about the shooting of General William Price Sanders. But I could not do it. I was still unable to fix on the facts that would help me get the answer to that lingering question: Was I or was I not the sharpshooter who shot General Sanders? So even as I hunt bear on Holston Mountain, I can't get out of the tower of Bleak House in Knoxville, where, in a fever, I got the general on a white horse in my sights.

All these years, I have tried to get him in my sights again. But what I *have* had in my sights for the past 50 years is photographs. And now I am moved to add here to other fragments you have found stuck away all over this cabin. Photographs come to me in memory the way actual events did, except the photographs are more persistent, sharper, make me remember other things, or imagine them, and think and feel more complicated feelings than my own few memories do (I was only 15 in the tower) so that now I can not always tell which is which, and don't usually care.

During the War, few people saw the photographs. Each photograph we saw in newspapers (captured Yankee papers because the blockade kept photographic supplies out of the South) was rendered in a technique of the ancient past—as a drawing; a reverse process, as if photography had not even been invented. They did not know how yet to print a photograph in a newspaper.

Not until about 1884 when the first book of them came out—*The Memorial War Book*. I look—no I *stare* at, gaze into, meditate on photographs. Still, like drawings on a cave wall.

The memory that stayed focused in the limbo years after the War was of the back of a black wagon, eye-like holes staring at me across the Rappahannock at Fredericksburg. I was in the bell tower of a church, on the sharp for Yankees putting a pontoon bridge together where we had burned the main bridge, and looking down saw, in my telescopic lens, these two black-rimmed eyes, as if in a mask. But I was not the sharpshooter who took a shot at the gleam on Mathew Brady's camera, mistaking it for gun-metal. I saw only the eyes of his "What's-it" wagon.

The sight of that wagon, an awkward mystery, awed the soldiers. I never got close to it, saw it only at a distance, for Confederates had no such wagons because the blockade made photographic supplies rare at the South. Remembering that black wagon, I always saw it in motion climbing a hill and dropping down on the other side out of sight. I remember now, though, that whenever I actually saw it, it was setting still.

Seeing the camera, with its black hunchback, mysterious, formidable, some Confederates believed it to be the great steam gun they had heard about, that could discharge 500 balls a minute, and some ran from it, as they say savages run from cameras. But some soldiers attacked this infernal machine. At Gettysburg, on Little Round Top where cannon had jolted, somebody later mounted a camera. The camera was like a weapon—"load, aim, shoot"—and a shroud in one, with the black hearse, the "What's-it" wagon, waiting nearby, the horse patient, the "undertaker" patient, alive under the shroud, captor of the image of the subject, who stands, as if embalmed, in front of the cannon lens. The camera, too, has a kind of fuse or trigger. Artists "sketch" you (quick as a skirmish), but photographers "shoot" you very slowly. A likeness as opposed to an exactness. The subject freezes, but the photographer is usually animated, running against the fading light, exposure time, and the subject's own inability to hold still for the five minutes the camera dictated, amid other distractions and hostile conditions, bullets, shells, bolting horses. All photographs are double exposures, the subject exposed to the light that simultaneously gives him life and fixes him as in death on the plate. In the aftermath of a battle, the photographer, under this black shroud, is an ogre on the landscape, making his afterimages.

My awareness of the photographer makes seeing more complex, more of a problem, than any awareness of a sketch artist. Whether the photographer's intent is sentimentality, nostalgia, maliciousness, satire, compassion, to expose or to reveal, behind all intentions lurks an evil eye. And we, too, cast an evil eye upon such scenes as we see what the photographer originally saw.

The photographs I saw, I kept in mind, and mulled over while hunting, walking the mountains, and sitting by winter fires, and while I gathered yarbs as skins played out. I put myself in the way of photograph books and actual photographs as often as I could. I could be looking right at you, and between you and me would jump a photograph. Until, of course, the images were *made* as much in my brain pan as in the original developing solutions, that painstaking process.

When I read a book, I feel that the author speaks directly to me as a universal reader. But when I scrutinize these photographs, I always feel unrelated to any community of viewers, estranged from them in fact. Looking at photographs makes me feel melancholy. Why is it that looking at drawings does not?

Seeing that the mask-like rear of that "What's-it" wagon was my most memorable picture of the War, why did I not remember until years later the day a southern photographer set up his camera in my sentinel box to shoot views of Andersonville Prison? Standing there again in 1876, ten years later, I remembered it all very clearly, and, looking out, saw what he must have seen—well, what we had both seen, standing almost hip to hip—then what he saw from under the black cloth, through the lens, before he slotted in the wet-plate and removed the lens-cap, and what he still later saw emerge in his wagon at the foot of the guard tower steps five minutes later.

When I finally saw a view of Andersonville, thousands of prisoners sprawled over a vast hillside, I remembered that photographer coming that day of good sunlight, climbing up and down from shots aimed north, east, south, west, for a panorama, like Barnard's views of Knoxville from the university cupola. I wondered, Am I that figure in the tower? I look for myself, as we all look for ourselves, proof that I was there, to show myself to myself and to know that others see me. Then I remembered we stood together while he shot the scene. Summer 1864, and hot, and thinking how hot the photographer must be under that black hood, framing his view.

I look for Cherokee in the photographs, as I had looked down from the guard tower one day and this big buck African was leaning his back against one of the deadline posts, reading a newspaper for all the world to wonder at. I thought he was putting on. No, he said, he had known how to read since he was 5 or 6. You lie. No lie. Let's hear it. He read off some of it as smooth as bear grease. No, he wasn't making it up as he went along.

He stood up and offered to pitch it up to me to prove it. I thought he was bluffing. I said, "Making fun of white boys who can't read any better than you, can get you shot." He laughed and danced around, not knowing how close he was to perdition. I called a halt to that, but he couldn't help himself, couldn't stop it, and even got me to laughing, and when he stopped, I believed him. Then it scalded my cheeks to know I was an illiterate who was looking at a Yankee African that could read. No, that wasn't so bad, because what did you expect of Yankees?

But as the days passed and he kept drifting over to my corner, it came out that before he was a Yankee, he was a Cherokee. I never learned his real name—I just called him Cherokee. He said his granddaddy's white master in North Carolina sold his granddaddy when he was a boy to an Indian living at Chota, the capitol of the Cherokee Nation, twenty or so miles from Knoxville.

When Cherokee's master's son set out for Memphis to join the Rebel army, he took a slave with him. "But he called me his brother," said Cherokee. "You know, they had slaves before the white man came and first enslaved some of *them*, but their own slaves were always enemies captured in battle."

At first it made me mad. I thought, well, hell's bells, if this damned Indian Sequoyah can bypass learning to speak, read, and write English by making up a whole new reading language all by his lonesome, even if it did take him twelve years to figure one out, is there any excuse for an illiterate white man, even if he is still just a boy, to stumble around unable to read the language he speaks?

"I'll teach you Cherokee!" he offered, to tease me.

To take the sting out of the teasing, I said, "You better, Cherokee," calling him by that name for the first time, "or I'll put a red frown between your black eyes!"

That tickled him, too, but he tossed the *Cherokee Advocate* (its new name since 1848) up to me and started lesson number one in the hot dust, reaching over the deadline, almost getting his arm shot off by an eleven year old warrior in the tower just north of mine.

Well, we got serious, and it was fun but hard, and we had time, so we used it, and after a few weeks, which proved I was dumber than Sequoyah's 5-year-old daughter, I was reading and writing Cherokee and speaking it with him.

Cherokee never asked me to help him escape, but not until he made the dash and I had shot him, did I realize he must have convinced himself that I would not shoot the man who had taught me how to read and write, even if it was only Cherokee.

Looking at photographs, I am always mindful of the point of view, the photographer's and the human subject's. What *I* see is not just in the eye of the beholder but also in the eye of the photographer and the subject, simultaneously.

In some way or ways, each of us—subject, photographer, and me—are aware of the points of view of the other two. Whatever the thing in itself is, its sun-painted image is fixed in no one of the three. Together, the three points of view convey the cruel radiance of what is.

Most of the photographs that I have seen and so imagined, or only heard about and imagined, seem as if they are views seen by an omniscient eye. Something about the height and angle of vision makes me feel the absence of a human eye—or rather the presence of an omniscient eye—in this view of Knoxville from the cupola of the university. That empty area below to the right suggests a lack of the usual human interest in people and things, and somehow makes me look upon the town more intently, though without human interest.

Barnard's views of Knoxville taken from the cupola of the university, looking east, west, north, south, a broken panorama, make the blood of battle seem as remote a few weeks after as it seems to most people over half a century later. That awareness released his pictures into the realm of the unknown, where, for me, they now float, no less vital, but much less anchored in time and place. But for me Barnard himself remains forever captive in the cupola, and I look at his pictures as if *all* were taken from up there. Seen first by a man, this view, in the photograph itself, becomes an omniscient view such as men in the War never had, not even, in the photograph's contemplative aspect, Generals. Not General Sanders riding high on his white horse, down Kingston Pike. Not my fevered eye in the tower of Bleak House where I did or did not get him in my telescopic sights.

The feeling of omniscient detachment and perspective is keener in Barnard's view of the garrison at Johnsonville, just as Thomas is pulling a federal battery out of there to go up against Hood at Nashville. It is shot from such an odd height, suggesting no man-made structure for tripod support, that I feel an omniscient eye gazes upon these men and caissons as they stand on wet surfaces, and General Forrest's entire career rushes into my mind's eye, for he assaulted this place like a natural force a month before this evacuation. The water and mud are November cold. The trees are all black columns, stripped by season and Forrest. The men wear new-looking caped overcoats. A wooden platform stretches from left to right in the foreground—five soldiers stand to the left, but a single soldier, looking down from the platform, lends to the scene a sense of imminent evacuation. Unable to imagine a human eye looking through a lens to produce this view, I feel a shiver, as if an All-Seeing Eye is looking over my shoulder.

And after 60 some odd years, I still can't shake the feeling that I, who fought with General Longstreet in all his campaigns except First Manassas, missed the War somehow.

A picture I go in search of, because it haunts me and I want to master it, is of the muskets of federal troops stacked beside the empty road the omniscient eye looks across in Petersburg. What haunts me is the fact that, like the photographer himself and all his viewers, the human subject is transitory; objects and landscapes seem permanent. The muskets are close enough to reach out

to, and they follow the curve of the road into the ruins of houses, though a white house still stands left of the road. Where are the soldiers? Where are the citizens of Petersburg? At this moment, as the omniscient eye stares at them, I get a sense of the omniscient intelligence's knowing exactly what each man, who is somewhere else, is thinking and feeling, the same eye that will look upon them in death or old age. The landscapes, often the architecture, sometimes in ruins, remain, as human subjects vanish. I think of Keats' "Ode on a Grecian Urn." "And what little town is emptied of this folk, this pious morn?" What wreck or ruin the human eye has seen can never be rebuilt.

Thousands of the glass negatives enhance the process of photosynthesis in green houses all over the country because many Civil War photographers sold

them to be used as panes. The sun in time bleached the images. One business man bought 100,000, scraped the images off to capture the silver. The glass itself ended up in gauges and meters. Glass from Mathew Brady's warehoused negatives were used in eyepieces in gas masks worn by soldiers in France. Through one of them I see Dunker Church at Sharpsburg.

I was so overwhelmed by the first great sudden shower of photographs in 1884 that it took a while for me to realize that the only Confederates I was seeing were the dead left on the battlefield—the army having marched away, the photographers having arrived—or of the captured, or simple portraits of the Generals. Most of the Civil War photographs were taken by Yankees in the South, a kind of wax-museum aftermath. Associated with those photographs are all the emotions that prompted that famous farmer Edmund Ruffin, who fired the first shot at Fort Sumter, to blow his brains out a few days after Appomattox.

The phantom circuits of light and time work differently in each region, from Knoxville to Gettysburg. American light: southern light, northern light, western light, maybe eastern. Polar light. Moon light. Nature exposes *in* time what the photographer's inner light has revealed about people and things and places exposed *to* time. The vision of the photographer works in and out of and with and against the light. Things—the church, the wheels, the corpses—give off a kind of light, lures set out by God.

Looking at photographs, I often get intimations of the fact that everything that exists gives off, as the mind gives off thought, a kind of radiance of which light cannot be the sole source. "Light is God's shadow." In light, the photograph captures a moment in life, but only for a moment. The image is a moment in and out of time, in and out of this world.

Looking at photographs makes me sensible of time in shifting perspectives. The element of time comes into the process with the exposure: all photographs are exposed in time, but a photograph shows only the present, that moment of time in which the subject was exposed in the light to time and to the sensitive plate or film. I get pleasure out of participating in this process of fragmenting time, and what I see is beautiful because I feel it made in time, just in time, at the very instant when the photographer decides to pull the trigger, the way my eyelid shutters to show me the image more clearly.

Things—people and animals and vehicles—temporarily stop—usually for 5 to 30 seconds now in these modern times—so a camera can permanently stop them. Sketch artists slowly stop everything so you can look at them, often in motion. Photographs could not back then catch action. But sketches adapted from photographs *could* catch action. The artist did not have to be at the scene. But photographs can be shot only there, at the place we see in the photograph.

Looking at Grant in a series of pictures taken from the tower of Bethesda Church near Cold Harbor, seemingly exposing his head to sniper fire, I feel the human subject caught, while the world keeps spinning and tilting toward light, toward darkness. Around this image fixed at an exact moment in an exact place, my consciousness moves in space, neither here nor there, in time, neither then nor now. In front of the trunks of two trees sits Grant on a church bench, smoking, as if withdrawn into himself. On five church benches sit all the other officers, including Meade, who studies a map. Surrounding the officers are attendants and waiting horses. In the second picture, Grant has moved over to Meade and leans over his shoulder, pointing to a place on the map. In the third picture, Grant sits in his original position, studying the map. A rare series of photographs of a council of war, but also rare in the way singly and together they convey a sense of the living Grant among other Generals who look and sit more like Generals than he. My imagination is more willfully at work in looking at this picture of Grant than in reading his memoirs. Things outside Grant's memoirs seldom intrude, but things outside this photograph affect my responses to it.

As we look at photographs, memory rises to consciousness, and we bring to each photograph our memories of other, similar or contrasting, photographs. Are all photographs memories, dreams, so that the photographer almost always shoots a memory of other photographs, not simply the subject before him? Is everyone who looks at photographs, where ever, even in newspapers and magazines, remembering, even dreaming? All these photographs

seem to have been taken inside my head where memories repose, rather than in the settings where I actually killed or waited to shoot.

All photographs call to mind the moment I first remembered seeing, or thought I did, General Sanders. As I stared the bear that day into focus, framed in my sights, and he got me in focus, hunter and prey became photographs to each other, and as other men or animals rose to the bear's consciousness, at the same moment, General Sanders rose to mine, caught in my sights, another photograph.

All photographs lie. I prefer "lie" over "deceive" because that word forces me to examine the problem. To regard the photograph as dealing with the actual, with reality, fact, truth, leaves me strangely uninformed, unmoved, unsatisfied. It is only when I regard the photograph as in its nature ambiguous, paradoxical, as a distortion, a deception, a lie that it deeply affects me.

Years ago, I used to redraw the drawings that had been made from photographs and published in *Harper's Weekly* and in books, like the one of the dead sharpshooter in Devil's Den at Gettysburg. There was something wrong in that scene. I used to try to put my finger on it.

When I visited Gettysburg, I met a man who caught a glimpse of my sketch of the dead sharpshooter, and he said he had seen the photograph itself, in a very expensive book published in Washington in 1866 by the photographer himself, Alexander Gardner, *not* Mathew Brady as the caption under the drawing had claimed. *A Photographic Sketchbook of the Civil War* it's called, the first published collection of Civil War photographs. Actual positive prints, each pasted in place—a portfolio. He described the mood of the photograph so sharply, I saw it myself and carried it around in my head as I wandered the battlefield that day. Drawing the scene from the picture in my head, I became aware what was wrong with it: the rifle is not a sharpshooter's rifle. Also soldiers would have taken that rifle; had they failed to see it, relic hunters would have found it. And burial details would have disposed of the body.

That photograph, which was only described to me, was more vivid than the photographs and drawings I had actually seen, and I saw it even more lucidly when I remembered it at *will* or involuntarily. Why did I then have a compulsion to draw it, too, again and again, looking, in memory, at the photograph as my Gettysburg host had only described it to me in 1876?

At Devil's Den, where many sight-lines had criss-crossed in battle three days before, the sight-lines of artists and photographers converged. I missed my own death in Devil's Den, but Timothy O'Sullivan and Alexander Gardner faked it, I know now, in one of the most famous photographs of the War: "The Home of a Rebel Sharpshooter, Gettysburg."

About to look at even a simple photograph—I get a different kind of chill of anticipation than when I ask someone to tell me a story. I hear voices, sense listening ears. I feel a compulsion to tell a story.

One charged image seems to ignite another. Each photograph leaves afterimages no closer to the actual event than our memory of an episode does. When I look at a particular photograph for the first time, I simultaneously see afterimages of other photographs. I can never see the photograph of the room in which Stonewall Jackson died at Guiney Station in its total living context. But I can imagine it. As I do the bridal suite of the Lamar House Hotel on Gay Street where the Bijou theater now stands, where I saw *The Birth of a Nation* and a newsreel of the war in Europe, where General Sanders lay in a fever of dying, without a photograph ever.

One source of this aura of richness is the power of the photograph to allude to more than it shows. It seems to be in the nature of a photograph that something unseen commands the attention of all our senses. Sometimes the photographer makes what is unseen the focal interest. It is especially true of photographs taken in the South, back then and now, that each gathers to itself a context that stirs the imagination, so that hovering around each photograph, I have a sense of the unseen, and so of the unspoken.

Even so, even so, a multitude of images have eluded us. I look in vain for civilians robbing the battlefield dead, the many camp scenes caught by artists (and so there is more variety among drawings; all scenes of action; all interiors, except the room where Stonewall Jackson died, flooded with direct light from bare windows; night scenes, which could not be captured, so that all photographs show people, places, and things in the hours of best light, no picture then of a pine tree burning to light a night march, nor of a sharpshooter up in a tree or up in a steeple.

The photographs I "take" in my head are as clear as Brady's, Barnard's, Gardner's, O'Sullivan's. I look at them. A bridge over a river burning. Soldiers meeting in the middle of a stream to exchange coffee and tobacco. The face of a soldier before battle and the same face at the moment he knows "it is finished." A general on a white horse in my sights. The doused ashes of a campfire, steaming, just before you turn away from it. Soldiers sleeping on their arms. General Longstreet among the women who walk among the gravestones in Hollywood Cemetery in Richmond. Grant looking up at O'Sullivan who looks down at him from the belfry of Bethesda Church. General Sanders dying in the bridal suite of the Lamar Hotel. A scarred drum head with a half-eaten hardtack lying on it. Myself, looking down into the Petersburg Crater, my face unclear. Orlando Poe at his friend General Sanders' grave in Knoxville, then the one in Chattanooga, then the one, still a mystery, where he came to rest at last. The painter standing before his unfinished fresco downstairs in Bleak House during the attack on General Sanders. General Forrest at the bedside of the dying officer he stabbed in self-defense. Alfred Waud standing on the Stone Bridge at Bull Run, revisiting it, the last year of his life. Trees burning in the Wilderness. A leg sticking up out of a ditch, telegraph wire taut across the ankle like a bow about to release an arrow at Fort Sanders. I see, close up, a soldier about to hang, and in another, far away on a hillside, a soldier already hanging, and I remember how close I came to that. A "What's-it Wagon" parked alongside Dunker Church, no dead in the yard. Cherokee leaning back against the deadline post at Andersonville, reading the *Cherokee Phoenix*. The one-legged Yankee vet posing as I draw his picture, honoring his request that I add his leg, the Vicksburg crater between us. Edmund Ruffin sitting in his chair, dead of the self-inflicted wound. A sharpshooter lying dead at the foot of an oak tree. The *Sultana* rests on the bottom of the Mississippi where almost 2,000 perished days after the end of the War, the worst maritime disaster in history. When I was a child sharpshooter observing events of the War, I was an ignorant eye, not knowing I was taking "photographs" and that I would tell you about them as I waited for the Messenger.

Hunting, for critters, or yarbs, keeps my memory sharp. A glance that tickets a healing or spicy yarb, a bead that drops a pheasant, bear being scarce in recent years, somehow triggers a picture in my head sharp and keen as frost on gun metal. Hunting, I see pictures, and seeing pictures when I'm not hunting makes me want to reach for my rifle and stalk. Every man knows you're most alive when you are stalking game, or, if you're a soldier, when you're thrust into action, but I never met a man who thrives as I do on pictures—not so much there in the books open on the table as there suddenly between you and the critter, your finger on the trigger, just about to squeeze.

But unlike the game that won't wait, pictures won't stay still. I mean not even there in the books open on the table. The more you stare, the more things you see, but you have the feeling you are missing some element that is not a thing, that is there somehow, or was there, or ought to be there. That's why, sometimes I don't look long at a photograph, I turn away from it before what I hope to see there vanishes on the page. I shut my eyes and expect it to show up like gold dust in my brain pan. I tell you what's the truth, it's so unsettling, I hesitate to take down my rifle anymore.

I *knew* I shot Cherokee, so he has been dead to me all these years. I remember him, but most often in that moment I squeezed the trigger. His story is too soon told.

But because I never knew for certain whether it was I who shot General William Price Sanders, he has remained alive in my imagination. It was as if imagining him, I created a General Sanders. But now I know too much, both facts and the seven contradictory eyewitness reports of his death. I must relinquish him.

And so I am left alone up here on Holston Mountain with Cherokee in my sights, always.

A Fever of Dying

Henrietta Ramsey Lenoir and General William Price Sanders

April 14, 1884
Written on Holston Mountain

In the Beginning was the Word. Parson Brownlow's words in the North, sparked by what he envisioned—a federal force penetrating East Tennessee—lent motive power, in a sense, even to General William Price Sanders' raid. General Sanders came down from Eastern Kentucky (before he became a General) to burn bridges, tear up railroads, and draw Confederate troops back to Knoxville, in preparation for Burnside's invasion, his mission not to take and hold, but to destroy.

A battle, even a raid, is so confusing to the ordinary soldier who is a living part of it and often to the commander who leads it that writing about a battle is even harder than fighting in it. I hear that Thomas William Humes, William Rule, and Oliver Temple down in Knoxville are writing books about Loyal Mountaineers of Tennessee. And it is known at Knoxville that before Doctor Ramsey left Charlotte and returned to Knoxville in 1872 he had finished his autobiography. I have not read it, of course, nor met anyone who has, for he intends it for his children and grandchildren, but I suppose he devotes space to Sanders' raid, and I often imagine how he, a historian, who did not witness it, for he was a fugitive from it, would write of it.

Here are the facts, as Parson Brownlow would say, and I give them as *he* would give them in the *Whig*, not unmixed with rhetoric and folklore, for I have read, I have listened, and I have meditated. I have heard eyewitnesses recount their experiences, laced with statistics, I have witnessed re-enactments by remnants of the old forces and their young relatives. Why did I feel nothing? Why did my imagination remain inert, my intellect stagnant? Something ought to be done. I will start with you and me. I hope I haven't missed anything. If this gets confusing, pay better attention.

Let me get my bearings: "Ever before" I spied General Sanders from the tower in Bleak House, many others got him in their sights. Through their eyes, I see him coming. Daily we see and are seen; we know that we see, but seldom know that we are seen. Sometimes we arrange *what we see*; seldom do we arrange *the ways we are seen*. To see, we must see ourselves as others see us, combine those images with the images of others that *we* see into a conception. Then as we *are* seen, we see; and all ambiguities are a natural part of a conception that we control.

I am always aware of the one *I* do not see seeing me.

On the evening of the seventeenth of June, some Rebel farmers saw General Sanders leading 1,500 mounted men into the vicinity of Montgomery, Tennessee, near Big Emory River.

Then a small party of Rebel soldiers stationed a mile east of Montgomery at Wartburg saw 400 of him, in the vital sense that a commander's men are, through his commands, an extension of himself. The 400 men he detached to surprise and capture those Rebels were successful, except for several who escaped to transmit their vision of him to Rebels in Kingston, Loudon, Knoxville, and other places, so that he was imagined lucidly by more people than actually ever saw him on this raid. Thus are we all seen, and never imagine that we are. As we pass, we are sketched, photographed.

At daylight of the 19th, three miles equidistant between Loudon and Lenoir's, a captured courier, carrying orders from the commanding officer at Loudon, saw him, watched him read the order directing forces from Kingston to combine with men from Lenoir already called to Loudon, where the most important bridge in the area was heavily fortified, in expectation of a raid by this expedition. The courier was taken with Sanders in the direction of the now unprotected Lenoir's.

I once heard how Doctor James Gettys McGready Ramsey's great-grandmother missed America. Imagining that he lay dreaming again of her, that morning in June in his daughter's house at Lenoir's, helps me somehow really to *see* Doctor Ramsey for the first time. In 1730, his Scotch-Irish Presbyterian great-grandparents, with their son, Reynolds Ramsey, set out from Ireland for New Castle, Delaware (where William Penn, not "by the way," first set foot on this soil). She fell into the Atlantic. The quilted dress that was the fashion in the high latitude they were leaving buoyed her above the waves, so that her husband and her son (and now her great-grandson, dreaming) watched her body float a long time, until she sank over the horizon. The sight young Reynolds witnessed in broad daylight on the Atlantic became, I would suppose, a nightmare image that he passed on in story to his son Francis Alexander who passed it on to James and his other children.

Knocking at the door woke Doctor Ramsey, and he heard his son-in-law, Doctor Lenoir, calling to him. "Wake up, Doctor, I must tell you something urgent."

"What is it, B.B.?"

"A neighbor has come to tell us that the Yankees were at Kingston last night."

"Thank you, B.B. I am getting up."

Seeing a Yankee officer leading his men in a violation of Tennessee soil, Doctor Ramsey's mind leapt up more quickly than his body. He was daily more aware that two separate sources of energy resided in him. The terror of the lifelong nightmare and the humidity of June in an upstairs bedroom had made his body moist. An effort of will shook off the effects of the dream, allowing the images of his daytime preoccupation for the past month to hover for attention: John Sevier and Andrew Jackson meet (as might Doctor Ramsey and Parson Brownlow) on Gay Street, Jackson saying again, "In view of my services to my country, I wonder at your criticisms of me," Sevier replying, "Services? I know of no great service you have rendered the country except taking a trip to Natchez with another man's wife." Buttoning his trousers, the historian smiled, even though the scene sometimes gave him pain, for John Sevier was the leather-shirt hero of his *Annals of Tennessee* to 1800 and General Andrew Jackson was taking shape as the hero of the sequel. He was glad Tennessee was spared the death that day on Gay Street in Knoxville of either man, or both men, for Jackson carried only his sword cane and Sevier his cutlass. (I see editor Brownlow and editor Landon Haynes in Jonesboro fighting in the street May 14, 1840.) The figure of the Yankee officer advancing toward Lenoir reminded Dr. Ramsey of his duties as State Director of the East Tennessee and Georgia Railroad and Confederate treasury agent for Tennessee.

Henrietta stood at the bottom of the stairs, setting her bonnet straight on her head. "What are you about, daughter?" he asked, descending toward her.

"I'm going on the cars with you as far as Concord."

"Even if I were indeed senile, I wouldn't permit it. I should stay and aid your husband in watching over *you* and the boys. But they won't linger here. Knoxville is their point of attack. And I must move the Confederate depository to Greeneville."

"Do you think I can let my father leave my house alone at a time like this? Father, the Yankees are finally *here*."

"Let me go with grandfather," said William.

"You and your brother are dearer to your mother than a legion of fathers," said Ramsey, smiling.

"Don't talk so," said Henrietta.

"Anyway, I can't wait for the passenger train. I must flag down the freight. It's due in a few minutes."

"I'll put my ear on the track," said William, "and tell you when I hear it."

"Who taught you that one?"

"James."

Ramsey imagined William's cheek on one rail, James' on the opposite rail, the engine named after himself bearing down on them. "William, did grandfather ever tell you about your great-great-great-grandmother who sailed from Ireland more than a century ago?"

"Father, must you?" asked Henrietta, shivering.

"No, tell me," said William.

"Good. I'll tell you a *better* story next time I come."

"I think I hear the train, father," said Henrietta.

"It's late. My watch is never tardy."

Doctor Ramsey bade Henrietta and Doctor Lenoir and his three grandchildren goodbye, walked down the short slope to the tracks and flagged down the freight train. As it chugged to a crawl, the engineer pulled him up into the cab. "You're not late are you, Fred?"

As the train pulled out of Lenoir's, Ramsey looked back at the Lenoir family standing on the long porch as they had done many times before, when Yankee raiders were *not* twelve miles north, heading south along the Great Trunk Lines up the Valley of East Tennessee.

"The track and the rolling stock has deteriorated, Doctor Ramsey. Yes, I am late. I reckon, I'll *be* late on the *next* run, too. Don't reckon you could scare up some Richmond money for the road, the way you done when it first got built? Didn't you even go up to New York and help sell some bonds?"

"Your information has some semblance of accuracy." *If there is any merit in having equipped so many miles with so little money*, Doctor Ramsey thought, *I claim it as my own. I,* egome—*my very self, did it all.*

"And now," Doctor Ramsey said, reaching for a chunk of wood as the engineer jerked open the fire door for him, "if overused equipment may be urged a little more forcibly, I must get to Knoxville." *And rescue my Confederate depository from the invading enemy.*

So the first time I truly *see* Doctor Ramsey, he, like Brownlow when I first conjured him, is on the run, in *medias res.*

From the porch, Henrietta watched the train until the caboose made the curve past the salt works and she could not see it any longer, except in her head as she turned to go into the house. The rooms through which she passed were cool and dark in the early morning and she listened to her dress move as she walked, and a pot clatter in the basement where the Negroes were getting up breakfast.

At 8:30, she opened the back porch door to see if the image of Confederate cavalry in her head was actually coming down the Kingston road yet.

She saw a cavalry force riding rapidly toward her gate in an escort of dust, still dense with night moisture.

She went out to the gate and called to one of the riders. "Are you escaping from the Yankees?"

"We *are* the Yankees."

She searched for the face of the man who spoke and recognized Colonel R. K. Byrd.

"We haven't seen you in several years, Mr. Byrd. We figured you were at the North."

"I have come home, Mrs. Lenoir. Let me put your mind at ease. You have no more to fear from me, and my comrades, today than you did before this revolution. I think I speak for my commander."

A tall officer of about 29 or 30 beside Colonel Byrd nodded politely and smiled. How did Colonel Sanders look to her? Handsome? Ugly? She didn't notice how he looked.

They rode on a little piece opposite the house, dismounted, and went inside the store and post office building.

Henrietta remembered that B.B. had opened the safe that morning—the key was still in its door. Without hesitation, she walked across the road to the store. She avoided Colonel Byrd and his commanding officer, and trusted her bonnet to conceal her face from my other soldiers native to this area who might recognize her.

Unrecognized, unmolested, she moved among the enemy, the first she had ever seen, and went directly to the safe, removed large parcels of money from the open shelves, tucked them in the bend of her thin arm, and in one motion as she rose, slipped two hanks of yarn from an open bale that set beside the safe over her arm. Passing out of the store, she was a quiet, contained storm of emotional energy. She crossed the great road faintly aware of Confederate soldiers under guard around a tree, passed through her back gate, passed some cavalry men decorously sprawled on her lawn, strode through the house out onto the front porch and down into the garden by the railroad tracks, where she deposited the money under the flowering rhododendron hedge. I impute to her my own reflection that even before Doctor Ramsey could get to Knoxville and transport the assets of the Bank of Tennessee and the Confederate Treasury beyond Yankee capture, even before his train reached Concord, his daughter had rescued the proceeds of her own family business.

As she walked up to the front porch (the front of the house faced the railroad, but long before the railroad came four years ago, the house was built to face Lenoir, North Carolina, where her husband's father, William Ballard Lenoir, the first, had built the first version of this house) she realized that not only had she not been the victim of monstrous Yankee atrocities, such as her men had long taught her to expect, but that no one had said more than a few words to her. Though she knew some had looked at her, covertly, it was as if she had been invisible, or they had been shadows of her imagination.

Looking out her parlor window, she saw that they were as real as the silver.

The small Confederate force that had left Lenoir to meet the Yankees on the Kingston Road last night was now captive there under her trees, some of them wounded, being attended to by her husband and others.

The young Yankee commander of the cavalry raiders stood in the road absently brushing dust from his sleeves, looking at her. A thrill rushed over her as the certainty that he knew what she had done struck her.

So General Sanders is real to her. But why is *she* more real to me than *he* is? Knowing from examining my own experience that the reader's imagination is not obliged to hew to the writing, I wonder if he is more real to *you*, reading, than he is now as I write. For me, he is a being struggling to get born.

I know that he made a terse, one-sentence report on his mission, when he got back into Kentucky; maybe, as is also the general procedure, a second brief report to Burnside. A few weeks later would have to come a fuller report, an actual copy of which is now being processed in Washington as part of a project that began in 1864, the first volumes of which will be published, we are told, in about 1888. Until then . . . I imagine . . .

Lexington, Ky.
July 26, 1863

General: I have the honor to report that, in obedience to special instructions from the General, I left Mount Vernon, Kentucky, June 14, 1863, with a force of 1,500 mounted men, composed of detachments of different regiments, for the East Tennessee and Virginia railroad. From Mount Vernon to Williamsburg, on the Cumberland River, a distance of 60 miles, a train of wagons containing forage and subsistence stores accompanied the expedition.

From this point, I followed the Marsh Creek road to near Huntsville, Tennessee, leaving that place a few miles to my left. On the evening of the 17th, we reached the vicinity of Montgomery, Tennessee (Morgan Court House on some maps). When I learned that a small party of Rebels were stationed one mile from Montgomery at Wartburg, I sent 400 men from the First East Tennessee to surprise and capture them.

An hour later, I followed with the remainder of the command. The surprise was complete, except for a small portion of this command, who were with their horses some distance from camp; they escaped and gave the first notice of our approach at Knoxville, Kingston, Loudon, and other places. We captured at Wartburg 102 enlisted men and 2 officers (one of them an aide to

General Pegram), together with a large number of horses, 60 boxes of artillery ammunition, several thousand pounds of salt, meal, flour, bacon, some corn, 500 spades, 100 picks, besides a large quantity of other public stores, and 6 wagons with mule teams. I paroled the prisoners and destroyed the property.

From this point, I marched toward Kingston. When within 8 miles of that place, I learned that Scott's brigade and one battery guarded the ford of Clinch River there. For this reason, leaving Kingston to my right, I crossed the river at Waller's Ford eight miles above, which is on the direct road to Loudon.

At daylight on the 19th, I was three miles equidistant between Loudon and Lenoir's. Here I learned that a force of three regiments was at the Loudon Bridge, with eight pieces of artillery, and that the Rebels had been digging rifle-pits, ditches, etc., at that place for two weeks. A captured courier of the commanding officer carried dispatches ordering the forces from Kingston to follow in my rear; the order states that the troops from Lenoir's had already been ordered to join them. I determined on this intelligence to avoid Loudon, and started immediately for Lenoir's Station, which place I reached about 8 a.m., some thirty minutes after the Rebel troops had departed. (Does the fact he makes no mention of Henrietta make this a false report?) At this station I captured a detachment of artillerymen, with three 6-pounder iron guns, 8 officers, and 57 enlisted men. Burned the depot, a large brick building, which contained five pieces of artillery, harness and saddles, two thousand five hundred stand of small-arms, large amount of artillery and musket ammunition, artillery and cavalry equipments. We also captured some 75 Confederate States mules and horses.

There was a large cotton factory owned by Dr. Lenoir and a large amount of cotton at this place, but I ordered that it should not be burned, as it furnished the Union citizens of the surrounding country with their only material for making cloth, but have since learned that it was burned by mistake or accidentally.

From Lenoir Station to Knoxville, 22 miles east, I had the telegraph wire cut and the railroad destroyed at points about 1 mile apart. (He comes in from the West along Kingston Road. Through the scope of my sharpshooter's rifle, I look down on him from the tower, even though on that occasion I was far from the tower, with no conception of it or of him. That evening at dusk, the Confederate pickets were waiting for him on the hill down from Bleak House, across the road.) At about 7 p.m. we met the enemy's pickets at Knoxville and drove them to within a mile of the city.

As soon as it was full dark, I left a portion of the First Kentucky Cavalry on this side of town and moved the rest of the command by another road entirely around to the other side, driving in the pickets at several places. To prevent the sending of troops to the bridges above, I cut the railroad. At day light, on the Tazewell road, I moved up to the city. I found the enemy well-posted on the heights and in the adjacent buildings, with eight or nine pieces of artillery. The enemy had protected the batteries and barricaded the streets with cotton bales. Their force was estimated at 3,000, including citizens who were impressed into service. After about one hour's skirmishing, I withdrew. Just east of the city, I captured two pieces of artillery and all the camp equipage of a regiment of conscripts who had joined the defending force in the city, and about 80 horses and 31 prisoners.

I then started for Strawberry Plains, following the railroad. I destroyed all the small bridges and depots to within 4 miles. At Flat Creek I burned a finely built covered bridge and also a county bridge. The guard had retreated. Three miles below Strawberry Plains, I left the railroad and crossed the Holston River, so as to attack the bridge on the same side the enemy were.

As soon as we came in sight, they opened on the advance with four pieces of artillery. I dismounted the infantry and sent the Forty-fourth Ohio, under Major Moore, up the river, and the rest, under Colonel Byrd and Major Dow, to get in their rear. After about an hour's skirmishing, the enemy were driven off, and having a train and locomotive, with steam up, in waiting, a portion of them escaped, leaving all their guns (five), 137 enlisted men and 2 officers as prisoners, a vast amount of stores, equipage and ammunition, in our possession. I remained at this place all night, and destroyed the splendid bridge over the Holston River, over 1,600 feet long, built on eleven piers. The trestle-work included, this bridge was 2,100 feet in length, the most important on the East Tennessee and Virginia line.

At daylight on the 21st of June I started up the railroad for Mossy Creek, New Market, and vicinity. I captured 120 prisoners and destroyed several cars and a large quantity of stores, I burned the fine bridge at Mossy Creek, over 300 feet long. Near this place I also destroyed the machinery of a gun factory and a saltpeter factory.

As I knew the enemy was making every effort to capture my command, I determined to leave the railroad here and endeavor to cross the mountains at Roger's Gap. Fording the Holston at Hayworth's Bend, I started for the Powder Springs Gap of Clinch Mountain. Here a large force opposed me directly in my front, and another strong force overtook and commenced skirmishing with my rear guard. But with all this force in my rear, I took country roads and got into the gap. A mile and half from Roger's Gap, I found that it was blockaded by fallen timber and strongly guarded by artillery and infantry. All the other practical Gaps were obstructed and guarded in a similar manner.

I determined to destroy and abandon my artillery and move by a wood path to Smith's Gap, 3 miles from Rogers' Gap. I now opposed a large force both in front and rear and could avoid capture only by getting into the mountains, placing all of them in my rear. After driving a regiment of cavalry from Smith's Gap, I was able to execute my plan. The road through this pass is only a bridle-path, and very rough. I did not get up the mountain until after night. About 170 of my men and officers got on the wrong road and did not join the command until we reached Kentucky.

Owing to the continued march, many horses gave out and were left, and although we captured several hundred on the march, there were not enough to supply all the men. We reached Boston, Kentucky, on the 24th. Our loss was 2 killed, 4 wounded, and 13 missing, several drowned. I enclose an abstract of these. I also enclose the parole of 461 prisoners.

Colonel William Price Sanders

Missing from the report would be the fact that he sent to Major Haynes, commanding at Knoxville in the absence of General Buckner, by a Lieutenant Luttrell, a paroled prisoner, this note: "I send you my compliments, and say that but for the admirable manner with which you managed your artillery I would have taken Knoxville today."

For Colonel Sanders, soon promoted to General, was a Southerner, born in Frankfort, Kentucky, raised in Natchez, Mississippi, a cousin of Jefferson Davis, who had interceded when Cadet Sanders was about to be dismissed in 1853 from West Point for deficiency in language. Had it not been for his cousin's devotion, he would not have graduated and gone on the Utah expedition, defended Washington against his own people, served on the Peninsula at Yorktown and Williamsburg, and at Mechanicsville and Hanover Courthouse, putting his cousin's capital in jeopardy, made a raid into Knoxville and invaded East Tennessee with Burnside, and ridden a white horse on the Kingston Road within view of the windows of Bleak House's tower.

Autumn 1863

Mrs. Lenoir's face was not at the window, but that made General Sanders see all the more lucidly, made him feel her presence fill the house, giving him a sense of all its rooms simultaneously.

Most of the trees within sight were stumps now, cut down, and buildings dismantled for firewood and to erect villas of cabins in the fertile fields. The black ruins of the cotton factory. He had been the first to use her property, but only for resting his men. Other officers, General Shackleford most recently, had come after him, had established headquarters in Doctor Lenoir's office. Two brigades, usually, at a given time, were camped on the place. The officer's tents were pitched in the yard and gardens around the house.

As he instructed his officers, he placed himself in view of the windows that faced the road, hoping she would see him.

Finally, he sent Captain Brill to ask Dr. Lenoir to prepare a room for him in the house. The Captain returned 15 minutes later to inform him that the Lenoirs were ready to receive him, that supper was on the table.

Doctor Lenoir greeted him at the door and showed him into the dining room, and introduced him to Mrs. J. G. M. Ramsey, wife of the historian of Tennessee, to Elizabeth Breck, his widowed daughter, to Susan Ramsey, to young Arthur Ramsey, saying that the babe in Mrs. Breck's arms was his youngest child. One chair was empty. "Is Mrs. Lenoir not joining us?"

"She is ill. She hasn't come to the table in several weeks. We lost two of our boys in a single night to fever."

"I am very sorry to hear that, sir."

"Is there anything I can do for you, Mrs. Ramsey?" he asked.

"Mother, why don't you ask General Sanders," said Susan, "if he would rebuild our house at Mecklenburg and restore from the ashes father's books and research material for his sequel to *The Annals of Tennessee*?" Susan turned as much of her back toward him as she could.

"Forgive my daughter, General, for reasons that should be obvious to a cousin of *our* President."

He nodded, and moved his gaze a little over the heads of the family, falling upon the doors as a Negress very gently slid them open, and Henrietta walked very slowly into the room.

General Sanders rose and held her chair. She smelled of crushed lavender and musk, like something put away in an armoire for weeks. He sat down again and looked into her face. Her eyes were full of death-before-death.

The food sickened him, but not because it was bad.

Throughout the meal, he knew that she had come to the table just to sit with him. They were alone together. She hardly *looked* at the others, and she *spoke* to no one.

But young Arthur had looked at her from the moment she came in and he was aware that it was obvious to everyone that he was staring at her, to everyone but Henrietta.

"I miss Sister Charlotte," Arthur murmured, still gazing at Henrietta.

"Charlotte," explained Dr. Lenoir, realizing that all the others were too moved to explain to him, "died early in the War of typhus fever."

"A dutiful daughter," said Mrs. Ramsey, "an affectionate sister, a patriotic and humane girl, a humble Christian."

"Doctor Curry said, 'She bade adieu to Earth's transience, and went to Heaven.'"

"Don't you know," his mother said to Arthur, "it's no more complicated than that?"

Arthur seemed to have caught a glimpse of God's design, how things only *appear* without connection. His brothers were all in the Confederate army, he was not yet seventeen, and had an irrepressible desire to join them and share their fate even though looking at Henrietta, remembering Charlotte, he had sensed for the first time what life came to. He was clearly affectionate and devoted to his mother and sisters. It would be hard to leave them and go into the camps.

"Doctor Curry wrote a beautiful tribute to Charlotte's memory," said Mrs. Breck, "'No one of her age was more highly esteemed, none more cordially loved.'"

"It's made an irreparable chasm in our family," said Mrs. Ramsey, "which amid war is otherwise whole. Henrietta . . . She does not hear me," she said, to *the family*. Henrietta seemed more of Charlotte's company than theirs. "Henrietta." She looked up. "Mind your duty to God to mind your health. You must eat."

Henrietta's faint nod of filial obedience was reassuring to no one.

As each person left the room, General Sanders dreaded the moment when Arthur would rise to go, and he would have to look and speak directly to him. He remembered the story he had heard of General Sherman saying goodbye to his cadets in Alexandria, Louisiana, when word came of Fort Sumter. With tears in his eyes, he had said to them, "I may have to meet you again on the battlefield." He imagined himself on a horse somewhere, caught in this boy's sights, the boy himself fixed in the sights of one of the sharpshooters under his own command—all these assembled here mourning the death of the boy, celebrating his own death. Either was always both victory and defeat, a Janus-faced event.

After a while, after several had excused themselves from the table, he saw that deep inside, beneath the look of death in Mrs. Lenoir's eyes, something came alive and glowed.

Finally, even Doctor Lenoir left the room, and they were literally alone.

"I knew you hid the silver from me that first time we camped here."

She nodded. "I saw in your face, as you looked up at me when I stood at the window, that you knew."

He shared with her the sense of certainty that there was no need to explain why he didn't confiscate the silver, and that both knew it was still there under the rhododendron hedge.

Watching her grow weaker, he said, "I must go to my room, so you can rest."

"Have they told you? That my two boys——"

"Yes. You have surrendered, Mrs. Lenoir," he said, trying to soften the tone of admonishment.

"I am lingering, I am only lingering."

"No one can help you. I see that. And I am very sad."

"I want you to be sad."

"Because I am the enemy?"

"You are not the enemy. There *is* no enemy."

"I must continue to pretend that there is."

"I am sorry that you must."

"How did you and I come to be sitting here like this?"

"For me, there is only the *question*. Do you have an *answer*?"

"No."

General Sanders rose.

Henrietta looked up at him. "Goodbye, General Sanders."

"Goodbye, Mrs. Lenoir."

Lying on the bed that had belonged, Doctor Lenoir had told him, "To my Grandfather," the bed that the Negress, who seemed paralyzed between devotion to the family to which she was enslaved and devotion to an abstract ideal of freedom that her own grandfather had perhaps known but that she had perhaps not known, told him Doctor Ramsey always slept in when he stayed at Lenoir's, he imagined how the old historian must have felt lying here the night his daughter had told him about how the raiders had passed her house on the morning of 19th of June, how she had concealed the silver from the store safe under her shawl. His daughter had acted the lady and the heroine, and Doctor Ramsey had gone to sleep here very proud of her. The old historian had lain here again in fitful sleep, he imagined, when he visited more recently, more in danger of capture by his enemies, and seen her contrasting mood all the more vividly: sad, disconsolate, uneasy about the situation, anxious about the exposure of the family at Mecklenburg, about the exposure of her own family here at Lenoir's. Dejected, she must have conveyed a sense of how she felt, an ominous presentiment of future disaster and of cause for overwhelming bereavement. Voicing none of it. The old historian being able plainly to discern what she apprehended and felt. So that he had lingered with her until the hour grew late, then gotten up the next morning to ride across his favorite bridge with his son, the last to cross before they had to burn it. Not knowing how efficiently Orlando Poe could on that site put out his pontoon bridge.

The General became aware of his own heavy breathing, and gradually of the breathing of all those asleep in the house, except Henrietta's, for the house itself seemed only an *image* in *her* mind, transfixed but palpitating in a prolonged fever of dying.

Willis Carr

The Incendiary at the Forks of the River

"Can you tell me the way to Mecklenburg?" the Yankee soldier asked a man on Gay Street in front of the Lamar House.

"Why do you want to know?"

"You aren't a Rebel, are you?"

"First, may I ask what *you* are?"

"My uniform tells my story."

"Only to the naked eye, not what might be beneath."

"Then you aren't going to tell me? I only want to deliver a message."

"From friend or foe?"

"Neutral."

"A Frenchman, then?"

"You aren't going to tell me, are you? I will ask someone else."

"No, it's just that Doctor Ramsey has friends on both sides. There's nobody out there to deliver a message to. It's deserted."

"Where?"

"At the Forks on the River."

"Upstream or downstream?"

The man pointed upstream.

"Thank you . . . In Michigan, you *ask* in one word and are *told* in one word."

"Michigan ain't far, if you get an early start."

The soldier found a road going in the direction of the citizen's pointed finger and followed it across a bridge over a creek, up a hill, past a church, and on out along a bluff into the country, hearing over and over Parson Brownlow's answer to his, "What must I do?" after his oration in Pike's Opera House. "What must you *do*? My friend, when Burnside gets you to Knoxville, burn the house belonging to that vain old historian, Ramsey, at Mecklenburg in the forks of the Holston and the French Broad Rivers . . . I say, Ramsey, Mecklenburg, the forks of the river. Yes. Ramsey, Mecklenburg, the forks."

Ramsey, Mecklenburg, the forks of the river, Fighting Parson Brownlow's voice, his face looking back over his shoulder, chanted in the soldier's head as he executed his solitary march.

Under a bluff on which stood a mansion, he looked out at the forks of two rivers that made the Tennessee River that flowed past Knoxville. He saw a ferry, an old station, a mound, and a large house on a slope, above which set a church and a graveyard, and behind it, another bluff with outcroppings of rock, like marble.

"Ramsey, Mecklenburg, the forks of the river. Okay. This is it," he said aloud, now that he was alone, having been in the middle of a moving army since that night in Pike's Opera House in Cincinnati in 1862. He had done nothing in battle. This was something he could do, and now, wading into the river, *wanted* to do, the matches clenched between his teeth.

People were out, here and there, coming and going, or sitting, or out in skiffs on the rivers, and the ferryman was at work.

The ferry was not necessary. *He* was the Union army, all of it, and General Burnside and President Lincoln, too, concentrated in him, their representative, and Fighting Parson Brownlow's, even John Brown's. He was a *messenger* in whom the words—he liked words, he admired the Parson, but he hated to have to *use* words, reading, writing, or speaking—and the weapons—he liked the noise and the shattering, but hated to use the rifles, the bullets, the bayonets, and, when he could bring it off, didn't—were fused together.

The matches between his clenched teeth were his own personal representatives. He wished he could do it with his breath alone: Blow on wood, inhale the smoke, step back from the first combustion and watch the flames spread the Parson's message to Doctor Ramsey, "that vain old historian at the Forks of the River."

Drenched in the river water, dripping, slogging, smelling of the river, he started up the bank, gritting his teeth as he had done a thousand times against the sunglare that only an infantryman feels.

As he gathered dry brush and piled it on the porch of the big house, he realized that he was attracting the attention of Ramsey's neighbors, all of whom would be Unionists and as eager to see it as he was to have it *done*. A promise he had made, an obligation he was discharging.

As he struck a match and put it to the brush, the people who had gathered broke into the house through every window and door almost at once, and before the smoke got to the nostrils, he caught the wafting smell of a shut-up house, mingled with a smell he only later, as they came out hauling the stuff, knew was old books.

So that when he put the "torch of the incendiary" to the smaller house by the mound, that he heard someone call "the old Indian Mount," he recognized the smell of old books as soon as someone kicked open the door where he squatted, blowing at the smoke to get fire.

"He's going to the smokehouse!"

"He's going to the cribs!"

"He's going to the barns!" they yelled, each time he moved on, until they ran there before him, then waited for him to catch up, in his slow, deliberate walk, not speaking to any of them.

He had not come to loot. They did not offer him anything, as if they thought he had been sent by order, to make available to this neighborhood the goods of Rebels who had fled. He was, he knew he *looked*, brisk, efficient, deliberate, resolute. He had never burned anything in his life that was not meant to cook his food or warm his body.

This fire, these fires, were drying his river-wet uniform, and as he stepped back from the final building, he realized he was dry, and getting hot.

He walked back down to the ferry crossing. He had earned a crossing.

"It's mine now," said the ferryman, pointing at the ferry underfoot. "Ramsey went off and left it."

Another man, who must have been visiting on this side, sat on some books and some strange objects, relics perhaps, that seemed to have survived another time, another world, grinning, "I can sell them in town to the Yankees. They'll buy anything that's a souvenir." He tried to sell some to the Incendiary.

As the ferry reached the middle of the river where the currents of the two rivers mingled and thrust the larger river towards Knoxville, the Incendiary looked up at the bluff: Three women stood at a fence, a mansion behind, looking down on the burning place. Perhaps they were the "vain old historian's" relatives. Now that he had delivered the message he had carried for almost two years, he felt like a new person, inclined to indulge in curiosity.

He camped on the Knoxville side above the ferry slip, among the trees, up under the rocks on the bluff where he had left his knapsack and more matches.

Early next morning, a woman's clear voice, close by, calling to the ferryman to wake him up, woke the Incendiary. He saw a young woman, obviously imitating the way her big brother would call to or whistle for the ferryman. Standing with her on the bank were an older woman and two women closer to her age. The four women carried empty baskets and a blanket. He could discern by the set of their backs that they had seen him sleeping, and were rigidly ignoring him. That was not a good feeling. He wished they would look at him.

"Hey! Ladies!" He felt as if he were a bothersome fly they were ignoring, as if they were at prayer. The ferry was crossing towards them.

After they had stepped onto the ferry, he went down towards them, kicking rocks to draw attention, and they all turned at once and looked up the slope at the Incendiary, and he looked down at his feet. He scarcely saw the ferry push off to go over to Mecklenburg.

When the four men walked up the slope on the other bank, past the station at the Indian Mount, he got down to the river, and watched them pick among the smoking ruins, and as they hauled what they had salvaged, the young one leading a horse, back down to the ferry, where the ferryman stood, arms crossed, legs spread defiantly, tugging at his beard, the Incendiary said to himself, "How do you know I won't climb this bluff and burn your other mansion on this side?"

He repeated that, yelling it across, for them. They ignored him.

As the ferry headed back, he imagined meeting the youngest lady face to face, mounted on her horse.

The Incendiary got back on the road and headed for Knoxville, for Gay Street, to return to his place in Burnside's "Wandering Corps."

By Willis Carr

Fragments Found on the Field

Parson Brownlow and Dr. James Gettys Ramsey

Started February 1, 1893
Still on Holston Mountain

These sketches and memoirs that I have been writing over the past twenty years are inert fragments lying around the cabin, waiting to be assembled. Having read them over, I now want these fragments to go together in some way

I am 45 and have a sense that it is all ending now. Many men are long dead.

Later, I will work on them, make them go together.

(1927, 34 years later: I never did this. What I know now, feel, think, imagine—I would like to write a book now. But it's too late. I once started to write "A Boy's History of the Civil War" by a Boy Sharpshooter, anonymous, but gave it up.)

Long, long ago, an editor down at the Elizabethton newspaper said, "Mr. Carr, why don't you write that book I keep hearing about?"

I said I would, one of these days.

He said, "You're already 50."

I said, no, 40.

"What keeps you from it?"

I said, "It has to be put together just the way they want it, like all the others, and I can't get interested in that."

"Like what?"

"Like putting in the love element, as they call it. I never had any. I mean *book* romance. Somebody once said that the women of Carter County are ugly beyond human conception. Maybe so. I don't compare. I'm not in a position to, looking myself like a cross between Parson Brownlow and Edwin

Booth—when I was young. I'm grateful for the ones that do take up with me around here. Always have been ones that will. But that ain't a love element," I told him.

Folks back in those days, on august occasions, were very fond of the phrase "The Right Man at the Right Time in the Right Place"—they said that of Jefferson Davis and later of Lincoln. Brownlow even said that of Military Governor Andrew Johnson when the parson arrived in Nashville, and when he became Governor himself, folks said Brownlow was "the Wrong Man in the Wrong Place at the Wrong Time." Scaled down to myself, a commoner, how might that phrase, and on what occasions, apply?

If you understood the words you live and mayhap die by, doesn't that make your experience different from that of folks who know the words a different way? "Sharpshooter," for instance. "Civil War." Others.

As I align my right eye, my sights, with General Sanders' heart, I cast light upon him, for is not the light of the body the eye? I fire. But my eye is creative. Thus, I think in images. And as I write, "Words become one with things," so sayeth Emerson. Having made words one with things, I think in images, more lucidly.

In the beginning were the words. Out of the words, the War. The battles are over and lost, but the words, though spoken, are also printed, and remain.

So much has been said and written about the War, I am stuck dumb. "What you have received as an inheritance from your fathers," we learn from Goethe, "you must possess again in order to make it your own."

As I read a veteran's memoir, I hear his voice distinctly. "Speak," I say to the book. "I'm listening." What I want, sometimes expect, but less and less often hope to hear, is a voice that will not just tell me what happened, for now I know it is all a blend of facts and illusions, willful and involuntary falsehoods, but some unexpected way of looking at that time—a voice shedding its light.

I own no books, except *Pilgrim's Progress*, *The Works of Milton*, *The Works of Shakespeare*, *Robinson Crusoe*, *Parson Brownlow's Book*, and *The Bible*. For other books, I am a patron of public libraries, hither and yon I borrow from the Lawson McGhee Library in Knoxville that Judge Oliver Temple and the Reverend Thomas Humes—both historians—in concert with others set up in 1886. It's a long trip, so sometimes I have to pay fines for tardy returns. And some few I borrow from Washington College at Limestone and a few from the obliging powers down about Elizabethton—the Carters, the Taylors, and the Stovers.

I have read now all those books about Tennessee that our historian Doctor James Gettys Ramsey read, by Timberlake, Adair, Judge Haywood, Putnam, Lyman Draper, Breazeale, and John Carr (I *am*, or was, or will be each of those men). And I have read Doctor Ramsey's book, and now I am making a book. Another god-damned book. To recapture, to redeem. (But never to vindicate.)

I keep going back to Adair's *History of the American Indians*, of 1775. It's not so much for his history of the American Indians—from which all tribes are missing except those of the Southeast which he actually knew—but for the 200 pages (half the book) in which he advances 23 arguments for the Indian tribes having descended from the Hebrew tribes that I read him.

All that I read again and again, as romance. But I see with some force that in following another man's romantic obsession as he argues for its actuality, the facts he enlists come clearer than if I had gotten them straight, undiluted by romantic vision, and that I am simultaneously transported as no blatant romance in itself has ever done.

Where do *my* fragments fit in? A contribution or a distraction?

The historian plunges into the unknown, sometimes the bizarre, because what is unknown and bizarre attracts him, but then all his effort are to domesticate it. Too many historians have the minds of public accountants. Knowing the end of each episode, the historian, no less than the fictioneer, pretends, thus distorts, while claiming objectivity. History, as I read it on the mountain, is replete with splendid irrelevancies and unactualized possibilities.

It is strange—how can it ever be familiar?—to stand in a library on your own two feet and face one hundred and twenty eight volumes of *War of the Rebellion: Official Records* and realize that all of it is *there*, there it all is, what the War generated, day by day, but no one man had it all at his command, not even Lincoln, certainly not the generals, most of them dead before the first five volumes appeared in 1880, even more absolutely not the soldier in the ranks, few of whom live today to gaze upon the row on row of thick tomes. More volumes came out in 1890–1891 and the rest will come out in 1901, complete. The official facts—even so, too many wrong, distorted, unverifiable, some adrift, like smoke thinning over a battlefield.

But there we had it at last, and the impact of those 128 volumes was to shatter many memoirs as basic authorities for historians. The editors had omnipotence when they commenced to hand us the day's mail, for each day, enabling us to hear the voices of the officers and statesmen (Reverend William Blount Carter's, Doctor Ramsey's, Parson Brownlow's, General Sanders'—though not Cherokee's, the slave I shot, not mine) as God heard them, to see the War day by day as God saw it. But they willed to give it all to us in pigeon-holes, departments, compartments, according to campaigns, battles, et cetera, and then the historians come along and put all that stuff in their own departments and compartments.

When I can get my hands on them, I roam through them, and I want to read each of those 128 volumes, I am indeed mesmerized, but I always leave them with a feeling of profound dissatisfaction that soon turns to melancholy. They are a melancholy necessity.

Brownlow's newspapers, books, diary, letters, and Ramsey's history, autobiography, and letters, among with my own scraps, fragments, and sketches, are talking leaves, making rustling sounds that conjure echoes and images of Sequoyah, the silversmith-wordsmith, lost in Mexico, and Cherokee, reading his Phoenix newspaper in Cherokee language in the sun on the dead-line at Andersonville.

I tried to meet Parson Brownlow (the prison encounter doesn't count). I tried to meet Doctor Ramsey.

Then I got to where I did not want to anymore. Fear, I reckon. Then it was too late. One morning in 1877, Parson Brownlow supervised repair on his back porch on East Cumberland and lay down to rest and never got up. He died April 29, at the age of 72. Seven years later, in 1884, Doctor Ramsey, at New Mecklenburg, a few blocks above Brownlow on East Main Street, died on April 11, at the age of 87, from "advanced age, together with injuries he received by being thrown from a horse some ten years ago." "Too late" is a phrase I hear more and more often.

Doctor Ramsey is buried where he planned to be, and ought to be, among his family, in the cemetery of the church of Lebanon in the Forks, and Brownlow is buried ambiguously in Old Gray Cemetery, where lies Ramsey's son Crozier, arch enemy of Brownlow, and perhaps a few other Confederate soldiers.

Came in a dream last night, this phrase, which I will simply set down: "Whereas whistling is darkness made visible, death is . . . "

That interests me, how people you never meet affect you, as much as, perhaps more than, the soldiers you clashed with on the Sunken Road, in the Bloody Angle, in the Hornet's Nest, on the ice-slick slopes of Fort Sanders. Davis and

Lincoln obviously. Generals Lee and Grant, obviously. General Longstreet and General Sanders. But what about all the others? They all determine who you were. But only if one day you come to know it, before it really is too late. Doesn't it amaze you that General Lee, who knew Generals Stonewall Jackson, Jeb Stuart, and Old Pete Longstreet, and "Little Powell" Hill, would answer the question, "Who was the greatest soldier in the Southern Army?" by saying. "A man I have never seen. His name is Forrest."

I can see clearly in my thinking, if not my life, the hand of Brownlow the journalist, of Doctor Ramsey the Historian, of Sequoyah the language-maker, of Brownlow the Orator.

Something in me leaned toward Brownlow and his newspaper shop, and then when I began to hear about Doctor Ramsey, something in me leaned toward Mecklenburg, Lebanon in the Forks. The Carter County bridge burners led me to Brownlow, the Fighting Parson. I discovered Ramsey gradually, as I went along, and as I began to piece my own life together, I inclined toward "the vain old historian," Ramsey before 1845, of that Golden Age, 1815–1845, before the Mexican War. But his other roles stirred my imagination too: farmer, banker, railroad man, doctor, wandering treasurer of the Confederacy.

Parson Brownlow and Doctor Ramsey walked toward me on Gay Street as grandfathers, and as I grew older, they became fathers, and then they died—"when the father dies the son becomes mortal"—and so they, both now long dead, will one day in the future be my brothers.

I am, like Orlando Poe and Jedediah Hotchkiss, a Map-Maker, like Bernard and Gardner and O'Sullivan, a photographer, like Alfred Waud and Winslow Homer, an artist. All Yankees.

That it was a young man's war seems to interest people, though we who were very young then understood so little of how the old folks got us into it. People like to point at the youngest soldier wounded or killed, and you can see them pictured in Miller's *The Photographic History of the Civil War* and hear them set to verse or song here and there.

The Old Men sow seeds that the young men reap in war. (1927: I have seen it since, in 1898, the Spanish-American War, and in 1914, the Great World War.)

Doctor Ramsey and Parson Brownlow moved up and down Gay Street like two planets. Knoxville was the hub of Brownlow's newspaper and Ramsey's banking ventures. Ramsey and Brownlow exemplify polar opposite traits in the divided character of East Tennesseans. Someday, I will show you exactly what I mean.

This image haunts Ramsey: his great-grandmother on his father's side was washed overboard and lost when she and her husband sailed for America from Scotland. No image haunts Brownlow.

I have meditated on words: on writings about the War, on books in general, on my own writings as re-read and as in progress. Reckon they will let me read out all I have written here to them between the speeches of the Generals? I missed the Fort Sanders reunion of 1890 at Knoxville and the one at Bethel Cemetery in Knoxville this year. But somewhere, there will be another one, soon.

As I read the Civil War memoirs, I look for a passage, a line, a footnote that sparks me as I was, or *maybe* was, or may have been. Survivors, marching without direction back and forth over these fields of print. These books are reunions and memorials.

North and South, like Brownlow and Ramsey, cite the same passages from the Bible, as if God were glib. Walking the mountain at twilight, they might hear God's voice, very faintly, "I am not what you think I am."

In uses of God's Word, this War between brothers was a gang rape of God.

In my own vision, Brownlow the fire-eater started out as Lucifer, while Ramsey the old Southern Gentleman, started out as Christ. Came a time when I began to see how their qualities were mixed.

Ramsey and Brownlow each in his own way strove to put death in its Place. Ramsey felt certain he lived in a place. Brownlow lived only in his description of a place. (Home, Knoxville, the Union.) He *was* the descriptions he cast out to the public. He existed in what *seemed*. He fabricated the world. Ramsey looked upon the world as a thing already made, by God. The War stripped away the placeness of Ramsey's life, but Brownlow, whose place was the creation of his own seemings and his own descriptions, was unchanged; peace and war to Brownlow were of the same process, with only word distinctions.

For Ramsey, Christ was alive in every moment, in all life's forms, rituals, offices, relations, family, et cetera. He is continuously there. For Brownlow, Christ was alive only when spoken of—he is newly risen from the dead in the Word spoken. The Word proves he has risen.

Ramsey sees manifestations of God, and in the work of his own hand feels the presence of God. Brownlow feels God only in his own mouth and in his own ear, magnified by other ears hearing him, or by hearing other mouths like his own.

Place, and life in it, ceases to be mundane for Brownlow during moments of fiery speech. For Ramsey, place, and life in it, is always momentous.

For Ramsey, the body of Christ and of history is *there* and language describes it, but for Brownlow until words are spoken, turning words into body, there is no body. That is why meditation on the made-world is Ramsey's mode, while constant speaking is Brownlow's.

Brownlow thinks he can talk his way out of being an animal. Ramsey's meditation tells him that he has never been an animal.

Both men fail repeatedly, but try again, condemned to create.

The god-like Generals were often petty. But so were the Greek Gods. Wasn't that part of their appeal? That they raised "life" to a higher plane? A petty God is higher than a petty mortal.

Good is the ambience of all human action. Evil exists only *in* isolated acts of good.

God is simultaneously the infinite extension of the finite, the finite inversion of the infinite. God is the infinite finite. Everywhere I walk on this mountain, I see evidence of that.

Cherokee, sometimes I wish you had never taught me to read and write, so that I would be forced to draw pictures.

I could capture it all best, image and emotion and idea, in Chinese ideograms, but you can't read them, and I can't draw them. Still, it's the primacy of the image.

Parson Brownlow was like John Randolph, in a backwoods way, totally individualist, Davy Crockett, a braggart always ready to go, Mike Fink, folk hero, Sut Lovingood, the wise rube, Lincoln, the folksy President, Andrew Johnson, the combative President, St. John, "the Word made flesh."

Doctor Ramsey was like General Lee, the gentleman bound to duty, Calhoun, the defender of states' rights, St. Paul, the thought is the same as the deed, Job, the sufferer of great calamities, modified by the Presbyterian injunction not to murmur.

I see in Brownlow's life a demonstration of the destiny of Western Man, who is condemned to respond to objects. I feel the pathos of strictly utilitarian objects that are still useful but remain unused: A bridge. A church. A graveyard.

A furnace. A hammer. A flute. Brownlow at 72. A locomotive. A photo negative. A telescopic lens, detached.

In half sleep came the phrase "a Separational Unity." Does that phrase describe the relation of North and South from the start?

What does that mean—the shoe is on the other foot? Is anything ever really alien? I read somewhere that every left-handed person lost a twin in the womb, and that the twin was absorbed into the mother, leaving an empty sack. Ramsey and Brownlow—did one of them *almost* stay enwombed?

I have made a list of the histories of the War that I intend to find and read, and beside the ones that sound the best, I have made a cross mark.

+ *Battles and Leaders*, 1887
+ Alfred I. Bledsoe, *Is Davis a Traitor?* 1866
Jefferson Davis, *The Rise and Fall of the Confederate Government*, 1881

Some biographies:

+ John J. Craven, *The Prison Life of Jefferson Davis*, 1866
R. L. Dabney, *Life and Campaigns of Lieutenant General Thomas J. Jackson*, 1866
H. B. McClellan, *The Life and Campaigns of J. E. B. Stuart*, 1885

Autobiographies of Generals and Privates now get into the act:

John B. Hood, *Advance and Retreat*, 1880
+ Basil Duke, *History of Morgan's Calvary*, 1866
Joseph E. Johnston, *Narrative of Military Operations*, 1874
+ J. B. Jones, *A Rebel War Clerk's Diary*, 1866
+ Sam R. Watkins, *"Co. Aytch,"* or *A Side Show of the Big Show*
+ Phoebe Pember, *A Southern Woman's Story*, 1879
+ Belle Boyd, *In Camp and Prison*, 1865
John Esten Cooke, *Wearing of the Gray*, 1867
J. William Jones, *Christ in the Camp*, 1888
J. Thomas Scharf, *History of the Confederate States Navy*, 1887 (I missed that part totally)

Can you simultaneously think of a chair as molecules—though that was not possible before 1811—*and* sit on it? History is land-locked water in which I am a sponge. History is the dialectic of the living and the dead. Count the votes of the dead at unwatched polling places. Do I have, among all these fragments the years have left behind, a synthesis?

The historical self is mere chance. In the re-creation of others, I become my-self. The personal rots. I am what survives me. To act is to witness, to witness is to act. Then, the emphasis was on the act. Now, the emphasis is on witness-ing. Then and now, I act and witness simultaneously.

I sometimes see the image of the naked body, male not female, why is that? and think of the phrase "the body politic."

This I know: God is in nature and man is made in nature's image. Man is shaped like a five-pointed star: a head, two arms, two legs. The head itself is a star composed of five parts, too: skull, eyes, ears, nose, mouth. Each hand, each foot has five points. Each hand may reach for the stars, even as each foot treads the ground. Star-shaped man simultaneously is also cross-shaped. Man has two of everything: eyes, ears, nostrils, mouth and bung-hole are further apart, two arms, hands, legs, feet, except, only one head, one private. All the elements of nature are alive in man: air, water, earth, fire enter through the mouth, exit through the bung and the dong. Sounds enter, fumes enter, and through the eyes, the windows of the soul, light enters. The anus mimics hell, the heart is emblematic of heaven, the guts are the labyrinth of Crete, and the genitals re-create man even as they excrete man's waste. The right hand is fact, pulls the trigger. The left hand is imagination. We have two opposable thumbs, each of which is a machine, which together make up a super machine. Writing, it seems odd that one thumb must lie useless as the other converts a piece of wood-encased lead into a machine that records the body's own description.

Is slavery an inflammation of the body politic? Cherokee.

When the Confederates occupied Knoxville, Ramsey was influential; when the Union occupied it, he was exiled. The Confederates jailed and exiled Brownlow; the Union made him a powerful administrator.

I see parallel images of their wandering. At different periods, each was on the run: Ramsey on back roads in the mountains and in many cities carrying deposits for the bank of Tennessee and of the Confederacy, on trains, horses, on foot, in wagons. Brownlow is a fugitive in the mountains, then he tours the cities of the North as exile, also gathering (but not, like Ramsey, dispersing) money or the cause, his own cause, his newspaper, so that he can serve the larger cause, the Union, which is another way of serving his personal cause.

Warm-hearted among family and friends, Brownlow made many enemies and engaged in a few street fights and was once ambushed at night. A club wound on his head affected his behavior thereafter. He was fearless and reckless. He once wrote to a friend about attending a religious conference. "Should they not kill me, I will leave for the Convention Thursday next." A friend once asked his advice in dealing with a foe: "Lather him with nitric acid and shave him with a hand saw."

Ramsey never becomes violent, although his soldier sons, especially Robert, do; Brownlow, physically, is seldom violent but his violent utterances and publications incite all kinds of violence. Ramsey does incite violence against Brownlow, and Brownlow against him. They seldom mention each other in public, although Brownlow attacks Ramsey's sons and other relatives; and Ramsey's sons and relatives attack him. Brownlow always carried a pistol and kept one in his desk at the newspaper but never shot a man. He always tried to kill the soul of his enemies with fear; psychological terror made of Tennesseans for four years nervous wrecks. He preached vengeance instead of orderly development. Violence as a community effort becomes an extra community in itself.

Brownlow boasts that he never drank, chewed, smoked, attended theaters or race tracks, that he courted only one woman and "her I married." He was always ready to step forward as a character reference for himself. Brownlow was accused of many crimes but never of personal dishonesty, drunkenness, or licentiousness. "He could express more vituperation and scorching hate than any half a dozen men that ever appeared in American politics," an historian said of him. "The man was a strange compound, and there are no more like him." "In politics, religion, journalism his work and his fame were temporary. He was a product of his times, but his times produced no one like him. His style of journalism passed before he did." He wronged many individuals, "dropped the bitterness of gall into many a cup of happiness," caused many a wreck of hopes and ambition. But some say he had high moral, arid intellectual qualities, though no sense of fitness or taste. Ramsey had innate good taste. If, as some say, a man's character is revealed in his choice of jokes (and his sense of humor), what am I to say of Ramsey, who had one, and of Brownlow, who had none? The comic figure is unshockable.

As polar parts of the body politic, Ramsey inhales life, but Brownlow exhales—an action like birth, like cannon.

Ramsey is a meditative person whose actions are clearly directed and succinctly executed—a man of action in the most civilized sense. Brownlow is an imaginative person who hardly acts at all—his utterances are his acts, like rocks breaking windows. Brownlow is sometimes like a ventriloquist's dummy for which he is his own ventriloquist. When he ruins his voice from too much loud speechifying, someone has to read his speeches while he sits or stands on the platform. In a sense, his newspapers and his books are dummies, through which he speaks, in a style that is more oral than literary. This compulsion of mine to picture things, I share with Brownlow, to reason, I share with Ramsey. Brownlow had a naive wisdom that I sometimes share.

Today I am 46. I have just re-read all these fragments. I have decided to quit making these stabs at the bull's eye. No more. It is over with.

I have made a list of Novels and Romances about the War that I plan to read.

+ = The ones that sound the best

Augusta Evans, *Micaria, or Altars of Sacrifice*, 1864
+ John Townsend Trowbridge, *Cudjo's Cave*, 1864
+ John Esten Cooke, *Surrey of Eagle's Nest, or, The Memoirs of a Staff Officer Serving in Virginia*, 1866
+ Sidney Lanier, *Tiger-lilies*, 1867 (set at Mountvale in the Smokies)
John William De Forrest, *Miss Ravenel's Conversion from Secession to Loyalty*, 1867
+ Albion Winegar Tourgee, *A Fool's Errand by One of the Fools*, 1879
E. P. Roe, *His Sombre Rivals*, 1883
+ Charles Egbert Craddock (really Mary Noailles Murfree of Murfreesboro, a lame spinster), *Where the Battle Was Fought*, 1884
George Washington Cable, *Dr. Sevier*, 1885
Stephen Crane, *The Red Badge of Courage*, 1885
+ Virginius Dabney, *The Story of Don Miff, as Told by His Friend John Bouche Whacker: A Symphony of Life*, 1886
+ Ambrose Bierce, *Tales of Soldiers and Civilians*, 1891
Joel Chandler Harris, *On the Plantation: A Story of a Georgia Boy's Adventures during the War*, 1892

It is the union of memory and reason, controlling emotion, that unites the past and the present, and no book I have read has done that. Facts help to discipline not only the intellect but emotion and imagination, too. It is the public's impassioned memory that transforms facts into myth. We have not developed an image of our public experience in the War because scholars fear the emotions and the imagination, and fiction writers fear the intellect, and each man knows not how to balance emotion and intellect to discipline the imagination. Memoirs and novels are part of the popular ceremonies that unify us as a nation. All this is theory-thinking and theory is cold. But why is my brain-pan smoking?

Oh, yes, the War was *The Iliad* and *The Odyssey* and *The Aeneid*, Homer and Virgil, all over again. Many say so. Often. What the Greeks set in motion can never be still. The patterns, the parallels are all laid out, unalterable, irreversible, predictable. Cassandra was not silent this time either. This time, the slave girl Helen wore deadly blackface. How do you recapture lost times, if you just keep seeing these god-damned parallels to *The Bible*, Old and New Testament, to Homer, to Virgil, to Milton, to plots laid down in old books? And it's only half-finished, over. Like Dickens—to be continued. A man must resist the strong temptation to drift into allegory. Because allegory does not thrive on multiple interpretations. Satire seems inappropriate. The War will not be mocked.

Books get hell from everybody, readers and writers right along with illiterates. Schools and books lose out to the college of hard knocks. But by now most of the War is only in books, "eyewitlesses," and imaginary accounts, and in the memories of survivors, most of whom are in their 50s. But most memories are inaccessible, even now. And what happens when us veterans are all dead? Then it's all romances—the repetition of stories veterans told, and of books before and to come. If fragments of facts and romantic vapors are all that are left, the War is missing, or seen in fits and starts, epileptically.

I'm the last of the Willises, so when I go down, these fragments are all that's left—and maybe glimpses of me in books by other men I know not of.

I set down here words that came in a dream: "The first to declare no clear air marked your word."

For Ramsey, first the deed, then the Word. He writes the fragments of his autobiography five years after the events of the War. One senses his classical training. His narrative is full of incident but immersed in meditation. Brownlow's words, spoken in debate or written, are his deeds—thus he writes his first autobiography when he is 37, and writes two more during the War, in all three instances attached to polemics on religious or political issues and always made up of fragments of previous writings. I see the influence of backwoods evangelical rhetoric combined with flowery Elizabethan and Miltonic style, and the influence of stump politics and yellow journalism. His narratives lack incident except to illustrate issues, and is immersed in epithets. Ramsey writes in the tradition of Homer and the Bible—to pay homage to ancestors and provide continuity for those who come after him.

The Civil War action was a kind of violent rhetoric, but after the War, it was rhetoric that made it real to both participants and nonparticipants. Since the masters Aristotle and Cicero formulated the methods, four notions of rhetoric have evolved. The public concept is that the purpose of rhetoric, as in Brownlow's use of it, is to obscure reality. That, of course, is bad rhetoric. Ramsey would say that good rhetoric reveals or reflects reality.

Rhetoric is an essential art, for it can change minds and thus change reality through the techniques of persuasion, mutual inquiry (forensic); it can change our sense of past, present, and future. We must distinguish among the kinds of things rhetoric makes. The future is made in how we talk about it now. Rhetoric can be like bullets, determining who lives, who dies. There is practical, pragmatic discourse to deal with realities.

Ramsey is a private person duty-bound to public service, a contributor to the historical process. Brownlow is a totally public person, from whom all issues flow. Brownlow made historical events, religious and political, so personal, he was, in a sense, outside history.

The head and shoulders of Doctor Ramsey, painted in 1877, the year Parson Brownlow died, by Lloyd Branson, hung in Mecklenburg Place on Main Street. The larger-than-life, full-length portrait of Governor Brownlow, artist unknown, painted in 1866 at the expense of $1,000 to the taxpayers, hangs still in the State Capitol Building at Nashville. Lawmakers still spit tobacco juice on it, and people of the area, including some of the old mountain Unionists who turned on him when he ran over them, spit on it.

I heard a boy in Carter County ask his pap, "Who won the War?" His pap said, "Son, it don't really make much difference who won the whole War. In East Tennessee, everybody lost!"

And I am not the only American who lost the War, and is still looking for it.

People seem to love to reach for odd facts about the War. That the accuracy of both Rebels and Yankees, for instance, was so poor it took about a man's body weight in lead to kill each soldier. Now here's something not many people remember: The last shot of the War was fired by a Confederate steamer at a Yankee whaler in the Bering Straits where you enter the Arctic Ocean—three months after surrender at Appomattox—a blank. Do you remember that? Did you ever know it? I didn't.

And they love to ponder all kinds of "What if . . . ?" questions about the War. "What if General Longstreet had taken Doctor Ramsey's advice as to the actual position on the French Broad's confluence with the Holston River?" That "What if" is obliterated when you ask, "What if Sherman had allowed

Thomas to invade East Tennessee, as planned, after the burning of the bridges in the Great Valley?" Why are they so eager to get the facts, individually and sectionally and nationally? So it will end at last? Then why for me has it yet to begin?

In a copy of *Parson Brownlow's Book*, I found the former owner's marginal comment: "When I heard Parson Brownlow tell all this in his orations at Cincinnati, I took all this as Gospel Truth, but I know now much of it is lies and the rest is gross distortion." He does not go on to state, because he probably does not perceive, that the orations, given backbone by the book after, made everything so real that the so-called facts were part of nobody's experience. What is this man's afterthought compared with the burning moment of "Gospel Truth"? To deny or reject the facts of imagination is the dim-wittest kind of romancing of facts.

The romantic ivy pulls down the house in time. Is that how it should be?

The phrase "common sense" is a contradiction. Reality is overrated, passé. Most of the pleasures of this world are imaginary. The rest are merely actual. Not the bear I find, but the bear I hunt. I am not what I eat, I am what I *imagine*. Is there then no reality, only various and workable fictions?

Memory is imagination. What I felt then will never return. But what I feel about what I imagine . . . The mysterious ways the imagination works. As if a man writes a letter to a man across the world, not knowing that the man is already dead, and then the writer dies before the letter reaches the address of the dead man, but somehow the letter comes into *my* hands and I read it and it changes my life. Thinking sets off an explosion of possibilities, the fragments fall where they may. Emotions root me, imagination and intellect transport me. I still stand in awe and wonderment before it all.

As events occurred, something kept me from experiencing them. Now that those events are memories, they are much more accessible, affect me much more piercingly like a pin-prick or a toothache or striking my crazy bone.

Sometimes, things I remember that I actually did or saw, I mistakenly think I only imagined while in the Tower.

I forgot to put this one in The Annals, thinks Doctor Ramsey. Mr. Audubon tells of the time Daniel Boone told him of an instance of his remarkable memory. He had been captured in the Green River Area of Kentucky by Indians, who got drunk on his own whiskey, so that he was able to slip away, but first he hacked three knotches in an ash tree to mark the spot.

Twenty years later, a friend told him he was having trouble establishing the boundary of some land he was claiming in court but that some men who lived nearby had told him that Boone had marked an ash tree right on the boundary years ago, so he asked Boone to come and go with him to the spot. The landscape had changed greatly, and Boone was sad to see the disappearance of deer and buffalo in that area. But he felt as if he were still a captive of the Indians, his memory was so lucid. The tree showed no signs of knotches, but Boone took an ax from one of the men who had accompanied him and his friend and began to scrape away at the bark. Slowly, the three distinct knotches were revealed. *I think I would not forget where I buried the depository of the Confederacy, even twenty years from now*, thinks Doctor Ramsey.

Lost Cause? Since the War, mostly Virginia has kept that up, focusing on Lee. But there never was a Cause for me, or for other East Tennesseans, certainly not for the Mountain North Carolinians, who died 4 to 1 compared with any other state (six times more than Tennessee). We fought to maintain the honor and wealth of the Old Virginia Dominion that had already faded into the past and for the new Cotton South's money.

One fact too many and the imagination balks, one feels atrophy in the brain. The problem is not so much an inability to experience the holocaust of that war as a failure in the aftermath to imagine it.

While the battle of Gettysburg—the high tide of the Confederacy—was going on, two tribes in Africa were slaughtering each other—the map screams of it. They, too, must have an historian. But how can I make of their event something significant, as Marx, a Russian writer, was readily able to make of the American Civil War in his articles for the New York *Daily Tribune* and a Vienna newspaper.

And in the Makan desert of China nothing was happening.

I'm not trying to be elusive—allusive, yes. So much eludes me that . . .

Perhaps we should, in fact, *say* those things that, we say, *go without* saying.

Parson Brownlow missed the bridge burning, as I did.

Both Brownlow and Doctor Ramsey missed General Sanders' Raid and the Siege of Knoxville.

Both Parson Brownlow and Doctor Ramsey missed the War.

They're both whirling in their graves as Knoxville changes from year to year.

Missing in action? They'll deal you the statistics. But weren't we all? Even Grant? Read his memoirs, the best of the bunch. Even he is missing in action. Jeff Davis was missing since Buena Vista. Bragg since West Point. Well, I exaggerate.

The sense of having missed myself plagued me all across the plains. When I reached the Rockies, it was like Shelley coming around the corner of his house on the balcony at Lerici and meeting himself.

Obsessed with this sense of having missed the War, I turned to the man I thought I had killed. But General Sanders was elusive, so I reached for Reverend Carter, and Brownlow, and then for Doctor Ramsey.

Charged image clichés first attracted me to Sanders, to Carter, to Brownlow, and Ramsey. Brownlow's voice, hot in my ear. The sense of Ramsey's omniscience as an historian. The man-of-action image of Reverend Carter, firing the bridges.

I knew I had fought in the War, but as I learned that I knew nothing about it, animal curiosity took hold of me. The discovery that I might have killed General Sanders . . . And through him, I became curious about Carter, Brownlow, and Ramsey. From general curiosity, I moved into guilt, a motive for repossessing the events, the specific events of his death, to general events. And then, compulsion to experience it all, see it, beyond curiosity, guilt, nostalgia. I passed through moods of cynicism, even pessimism, and then of Rabelaisian mockery, like Sut Lovingood. But over all—this compulsion to repossess those years.

I want to look at it every way there is to look at it. Look at it this way: General Sanders' circulatory system could encircle the world four times—and, mine, of course, and yours.

I think of the many men who sent substitutes and so missed the War.

Is it any wonder so many missed so much of the War? Somebody, I forget who, asked, "Can you count the spokes, of a turning wheel?" Of whom did he ask that question? Regarding what? And when? And why?

Forgiveness restores innocence for a moment, and to be innocent is to begin again. Better the certainty of experience than beginning again.

I'm still not certain. If the hand that shot General Sanders had become like the dyer's hand, red always, I would have known the first time the question was raised, but I would, if mine had not been red, have written none of these fragments, and I would have lived alone on this mountain or alone in some populous city.

The sense of everyone else dying in *my* death fills me more with compassion for all the others than with fear or pity for myself. I do not want to die, because when I die, I feel, the whole world dies with me. I feel pathos for the death of everyone but myself. That is only *two* ways of saying the same thing.

Each of these writings is a shell fragment, a nail in one of these cluster bombs.

If we are not mute, but speak, if we can read and write, are we condemned by words to create?

Remember. Repent. Return.

Of course, what is most important remains unwritten.

Brownlow's Knoxville *Whigs* are no more. They caught fire somehow and, being dry and brittle, almost burned down my cabin, but I went tearing out the front door with my arms full of them and tossed them like a flock of burning birds into the air, risking burning the whole mountain, for the slopes are dry and brittle, too, in September.

Only voices now, only echoes.

I always intended all these fragments for my family, but I have never had any children. I am by my lonesome.

December 12, 1929

I'm ready, I think, to write about the shooting of General Sanders, but not about the shooting of Cherokee, who taught me how to read.

III

LINCOLN ON REMEMBRANCE AND PERSPECTIVE

Lincoln's Second Gettysburg Address

Performance Criticism, Lincoln Fellowship,
Luncheon Keynote Speaker, 133rd Gettysburg
Address Commemorative, Gettysburg,
Pennsylvania, November 19, 1996

A few weeks ago, having stayed up late considering my talk for you about the Lincoln poems of Walt Whitman, Carl Sandburg, Vachel Lindsay, and others, I woke just before daylight and lay there, imagining what Abraham Lincoln might have said to us this afternoon. The poets have fallen silent. I ask you to listen now to Lincoln's speech, as I imagined it.

Six score and thirteen years ago, I left my son on his sickbed and boarded the train for this place, with some "appropriate remarks" in my pocket.

"The world will little note nor long remember what we say here today." Time seems to have proven me wrong when I said that on this date back in 1863, but it is fitting that I repeat it over a century later, today. For this annual Gettysburg's Address Commemoration is a relatively modest affair.

I went on to say that "the world can never forget what they did here." The irony that gives me pause is that I and what I said are today far better remembered than the thousands of common men who are buried out there. The few generals who are buried out there *are* remembered, and "it is fitting and proper that we do so." Ironically, however, better remembered are those who did *not* die out there and were *not* buried out there. General Robert E. Lee did not die here. General George Meade did not die. General James Longstreet is not buried out there, nor George Pickett, nor Winfield Scott Hancock. During the past 133 years, I have had more than my full measure of monumentalization on the grand scale, in bronze, marble, music, and canvas, in the words of poets and playwrights. For all that and for this occasion I am not ungrateful.

Several famous poets have taken as their mission to depict my life as that of the archetypal common American who rises from obscurity to the presidency in a time of crisis and who bodies forth from that great height the qualities, virtues, and frailties of the common man. It is a melancholy irony that their success has been, finally, to turn *this* common man into a godlike creature, whose utterances, in my address out there, among other occasions, are often confused with scripture, and for that you can imagine the difficulties I have had in explaining myself to folks where my spirit otherwise rests in peace. Something deep in my spirit must turn away from all that respectful attention to actual scripture, to the invocation in Ecclesiasticus: "Let us now praise famous men" (44:1). The prophet does indeed praise "such as did bear rule in their kingdoms, men renowned for their power, giving counsel by their understanding, and declaring prophecies" (44:3). The world is populated with statues of such men. But, saith the prophet, "some there be which have no memorial; who perished, as though they had never been; and are become as though they had never been born; and their children after them" (44:9). We have given them here at Gettysburg a habitation and a name, but "in a larger sense," they are all missing.

Today, having paid homage both to leaders and to men of the rank and file, and having eaten food blessed by our Lord and having had fellowship together, let us go from this place, lifting our voices higher and louder and longer in praise of those legions of *other* "famous men."

Because the numbing irony is this: that although the world has forgotten—having, indeed, never truly known—the individual common men who died here, it has indeed not forgotten what happened here. In countless poems, novels, and works of history, this nation and the world have bodied forth this battle as an expression of the conflicting ideals and violent actions of the entire War. But the fate of each individual common man has been ever thus, to be, from the start and ever afterward—in the digging of tunnels, the raising of pyramids, the building of cathedrals, the erection of bridges, and the execution of great wars—overwhelmed and obscured by the magnificence of the things they made and the events they created.

Scores of years ago, I said out there that "in a larger sense, we cannot dedicate, we cannot consecrate, we cannot hallow, this ground." As I think about that oft-repeated sentence, I feel with a pang the implications of the sense of that phrase "larger sense." Indeed, it was a sense so "large" that I was forced to confront the brute fact that it was impossible to pay to each common man the homage we pay with relative ease to those famous men we regard as leaders. Mindful of this impotence of conception and language, I sometimes wonder whether the sentence that follows was not my rhetorical avoidance of that brute fact: "The brave men, living and dead, who struggled here, have consecrated it, far above our poor power to add or detract." True enough, in some sense, but given the almost biblical reverence accorded my speech over the century and more since that day, did I not, in that sentence, bury for myself and thus for you the corpse of my own impotence? Ecclesiasticus, it is true, assures us that the righteousness of those who have no memorial "hath not been forgotten," that "their name liveth for evermore" in the kingdom of heaven (44:10, 14). In a democracy, however, we have an obligation not to leave such remembrances to heaven alone but to search until we find a way to resurrect such men and to keep them alive in our private and public identities, day by day.

In the nation's capital, I haunted the telegraph office out of an acute sense of missing the War, day by day, desperate to experience it with the immediacy of the telegraph, as if feeling the pulse of the battle. It was the damned not knowing . . .

Even that one young foot soldier who marched to more battlefields than any other and who lived to be a hundred years old missed each of those battles and all the War because of the nature of battle, in which a man sees only fragments, with the disconnectedness of the pieces of an exploded shell.

And the generals standing on a hill or behind a hill or leading a charge against a hill missed the War because even with cavalry giving them eyes over the countryside and even with mapmakers giving them omniscient views as if from the sky, they saw little more than the soldier who sees the bent back of the man in front of him. And the talking wires of the telegraph told me only what the generals, with imperfect vision going into battle and imperfect comprehension afterward, could gather in nervous-quick time.

The reporters missed the War, the sketch artists who were eyewitnesses to the battles missed it, and the photographers who seldom arrived before most of the dead had been buried missed the War.

Civilians in all walks of life, men, women, and children, even those standing outside their burning homes, watching and wailing, missed the War, damned to know only their own limited fate and to pick up fragments from reporters and sketch artists.

Imagine the child's confused perception of the War, the different views of the children in the South from those in the North, and you begin to understand the scope and depth of what all who survived the War missed.

In the several decades after the War, men, women, and children saw more and more of the artists and finally the photographers' scenes; read the memoirs of the generals and officers; and heard the memorial speeches—Americans took in more facts, saw more images, stored them up, mulled them over, and then began the long forgetting, made more painful in the South by punitive Reconstruction, which was prolonged three times longer than the War itself. And still, each and all missed the War, because the pictures, the diaries, the memoirs, the histories, and the 128 volumes of *War of the Rebellion: Official Records of the Union and Confederates Armies* sift down finally to little more than fragments found on the field.

Then over the years, into the next century, into the hands of Americans came more and more of the common man's accounts: views from the battlefields, the hospitals, and the prisons. And more and more came the woman's perspective from the home front: the refugee's, the widow's, the spy's, the mother's, and the nurse's perspectives. And still, pervading all those testimonials is that nagging apprehensiveness that drove me to the telegraph office—I am missing the War, I am missing the War . . . I have missed the War.

But what of the historians and the biographers, trailing along behind, collecting, arranging, and filling in background? The fragments have insisted on remaining fragments—the whole, the vision of the whole, has remained unachieved, with so much missing.

Americans missed the War that most shaped its destiny by remaining mesmerized by the fragments they picked up, each individual from his or her own field of vision, isolated handfuls of facts about battles and leaders and this aspect or that aspect by, as a public, from generation to generation, remaining obsessed by the role of ancestors or by the look of artifacts, those literal fragments—swords, guns, bullets, uniforms, flags—found on the field.

I cannot brush away something I saw in the two hours I wandered the battlefield that morning here in Gettysburg and even as I listened to speeches and even as I spoke—the sight of the scavengers at Gettysburg, thrilled to pick up, possess, and count the value of fragments.

Americans have been immersed in seemingly endless talk, an endless stream of books, endless novels, and poems that repeat, and repeat, and repeat, as if damned to seek knowledge, understanding, and perhaps even the vision in the self-same icons, tokens, runes, and ruins. Everything collected together is still only a collection of fragments found on the field.

The painful paradox is that both the men who fought here and all people who have read about the battle of Gettysburg missed the War. For the War is not only the details of battles such as Gettysburg, the questions of strategy employed well or ill by the leaders in that battle, but also the meaning of the whole War as it reveals itself in each individual American, in each creative and destructive act from the day of my address to this day's commemoration of that address.

Because they are human beings, damned always to know far too little but aspiring to the vision of angels, Americans missed what matters most: the understanding and the vision that are the motive for action. Americans have failed to make the nature of this War and its lessons part of their everyday lives as they deal with America's problems. Let your vision henceforth be not to celebrate the War as an interesting time in history but to meditate on the War as a prelude to action.

Let us come to the realization at long last—six score and thirteen years later—that the task, long neglected through imperfect understanding, which must now be taken up, is to look at the War through fresh perspectives, through every conceivable perspective. Implore nurses, lawyers, physicians, journalists, dentists, teachers, merchants, laborers of every type, scientists of every type, engineers, geographers, secretaries, politicians, architects, teamsters, even optometrists to look at the War from their points of view and meditate on, talk about, and publish their visions.

Implore the Native American, the African American, and each of every other ethnic group—Irish, Jews, Asians—to look at the War from their own unique points of view. Implore women, black and white, of the North and the South, to filter the War through their perspective.

Most neglected are the children. Collect all those tiny, hidden, ignored fragments that reveal the plight and perception of children during the War and throughout all the years since. It's the damned not knowing, you see? . . .

The goal in the coming score of years is to help the nation achieve at long last an understanding of the War commensurate with its effect. The purpose is to miss the War no longer, by understanding more fully what caused the War; what the War in all its aspects was; what dark problems and bright prospects for America came out of the War; how Americans have been damned by the not knowing to repeat all the dark problems unto this day; and how Americans have been damned by the not knowing to fail to achieve the bright prospects that often come out of terrible calamities.

The task is to examine and understand all aspects of the War in such a way as to actively pursue solutions to the problems of today—violence, racism, mistrust of government. Because that task is so difficult to perform, I took then and Americans take now refuge in compensatory rhetoric. Democracy being, as we know, an unending experiment in problem solving, let us now search until we find ways to praise the common man—and not only those out there but also all the other men and women, black and white, who fought, suffered, endured the four most insane and most glorious years in American life.

I came here today to reiterate my challenge of six score and thirteen years ago: "It is for us, the living, rather, to be dedicated, here, to the great task remaining before us." Americans have indeed, from time to time, "resolved that these dead shall not have died in vain," and from time to time this nation has indeed had "a new birth of freedom" that "government of the people, by the people, for the people shall not perish from the earth." But in those bronze likenesses of myself found throughout this nation, you may have noticed that my hands seem a little restless. The sadness often remarked in my face is sometimes there in the palm of your hand. Because something is missing. Something essential is missing, and that is an answer—in a larger sense—to a question implicit in my address: "Can a nation so conceived and so dedicated long endure?" With all the progress and advances, prefigured to a great extent in the War itself, that this nation enjoys, the severe problems that have their roots in the War and Reconstruction continue to plague these United States. Let us now so remember the War as to reveal ways in which the bright prospects and the dark problems of the War evolved, directly and indirectly, out of the War and Reconstruction.

Because something has been missing. Something essential is still missing, not from the record, the written, photographed, drawn, mapped, and remembered record, but from our individual and national consciousnesses. What is missing is compassionate imagination. It is not dull facts alone that make history dull and forbidding to young minds; it is dull imaginations. Where imagination is dull, compassion is numb. The compassionate imagination is vibrant; it searches, and it aspires to a visionary truth that would suffuse our very identity, day by day. How do we arouse that now dormant compassionate imagination? We, as "a nation conceived in liberty and dedicated to the proposition that all men are created equal," must seize upon the enormous record of facts about the War and Reconstruction and subject that inert record to the life-giving force of imagination guided by compassion. Our goal is enlightenment, but our purpose is action guided by that enlightenment.

What enlightenment do I imagine? An enlightenment that comes from having recognized the problem: that Americans have not from the end of the War or ever after tried to examine all aspects of the War, succumbing instead to the lure of romantic battles and leaders. The fitful and fragmented attention given the War over the years and the prevalent emphasis on battles and leaders and memorials have prevented Americans, North and South, from achieving a coherent vision of the causes, consequences, and effects of the War. "The great task remaining before" you, "the living," "that cause" to which I referred in 1863, has been transmuted over scores of years into the task of achieving that all-encompassing vision of the War to which I have just referred.

Every aspect of the War and Reconstruction set in motion forces that determined all our dark problems and our bright prospects, and lack of understanding has darkened our prospects, or slowed our progress, and prevented us from solving our problems. Racism, violence, economic instability, mistrust of government—these lingering problems await solutions that can come only from a thorough, imaginative, compassionate understanding of the War and its aftermath. Reconstruction, more than the War itself, impeded action against our problems. Reconstruction prolonged and worsened the dark effects of the War and discouraged a more enlightened pursuit of our bright prospects. The action in which I urge you to become engaged is the solution of the problems of society today.

In the score of years to come, dedicate yourselves to the achievement at long last of a profound reconciliation of the men and women of the North and the South. During my time, the Emancipation Proclamation freed the slaves by law; in the next century, I implore all Americans to free ourselves of racism at the deepest level of the human spirit.

Is it too late? As St. Paul is fond of answering his own rhetorical questions, God forbid. May I urge you as leaders to reexamine, redefine, and revise your perspectives on this War? Encourage each American to look at the War first through the lens of his or her own occupation, profession, or discipline of knowledge. That act will help each person to become enlightened as to all the facets and meanings of the War, to make an understanding of the War a part of his or her own identity, day by day.

We know that in every War, given the nature of War, the common soldier in his way and the general in his way miss the War as it happens and recall it imperfectly. Do not then their children fill in the record and the vision? Let us turn again to Ecclesiasticus and listen again to the verse: "They are become as though they had never been born." It is the phrase that follows that renders my mind restless: "and their children after them." The children, too, became "as though they had never been born." Imagine the thousands of narrow graves out there on that battlefield filled also with all the forgotten children and descendants of the men who died here. Because they failed to see and understand and thus to shape their private and public identities in light of what was there to see and understand, the children and descendants of the common man also missed the War and are, in a "larger sense," missing in action, dead in vain.

The War did not end in the cemeteries, or with the publication of books; it went on through Reconstruction—up to this very day. The aftermath has yet to begin. Let it begin in the minds of the children of the common man. Let there come a day when Ecclesiasticus's lament will no longer apply: "some there be . . . who perished . . . as though they had never been born; and their children after them."

Notes

WILLIAM FAULKNER'S *ABSALOM, ABSALOM!* QUENTIN! LISTEN!

1. Ernest Hemingway, *Green Hills of Africa* (New York: Scribner, 1935), 22.

2. Frederick L. Gwynn and Joseph L. Blotner, eds., *Faulkner in the University* (Charlottesville: University Press of Virginia, 1959), 6, 263. Faulkner describes Caddy and her relationship with Quentin.

3. Faulkner disagrees, while stressing Quentin's importance. The argument may proceed not only from the author's intent in the novel but also from its effect. Gwynn and Blotner, *Faulkner in the University*, 71, 274–75.

4. One of the most recent examples is Dirk Kuyk Jr., *Sutpen's Design: Interpreting Faulkner's Absalom, Absalom!* (Charlottesville: University Press of Virginia, 1990). Cleanth Brooks is an earlier, salient example, even though he understood, as a New Critic, how point of view expresses essence in a work of fiction: *William Faulkner: The Yoknapatawpha Country* (New Haven, CT: Yale University Press, 1963), 295–324. See also his appendix B, "Notes to *Absalom, Absalom!*" in *Twentieth Century Interpretations of Absalom, Absalom! ed.* Arnold Goldman (Englewood Cliffs, NJ: Prentice-Hall, 1971), 107–13. In most of the essays in that collection, the emphasis is upon the importance of the Sutpen story, with no stress on its effect upon Quentin.

5. William Faulkner, *Absalom, Absalom!* (New York: Vintage, 1936; repr., corrected text, ed. Noel Polk, 1986), 166.

6. Cleanth Brooks is again a major example: "All the information the reader has comes through Quentin directly or through Quentin's conversations." Brooks fails to call attention to the omniscient narrator of the entire novel, Faulkner himself. *Twentieth Century Interpretations,* 107. In the same volume, Thomas E. Connolly instructs us that "Quentin" is "the principal narrator" (appendix A, "An Index to *Absalom, Absalom!*" 101). Also in that volume, Richard Poitier says much the same thing ("'Strange Gods' in Jefferson Mississippi," 12–13). This misunderstanding is frequently repeated elsewhere. Ambiguity may be the culprit. To distinguish between Faulkner as authorial

narrator and the characters he quotes telling old tales and talking, one should use the term "storyteller" for Quentin and others.

7. Gerald Langford, *Absalom, Absalom!* (Austin: University of Texas Press, 1971). See his introduction.

8. Joseph Blotner, *Faulkner: A Biography*, vol. 1 (New York: Random House, 1984), 348.

9. Langford, *Absalom, Absalom!* 3.

10. Gwynn and Blotner, *Faulkner in the University*, 274.

11. In Faulkner, *Absalom, Absalom!* a good example begins on page 148.

12. Blotner, *Faulkner*, 348–49.

13. Rollo May, Ernest Angel and Henri F. Ellenberger, eds., *Existence: A New Dimension in Psychiatry and Psychology* (New York: Basic, 1958), 50–54.

14. Among those critics who deal extensively with this question are John T. Irwin, *Doubling and Incest: Repetition and Revenge; A Speculative Reading of Faulkner* (Baltimore: Johns Hopkins University Press, 1975); Estella Schoenberg, *Old Tales and Talking: Quentin Compson in William Faulkner's Absalom, Absalom! and Related Works* (Jackson: University Press of Mississippi, 1977); and Michael Grimwood, *Heart in Conflict: Faulkner's Struggles with Vocation* (Athens: University of Georgia Press, 1987). In Arthur F. Kinney, ed., *Critical Essays on William Faulkner: The Compson Family* (Boston: G. K. Hall, 1982), several of the contributors take up the question. An interesting revelation of Faulkner's identification with Quentin is the fact that "he told Joan [Williams] to send her letters to Quentin Compson, General Delivery, in Oxford." Blotner, *Faulkner*, 520.

THE SIMULTANEOUS BURNING OF NINE BRIDGES IN EAST TENNESSEE

1. Oliver P. Temple, *East Tennessee and the Civil War* (Cincinnati: R. Clarke Company, 1899), 366–70; Charles F. Bryan Jr., "The Civil War in East Tennessee: A Social, Political, and Economic Study" (PhD diss., University of Tennessee, 1978), iii–iv; Jesse Burt, "East Tennessee, Lincoln, and Sherman," East Tennessee Historical Society's *Publications*, no. 34 (1962): 3–25; no. 35 (1963): 54–75; Eric R. Lacy, *Vanquished Volunteers* (Johnson City, TN: East Tennessee State University Press, 1965); Martha L. Turner, "The Cause of the Union in East Tennessee," *Tennessee Historical Quarterly* 40 (1981): 366–80.

2. Bryan, "Civil War in East Tennessee," 65.

3. Ibid., 71–72; William Rule, *The Loyalists of Tennessee in the Late War* (Cincinnati: H. C. Sherick & Co., 1887), 4.

4. William Gannaway Brownlow, *Sketches of the Rise, Progress, and Decline of Secession, with a Narrative of Personal Adventures among the Rebels* (Philadelphia: G. W. Childs, 1862), 134–40, 277–78, 299–301, 414; *War of the Rebellion: Official Records of the Union and Confederate Armies* (128 vols., Washington, DC: Government Printing Office, 1880–1901), vol. 1, pp. 911–12 (hereafter cited as *Official Records*).

5. *Official Records*, series 1, vol. 4, pp. 364–65.

6. *Official Records*, series 1, vol. 1, pp. 829–30; series 1, vol. 4, pp. 529–30, 824–37.

7. Oliver P. Temple, *Notable Men of Tennessee, from 1833 to 1875* (New York: Cosmopolitan Press, 1912), 88–90.

8. For more on Samuel Carter and his family, see William Garrett Piston, "Carter's Raid," East Tennessee Historical Society's *Publications*, no. 49 (1977): 61–76; no. 50 (1978): 31–57; John S. Goff, "Colonel James P. T. Carter of Carter County," *Tennessee Historical Quarterly* 26 (1967): 372–82; and Temple, *East Tennessee*, 376.

9. *Official Records*, series 1, vol. 1, p. 8.

10. Burt, "East Tennessee," 10–11; T. Harry Williams, *Lincoln and His Generals* (New York: Knopf, 1952), 23–24, 47–48.

11. Temple, *East Tennessee*, 370–72, 375–77.

12. *Official Records*, series 1, vol. 4, p. 317.

13. Ibid., 320.

14. Ibid. Ironically, information in Carter's postscript only lent credence to Sherman's conviction that an expedition into East Tennessee would weaken a more strategic concentration in the direction of Bowling Green.

15. Ibid., 318, 321, 325.

16. Temple, *Notable Men*, 85–87.

17. *Official Records*, series 1, vol. 4, p. 338.

18. Ibid., 343, 347. On the eve of the raid, General McClellan wrote to General Don Carlos Buell, who was to be appointed Sherman's successor on November 9 (to take command on the 15th) giving a long explanation about the importance of East Tennessee, stressing the political implications: "It so happens that a large majority of the inhabitants of East Tennessee are in favor of the Union. It therefore seems proper that you should remain on the defensive on the line from Louisville to Nashville while you throw the mass of your forces by rapid marches to Cumberland Gap or Walker's Gap on Knoxville in order to occupy the railroad at that point and thus enable the loyal citizens of Eastern Tennessee to rise while *you* at the same time cut off the railway communication between Eastern Virginia and Mississippi." The invasion McClellan was trying to persuade Buell to plan had already been formulated with Reverend Carter, Lincoln, and Seward, and the date had been set for the very next night. Ibid., 342.

19. Ibid., 300, 347.

20. Temple, *East Tennessee*, 380.

21. Ibid.

22. *Petition of A. M. Cate* (1871?), Special Collections, University of Tennessee Library, 1–4.

23. Ibid.

24. Ibid.

25. Ibid.

26. Ibid., 9.

27. Temple, *East Tennessee*, 381.

28. Ibid., 381–83.

29. Ibid. In 1862, Radford Gatlin, author of the *Confederate Spelling Book*, published a fourteen-page pamphlet that made the thirty-five-year-old guard, James Keelan, famous

throughout the South. He entitled it *The Parentage, Birth, Nativity and Exploits of the Immortal Hero James Keelan, Who Defended Successfully the Bridge at Strawberry Plains, and Alone, Put to Flight Fifteen Lincolnites on the Night of Eighth of November, A.D., 1861* (Atlanta: Stubley Printing, 1862, reissued 1932).

30. Temple, *East Tennessee*, 382–83.

31. Ibid.

32. *Official Records*, series 1, vol. 4, p. 862.

33. Abram Jobe, a Unionist from Carter County, recalled many years later that he had persuaded "the commander" of the men who were to burn the Carter's Depot bridge to spare it because he feared reprisals should Sherman fail to rescue East Tennessee loyalists. He stated that a Negro man had been offered his freedom the next morning if he would fire the bridge that night. Jobe to Oliver P. Temple, September 20, 1899, Temple Papers, Special Collections, University of Tennessee Library.

34. Temple, *East Tennessee*, 385.

35. Ibid.

36. Ibid.

37. Ibid.

38. Ibid., 386; Rule, *Loyalists of Tennessee*, 9–10. For letters concerning the exile of William Carter's wife and the wives of Horace Maynard, Andrew Johnson, and others, see *Official Records*, series 2, vol. 1, pp. 883–89.

39. *Petition of A. M. Cate*, 7. Temple does not cite this petition as one of his sources; he reports the total amount allocated to Carter as being only $2,500. The amount varies from one authority to another.

40. Temple, *Notable Men*, 87.

41. *Petition of A. M. Cate*, 11–12.

42. Temple, *East Tennessee*, 381.

43. *Official Records*, series 2, vol. 1, p. 881. For additional information concerning Fry, see pp. 862, 863, 882, 899; series 1, vol. 7, p. 147; Temple, *East Tennessee*, 400; Philip Shaw Paludan, *Victims: A True Story of the Civil War* (Knoxville: University of Tennessee Press, 1981), 65, 67, 128, 129.

44. Temple, *East Tennessee*, 383.

45. Rule, *Loyalists of Tennessee*, 11–12.

46. Temple, *East Tennessee*, 383.

47. *Official Records*, series 1, vol. 7, pp. 700–701; Bryan, "Civil War in East Tennessee," 91; Brownlow, *Sketches*, 311–12, 420–21.

48. Kermit Hall, "West H. Humphreys and the Crisis of the Union," *Tennessee Historical Quarterly* 34 (1975): 59–60; Brownlow, *Sketches*, 293; *Official Records*, series 1, vol. 7, p. 806. See also E. Merton Coulter, *William G. Brownlow: Fighting Parson of the Southern Highlands* (Chapel Hill: University of North Carolina Press, 1937), 154–207; and Steve Humphrey, *"That D——d Brownlow"* (Boone, NC: Appalachian Consortium Press, 1978), 218–53. For a curious, vivid, fictional account of the burning of the bridges and of events preceding and following, with some attention to Brownlow, see William E. Barton, *A Hero in Homespun* (Boston: Lamson, Wolffe, 1897). "The historical background," the author claims, "is believed to be true to fact" (vii).

49. *Official Records*, series 1, vol. 4, pp. 359–60. For more letters from Samuel Carter concerning the invasion of East Tennessee, see ibid., 361–70; series 2, vol. 1., pp. 892–94, 896–97, 899–900. In January 1862, Colonel Leadbetter reported that Holston Bridge at Union was still down. December 19 of that year, General Samuel Carter, Reverend Carter's brother, entered Tennessee east of Cumberland Gap and destroyed both bridges, the first Union cavalry operation in the West. After the war. Major General Carter reentered the navy and rose to the rank of rear admiral, reputedly the only man in U.S. history to rise to such eminence in both branches of the service. Piston, "Carter's Raid" (1978), 56; Temple, *Notable Men*, 92.

50. Temple, *East Tennessee*, 379; Temple, *Notable Men*, 92–93.

51. Rule, *Loyalists of Tennessee*, 10; Thomas William Humes, *The Loyal Mountaineers of Tennessee* (Knoxville, TN: Ogden Bros., 1888), 133; Temple, *East Tennessee*, 387; James Welch Patton, *Unionism and Reconstruction in Tennessee, 1860–1869* (Chapel Hill: University of North Carolina Press, 1934), 60; Bryan, "Civil War in East Tennessee," 87–91.

Acknowledgments

In different versions, the following essays and short stories appeared in the following publications:

"For the New Millennium, New Perspectives on the Civil War and Reconstruction." *National Forum* (*Phi Kappa Phi Journal*) 77, no. 3 (Summer 1997): 24–29.

Preface. In *Short History of the Civil War: Ordeal by Fire*, by Fletcher Pratt. Mineola, NY: Dover Books, 1997.

"On James McPherson's *For Cause and Comrades: Why Men Fought in the Civil War.*" *World and I* 12, no. 7 (1997): 273–79.

"Classics of Civil War Fiction." Preface in *Classics of Civil War Fiction*, edited by David Madden and Peggy Bach. Jackson: University Press of Mississippi, 1991; Tuscaloosa: University of Alabama Press, 2001.

"William Faulkner's *Absalom, Absalom!* Quentin! Listen!" In *Touching the Web of Southern Novelists*, 41–58. Knoxville: University of Tennessee Press, 2005.

"Rediscovering a Major Civil War Novel: Joseph Stanley Pennell's *The History of Rome Hanks and Kindred Matters*." In Madden and Bach, *Classics of Civil War Fiction*, 181–203.

"The Innocent Stare at the Civil War: Madison Jones's *Nashville 1864: The Dying of the Light*." In *Madison Jones' Garden of Innocence*, edited by Jan Nordby Gretlund, 125–39. Odense: University Press of Southern Denmark, 2005.

"The Last American Epic: The Civil War Novels of Father and Son, Michael and Jeff Shaara." *World and I*, 2004.

"The Simultaneous Burning of Nine Bridges in East Tennessee." Article published as "Unionist Resistance to Confederate Occupation: The Bridge Burners of East Tennessee." East Tennessee Historical Society's *Publications*, nos. 52 and 53 (1981 and 1982): 22–39.

"The Sinking of the Sultana: A Meditation on Loss and Forgetfulness." Foreword in *Loss of the Sultana and Reminiscences of Survivors*. Knoxville: University of Tennessee Press, 2005.

"Willis Carr, Sharpshooter, at Bleak House, Knoxville." *Southern Review* (Spring 1985): 522–33.

"Willis Carr Meditates on the Act of Sketching: Hair Trigger Pencil Lines." *Louisiana Cultural Vistas* (Spring 1994): 56–59.

"Willis Carr, Sharpshooter, Meditates on Photographs." *New Letters* 55 (Spring 1989): 55–78.

"A Fever of Dying: Henrietta Ramsey Lenoir and General William Price Sanders." In *Homewords: A Book of Tennessee Writers*, 116–27. Knoxville: University of Tennessee Press, 1986.

"The Incendiary at the Forks of the River." *Library Development Review*, University of Tennessee (2003–2004): 12–14.

"Fragments Found on the Field: Parson Brownlow and Dr. James Gettys Ramsey." In *Gulf Coast Collection of Stories and Poems*, edited by James P. White and Jeff Todd, 36–54. Montrose, AL: Texas Center for Writers Press, 1994.